DISCOVER AMERICAN TREES

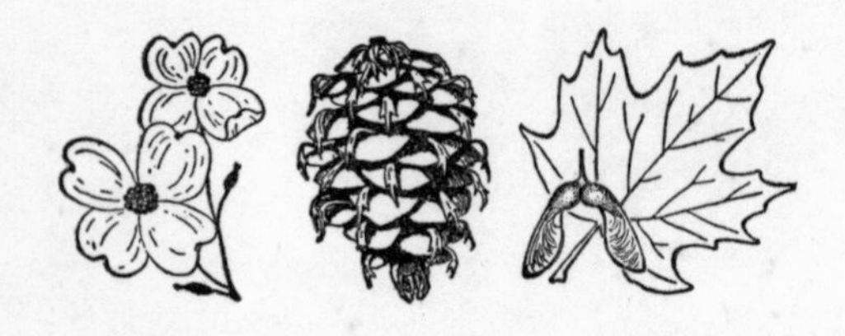

Also by Rutherford Platt:

THIS GREEN WORLD / THE WOODS OF TIME

THE GREAT AMERICAN FOREST

DISCOVER AMERICAN TREES

A Revised Edition of the Book Originally Published as
AMERICAN TREES

by Rutherford Platt

With drawings by Margaret L. Cosgrove

Photographs by the author

DODD, MEAD & COMPANY · New York · 1968

Library of Congress Catalog Card Number: 68-27440

Manufactured in the United States of America

DISCOVER AMERICAN TREES *is a revised edition of the book originally published as* AMERICAN TREES.

BUT *WHY* DISCOVER A TREE?

You will find a good answer to that question simply by flipping open this book at random. You may read (page 47) that the tulip tree stands on tiptoe! You may see (page 49) that linden seeds are carried by a helicopter. You may discover (page 97) why cones of white pine make such a cheery fire in your fireplace. You may find this bit of philosophy on page 167: "Whitebark pine taps the essence of eternal order to which all life must submit in order to be free." Or you may find yourself (page 201) in a redwood grove "where there is no hurry, no measure of time, no sound. A dog does not bark. A person whispers."

In this confused, overcrowded world in which we find ourselves, the discovery of trees is an utterly refreshing adventure. Even a single tree is a trail of wonder. Merely stretch out your hand to it. If the leaves are off the tree, look closely at the buds which stud the twigs. They are beautiful colors, many of them have bud scales in spirals, and each bud is an exquisite piece of architecture. In the spring watch the rhythmic way bud scales open and leaves and flowers pour out.

Nowadays, many people who scarcely noticed trees and have missed the pleasure of having them as personal friends are suddenly missing something from their lives, or sensing a loss in a neighborhood. This feeling is growing where trees, which were there last year, happened to be in the way of a shopping center or housing development, or a wide concrete carpet which "they" were laying for his Supreme Majesty the Car. Those who feel the loss of trees can take a step—a most enjoyable one—toward changing public opinion by personal discovery. In a small way, you will feel a strong sense of elation, it stretches the spirit and the mind, to discover what composes the art and architecture of trees, and to realize that you can tell the difference between a "white oak" and a "black oak", between a "spruce", "fir" and "pine."

To recognize a tree and call it by name is of course the first step toward discovery. So this book puts some emphasis on the details of trees that spell out their names. These details by themselves trigger a good deal of excitement.

With this in mind, I have not relied just on botanical characteristics for recognition. To that end, you will find delightful features like the flavor of a twig when you chew it (for example sweet birch, sassafras, black cherry), or the odor of crushed leaves or buds (sweetgum, balsam fir). And there is the flabby ribbon that makes the leaves of trembling aspen dance up and down and twinkle in the sunlight. The base of the sycamore leaf stem forms a little dunce cap over the bud—a most fanciful item. The shapes of leaves, the patterns of their veins, the teeth, lobes, and scallops of their margins, are revelations of a fantastically beautiful and diverse art exhibit filled with nature's sweeping harmonies and laws of symmetry—often drawn with deft eccentricities. Every scrub oak tree, in which no two leaves are ever alike, is an enticing display of abstract art. The tints and tones of leaves, bark, buds, acorns, and berries, are a palette mixed by air, water, and sunlight.

Thus, this book seeks to tell you the name of every tree you see in every part of the United States, from Canada to Key West, from New England to the marvelous forests of our Northwest, from the Atlantic edge of our Southern states across the Southwestern deserts (that also have trees) to the astonishing heritage of ancient trees along the California coast. This book groups American trees according to the regions where they grow, because most people find trees today when they go forth in their cars. This arrangement also underscores the word "discovery."

Recent News About Trees

With the original edition of this book I had the boastful thought that it included every tree that you might see anywhere in our country—except, of course, horticultural and rare kinds of trees in botanical gardens—but including introduced aliens which have become naturalized such as horsechestnut, eucalyptus, white mulberry, lombardy poplar, cedar of Lebanon. However, one important tree, not mentioned in the original edition, has made some dramatic headlines in recent years.

Bristlecone Pine. Some gnarled old skeletons of trees with trunks silvered by icy blasts where the bark has fallen off, with jagged broken branches stabbing out in all directions as though in the throes of a titanic struggle with the elements, are located about two miles high on the White Mountains of California, close to the California-Arizona state line. These are bristlecone pines, with lifespans measured—not in hundreds of years—but in *millennia!* While these incredible trees may appear to our eyes to be losing the battle for survival, they have doubtless looked like that ever since Columbus discovered America. They may well add another thousand years to the four thousand they have already lived.

In 1958, Dr. Edmund Shulman of the University of Arizona found that one of these trees named Methuselah is 4600 years old. It was a healthy young tree when the ancient Egyptians were building the pyramids in the fifteenth century B.C. This growth of bristlecone pines is now named the Ancient Bristlecone Pine Forest, located in the Inyo Forest of California and open to visitors from June 1 to October 30. Instructions for reaching this spectacular sanctuary can be obtained from the White Mountain Ranger Station, Bishop, California.

Let the record show an incident in the Snake Mountains in the eastern part of Nevada, where there is another grove of bristlecone pines. In 1964 a young scientist from an Eastern university, with the permission of the Forest Service, cut down a massive old patriarch in connection with a study of the distribution and age limits of these priceless antiques. The resulting report in a scientific journal stated that this tree was 4900 years old—300 years older than Methuselah—in truth the oldest living thing known to be growing on earth, with

The drawing of bristlecone pine on the facing page was made especially for this edition by Mrs. Esther D. Anderson.

E.P.A.

a lifespan as great as that of human history. The researcher might have used an ingenious instrument called an increment borer by which a slender pencil can be drawn out of the trunk of the tree with marks showing the annual rings that can be counted. This does not destroy the tree. By this means the age of Methuselah was established, as well as that of the General Sherman, big tree sequoia (see page 207).

In the Ancient Bristlecone Pine Forest, one sees those old warriors against elemental rocks, ice, and bitter winds, that seem to be wearing shining silver armor, still putting out fresh green needles every spring on scattered branches. And you will see that they have some young companions—another snowline tree of the Rocky Mountains called limber pine (page 169). You can tell the two kinds of pine trees apart by their needles. Limber pine needles appear as short tufts at the ends of twigs, while bristlecone needles grow along the length of the twig for four feet or more so they resemble big fox tails. You can also tell these two pines by their cones. Limber cones are smooth and green in summer, while bristlecone pinecones are purple with sharp bristles at the end of each cone scale.

With bristlecone pine America holds the title for the oldest living thing on earth for several reasons. First, this continent was not discovered until rather late in human history. By that time great forests in China and the Near East had been destroyed by ancient civilizations. Trees so often referred to in the Old Testament came from remnant forests whose seedling sprouts were trampled and eaten by the sheep and goats of the herdsmen.

The primitive tribes that first arrived on this continent

were hunters and pursuers of woodland game. They became the woodland Indians who were protected and nourished by the great forest that spread an unbroken ocean of leaves from the Atlantic Coast to the Mississippi River. That was the magnificent forest which the first settlers from Europe found, which played such a large part in American history and which seemed to be such an exhaustless heritage of timber and wildlife. This forest left us the trees you find in this book. Its remnants are being pulverized by bulldozers as this is written.

The bristlecones survived in America after "civilized people" spread from coast to coast, because they happened to occupy a site out of the reach of men. They grow serenely two miles high in the sky. They are so elemental, so isolated, they remained unknown and undisturbed until they were first announced in today's news reports on modern television. They are pristine and exciting, as were our oaks and maples and other trees when they were discovered by the pioneers.

So much for the title to the *oldest*—what about the *tallest?*

This brings us to another recent discovery. The title of the world's tallest tree has been a competition between Australia and America, like The America's Cup Race. The Australians claim that their graceful, towering eucalyptus must be taller than our redwoods. But at present America holds the trophy with an announcement by the National Geographic Society in July, 1964. Their scientists, using new techniques for measuring the height of a tree to a fraction of an inch, announced that a certain redwood is 349.3 feet tall. This tree is such a tall, straight column it seems to belong in a fairy story.

The circumference of the trunk (four feet above the ground) is 65 feet, yet it seems so slender and the trunk converges to a point like a railroad track running off into the distance. For more about the redwoods, see page 202.

The Discovery of the Redwoods

Redwood trees are first cousins of the big tree sequoias which live high up in mountains a hundred miles away (see page 204). These tree cousins are both called —*Sequoia.* Big tree is wide, with branches reaching far out and a "fatter" trunk. Redwood is a very tall column that reaches straight up into the sky as though trying to touch a cloud. This marvelous tree is born from a seed so tiny you could hold it on the tip of a finger. The sprout which comes out of that seed is delicate and soft for a few years, but if no animal steps on it and no accident happens to it in this delicate stage, it turns into a massive pillar of wood which keeps on going up and up. It does not grow old and die. If it is unhurt and left alone to grow in its own way, after a thousand years it may become like the redwoods which America is so proud of today.

The tallest redwoods grow in deep dark valleys with steep sides so that sunshine and light from the sky reaches the floor of that valley from directly overhead. All plants tend to reach toward light, so this special location makes redwoods grow straight up. Every night without fail, winds bringing moisture from the Pacific Ocean collide with the mountains where the redwoods are hidden and fill them with fog. Then the fog makes the branches of the redwoods drip, drip, drip, so the trees enjoy plenty of water.

The redwood giants might have been on another planet; they were undiscovered for a long time after settlers came to California. In their deep valleys they were out of sight of people who came by ships. Even after towns were established, people traveled by trails and rivers which did not go through the redwood valleys. Even Indian trails avoided them because they held so few game animals and birds compared to other forests. The floor of a redwood forest is mostly a beautiful carpet of red needles, with clumps of ferns. There are few springs and brooks with sapling trees like alder and birch where deer can browse on the branches. The lowest branches of the redwood towers are apt to be more than a hundred feet above the ground. A redwood valley is perpetual twilight between steep mountain sides; direct rays of the sun scarcely reach the forest floor. In the dim light there are few bushes with berries to tempt birds. A redwood forest is silent, protected from the wind by the steep walls of its valley. It is like a dimly-lighted cathedral.

In 1849, people from eastern United States were pouring into California to look for gold. There were no maps but they could follow rivers for hundreds of miles without getting lost. One party of goldminers from San Francisco went inland about a hundred miles and then traveled north on the Trinity River. They pushed on and on, hoping to see the yellow glint of gold in the sand around the next bend. This tempted them to go too far and stay too long.

In the first week of November it rained torrents, day after day. The river became a furious flood, carried away their supplies, and made it impossible to travel. It seemed that they could not get back to civilization before the following spring and they did not have supplies to stay all winter. They had a map showing their river and the coastline about fifty miles toward the west. In between the map was blank, where it was mountainous, unexplored. The only chance to survive was to cross that fifty miles on foot, reach the coast, and signal to a boat to pick them up. Even in rough country they should make it in five days.

So a party of eight men, led by L. K. Wood, started to cross the unexplored country by following an elk trail up a mountainside. The torrential rains continued. The desperate men were soon floundering around in mud where there were no animal trails. By heading toward the light of the setting sun they tried to keep going straight west, but this was impossible. They had to make big detours to get around steep mountains and to cross roaring streams. They plunged through snowfields on the ridges and slipped down stony, muddy mountainsides. For a few days they could hunt game for food, and then their ammunition was all gone. Weeks passed while they struggled on, barely able to average two miles a day. Now they were starving with only acorns and roots to eat. But they couldn't stop. They must still fight, through roaring streams, through deep snow on ridges, stumble among boulders. They were in a daze like that of an endless, horrible dream. They didn't talk to each other, but they kept going in silence, putting one foot in front of another, enduring for one day more, and then another day, and another.

Suddenly, after six weeks of this timeless torture,

they found themselves in a dark, deep valley, where the ground was a red carpet that was easy to walk on. And then they were sure they were out of their minds; this was not like any forest they knew—it was a nightmare. It was very quiet. They were no sounds of birds, no rushing water—and the trees were enormous, much too big to be real.

The fact is they had reached a redwood forest near the coast. It must have been like the valley of Muir Woods that tourists visit today just beyond the north end of the Golden Gate Bridge in San Francisco.

The report says that Mr. Wood wanted to linger among the amazing trees. His legs were weak from starvation but he paced off a fallen trunk and found that it was 300 feet long. The other men were mad at him for being excited about the phantom trees, and urged him to keep going. That same day they reached the ocean and were saved. Later Mr. Wood, leader who kept his head and who understood that the redwoods were marvelous, real trees and not a nightmare, wrote his report and told about his discovery.

What are your Five Favorite Trees?

Recently the editor of *American Forests* asked me—"What are your five favorite trees?" As I pondered this question it dawned on me that this is a fascinating game to play. Trees you take for granted in everyday life suddenly become vivid personalities crowding your thoughts in a lively contest.

Of course everyone will choose different trees. The key word in the game is "favorite," which makes this a most personal choice. A baseball fan might name white ash because its wood makes a tough springy bat. A yachtsman might choose Douglas fir, as this makes a tall mast that can bend in great winds without breaking. A woodsman might choose hickory, for an axe handle; a hunter, black walnut for a gun stock; a whittler, white pine or apple for its clean, straight-grained wood; a venetian blind manufacturer, basswood; a college crewman would choose western red cedar for lightness and because it makes a shell that will shoot through the water with little friction. A paper manufacturer would choose spruce.

I mention these choices because they suggest some of the countless ways that trees shape our daily lives. However, this book of discovery aims to discover only a few uses of trees. Its purpose is to help you make their acquaintance, to discover their points of special beauty and interest, and to find full enjoyment in them as you see them growing along a street, in your home yard, in a city park, or in remnants of the wilderness that still remain with their wildflowers and ferns and some of their animals and birds.

In choosing my five favorite trees I reluctantly turn away from the beautiful decorative trees such as dogwood, arching American elm, locust, delightful flowering trees such as hawthornes, flowering fruit trees, magnolias, and that trim decoration, red cedar. Also I ask to step aside some fine trees with a special distinction, such as live oak, holly, willow, basswood, hickory, bald cyprus, redwood, sycamore, walnut, and tulip tree.

My five favorite trees—not in order of importance—are as follows:

White Oak, for its strong, healthy personality and positive nature, revealed in durable, erect trunk and emphatic horizontal thrust of its branches. It ranges from Texas to Florida, from Maine to Minnesota. Where it stands solitary in a pasture as a shady spot for farm animals, it never looks lonely, it owns the field.

Sugar Maple. Its leaf, the emblem of Canada, is one of the most beautiful symmetries in all nature. Sugar maple is distinctly American. The Indians taught the first colonists in New England how to tap the trunk for maple sugar. Since then the mechanics of collecting maple sap and boiling it down has improved, but not the utterly delicious flavor of maple syrup and the natural quality of maple sugar. Sugar maple is a charter member of our eastern hardwood forest, found from Nova Scotia to Mississippi, from Texas to Manitoba.

Trembling Aspen. This bright, wide-awake poplar is the only native American tree that has traveled on the footsteps of its seeds all the way across the continent. It ranges naturally from Maine to California, from Alaska to Mexico. It is the only tree that can be clearly identified from a distance by the way its foliage quivers. It has been called a "weed tree" by some people because it grows so fast and its seedlings may crowd the ground like weeds. Yet for this reason it promptly repopulates burned-over ground, and tackles less fertile soil; it repairs and promotes forests. It is obviously a wide-awake tree.

Canoe Birch. You will find the commoner name, "paper birch," in this book, but I mention the older woodland name here because it tells of the American background of this beautiful tree with the white bark. Canoe birches standing at the top of a field on the edge of the woods in a sunset glow are lovely beyond words! Beside a blue pond they offer a picture famous in many paintings. This slender tree is so flexible that it can be bent over forming a beautiful loop with its top touching the ground, and when released it will snap upright again. As a boy in Maine, I swung on canoe birches with the other 12-year-olds. Perhaps that is one reason it is a personal favorite.

White Pine. This was the tree that provided the colonists who first landed in New England with tall masts for their ships. Its clean, white grain darkens exquisitely —making the famous fragrant pine paneling of colonial houses. White pine's silhouette is magnificent—a wide, solidly-anchored trunk sends out massive branches at right angles that are nicely graduated with the longest branches at the bottom, tapering with shorter branches to the top, giving the tree a rugged, triangular silhouette. Although most of the colonial monarchs are gone, except for a few solitary old field pines, white pine is very young at heart. It seeds rapidly and will quickly reforest an open field.

You will see from this list that my native land is in the Great American Woods in this book—the Eastern states and New England. Readers who live in the other six regions of tree discovery will have entirely different choices for their five favorite trees. It is a unique and glorious fact that American trees are dramatically different in each of the seven regions of tree discovery.

Trees exert various influences over the lives of the people living in those regions. What would our Northeastern states be like without maple, oak, elm, hickory, and dogwood? The South without palm trees, live oak, and magnolia? The desert needs saguaro and joshua tree to make people happy. Can you imagine California without sequoia, eucalyptus, and Monterey cypress? The dark forest of Douglas fir and Englemann spruce in the Northwest is a rugged symbol of the granduer and pride of America. There is nothing monotonous about trees.

Now you play the game. *What are your five favorite trees?*

TEST YOUR TREE KNOWLEDGE

What trees have funny faces? (page 26 and 30) What tree makes a good barbed wire fence? (page 111) What tree shoots out its seeds from a little howitzer? (page 65) What kind of pine tree has seeds good to eat? (page 225) What is the right way to tap a maple tree for maple sugar? (page 21) Why does bald cypress have knees? (page 122) What are the best trees for city streets? (page 87)

What tree has more peculiar surprises than any other tree of our land? (page 125) What is hickory tree's defense against squirrels? (page 31) What pine tree has *needles* up to 18 inches long? (page 135) What pine tree has *cones* up to 20 inches long? (page 164) What tree has leaves that make fine valentines? (page 73)

What tree has seeds like little canoe paddles? (page 42) What two trees have leaves with three different shapes? (page 64 and 91) What tree has a horizontal, instead of a vertical, trunk? (page 168) What tree in Alaska looks like a collapsed tent? (page 174) Why does trembling aspen shake its leaves? (page 58) What tree has upside-down leaves? (page 96)

What tree has bark that falls off in the shapes of whimsical little animals? (page 166) What tree has very poisonous sap? (page 148) What tree has the most delicious fragrance? (page 104) What tree has twigs with a bad odor? (page 102) What tree gave its name to a State? (page 71) What tree is a good one for a Park Commissioner to know about? (page 78) What tree has the biggest leaves of any any tree in the U.S.A.? (page 79)

THE SEVEN REGIONS OF TREE DISCOVERY

The trees of each of these regions are wonderfully different. This is one of the glories of our country.

Three stars before the name of a tree indicate that it is one of the fourteen keynote trees of the Great American Woods. Two stars and one star are used for the most outstanding trees in the areas where they grow.

THE OAKS

In landscaping the world, nature has used more kinds of oak than any other tree. All have acorns, and since no other tree produces this peculiar style of fruit, the acorn is the sure sign of an oak. All acorns have the cup and nut design, yet each is so different that it tells you at a glance what kind of oak it came from. This is seen in the depth of the cup—whether it is a shallow saucer, covers half of the nut, or all but encases the nut that peeks out at the top. The texture of the cup may be rough, spiney, or with smooth scales neatly overlapping. The nut may taper, be rounded, or be long and cylindrical. Color ranges from bright tan to rich mahogany, often seemingly varnished or waxed. The acorn is a masterpiece of finish, as well as a tough and efficient unit for reproduction.

The leaf of the white oak is so well known that people do not realize there are other entirely different shapes of oak leaves. Indeed, it takes mental effort for northerners visiting the South to look upon live oak and laurel oak with their smooth, evergreen, oval leaves as being true oaks at all. The familiar oak leaf deserves its fame. It is like looking from an airplane at an exciting coast with bays and fjords between long peninsulas. Shore lines are fluid; so are the margins of oak leaves. No two are precisely alike, for their deep bays and peninsulas have infinite variety.

The sovereign of the Great American Woods has perfected a body to live in cold or hot, wet or dry, stony place or loam—you see an oak almost everywhere you go. Oak is a positive tree, solidly engineered. Its beauty lies in health and strength, in the simplicity and quality of details.

Distinction goes right to the heart of oak. Its wood is recognizable even to people who pay little heed to the marvelous beauty of wood graining. This is due to vivid markings that swish through the wood, with an eccentric streaming scarcely described by the words "the grain of quartered oak." Their pattern is like that of the aurora borealis when broad glowing festoons of vertical lines dip and sway across the sky. These marks are rays, a feature of wood grain missing from pine. Oak rays are silvery ribbons, set vertically in the wood. They run like the spokes of a wheel from the center of the trunk to the bark. In a cross-cut stump, they form radiating straight lines. Silvery oak rays vary in width at every point, from a half-inch to five inches.

Oaks divide into two groups, the white oaks and the black oaks. It is an interesting sidelight on the mystery of trees that those of our white oak group will not live in Europe when planted there; those of our black oak group live in Europe with vigor. Your first step to enjoy oaks is to see which group your oak belongs to. The following oaks are found in the Great American Woods. See other oaks of the South, Middle West, and West.

WHITE OAK GROUP

Tips of leaf lobes are rounded and smooth, they do not come to a sharp point; and they lack a tiny bristle that black oaks have. Buds are blunt and, like all oaks, are crowded together at the end of their twig. You find few acorns, because they ripen and fall off in one season, and small animals make off with them quickly. Acorns of the White Oak Group are fairly good to eat when roasted. They were an important food of Indians, but we are more fastidious, and let hogs grow fat on them.

You are most likely to see the following white oaks:

★★★**White Oak** takes the least effort to see as it grows from Maine to Texas, and the least effort to call by name, as the bark is the lightest gray of any of the oaks. The white oak acorn is smooth and rounded at the tip like your little finger. You'll discover that same finger form also in the lobes of the white oak leaf. The light gray of the bark is reproduced on the cup of this handsome acorn. Such correspondence of the tints and shapes of different parts of a tree has no botanical importance but it does suggest what we might call a decorator's touch.

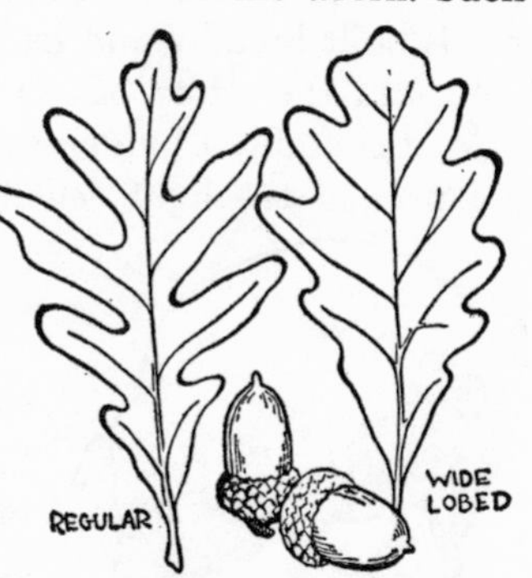

The wide lobe is frequent around New York City.

People seldom see a perfect white oak acorn (if you find one, you're entitled to be excited). They grow and fall off in a few months and break up rapidly, to vanish into the soil, returning the loan of nourishment which the tree borrowed from the ground and packed into them. This disappearance is assisted by blue jays, crows, squirrels, mice, who find the white oak acorn meat sweet, and eat or hide the acorns as soon as they fall. Another reason for acorn scarcity is that it takes some 50 years for this tree to mature and bear acorns.

Everyone who thinks when he looks can see that trees come in two styles. Trees with needles (usually evergreen) and trees with broad leaves (usually dropping in winter). If the broad-leafed race elected an elder statesman, the white oak should win. It has all the best qualities that we associate with trees. It forms clean woods without black shadows but luminous with filtered sunlight. In these woods the white oak bole reaches high to get its leaves up to unobstructed sunshine.

In the open field the white oak takes an entirely different form. The trunk is short and heavy, solidly engineered to support mighty, horizontal limbs. Thus the tree is built broadly and looks as a monarch tree should look. And the white oak is not only majestic on a big scale, it contains a hidden star. Cut a twig cleanly across and peer at the light center of the wood which is the pith. This cross section is not round but star-shaped.

Put the white oak on your calendar for mid-spring when the sun is bright, and see in a brief space of two or three days a color effect that is unparalleled among trees. The tiny, opening leaves are a blend of bright pink and silver hairs. The twigs sprout tassels, three to six inches long, that are creamy green. These tassels, tinting the tree with gauzy chartreuse, are the male flowers.

Pioneers looked for the white oak as indicating the best place to build their homes, for its roots go deep and it enjoys rich soil. They followed its advice also in planting corn, knowing that the last frost is over when the pink and silver leaves are the size of the ear of a mouse.

As it's both strong and beautiful, there are more uses for white oak wood than any other timber in the world. It's built into ships, trestles and ties; the oldest whiskey is matured in charred white oak barrels; plank oak floors, paneling, and furniture reveal beautiful graining when they are polished. *Quercus alba*

The next three trees give you a chance to make some real tree discoveries, and there's definite pride in knowing these when most people don't. All three belong to the White Oak Group, and that is why they are often confused with the white oak described above.

First, get the "feel" of the kind of a spot they grow in. For example, post oak likes the edge of woods, where it's sandy, gravelly, sunny, hot. Chestnut oak (not to be confused with chestnut) likes cool, shadowy ravines, steep rocky places. Swamp white oak likes low wet places.

Post Oak presents an eye-catching leaf with three big squarish lobes like a Maltese cross at the top. The wonder of such a leaf is the way it suggests the shapes of interesting things. Hold it one way—you have a violoncello. The other way it's a dancing doll with big sleeves. This tree's strong wood used to be used for fence posts, but oak lumber is too valuable today. Most of the 600 million fence posts in our country are now red cedar, cypress, black locust. Red hairs grow on under surface of leaf in minute star-shapes, but this takes a lens to see. Post oak gets more common toward the Southwest–abundant in eastern Texas.

Quercus stellata (means star after hairs on leaf)

Chestnut Oak is the big, tough-looking tree with bark in heavy ridges. At the bottom of the furrows between ridges, bark is cinnamon-red. Chestnut oak has largest acorns known on oaks –1½ inches or even 2 inches. This is the acorn to roast and eat. It's the sweetest of all the northern oaks. Look for orange-brown twigs that are not round but angled in an interesting way. Name comes from resemblance to chestnut leaves–large ovals with wavy edges; one of the most beautiful of oak leaves.

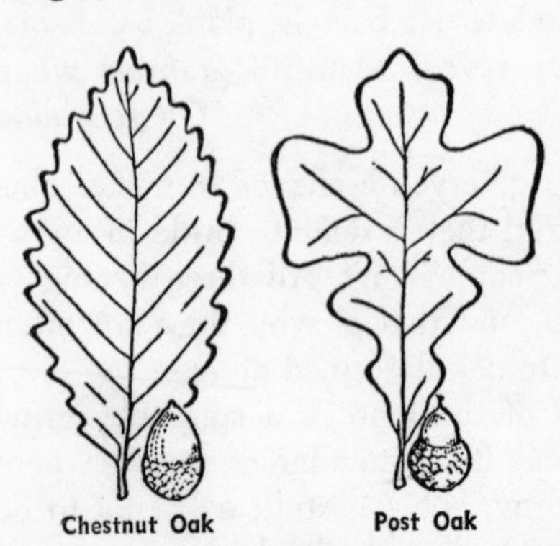

Quercus montana (means mountain, grows high)

Swamp White Oak is the shaggy tree with long-reaching, ungainly limbs. Its bark is loose and sheds in little pieces. Stand off and see the form of this tree. Below the main limbs of the crown there are crooked, down-turned branches covered with leaves throughout their length. These with their bark help to give the shaggy look. Leaf is kite-shaped, wavy around the top like chestnut oak, wedge-shaped near the base like the white oak.

Quercus bicolor

BLACK OAK GROUP

Leaves have sharp angles, lobes are sharp-tipped, bear a tiny bristle. Buds, too, are sharp. You find plenty of acorns because they take two years to ripen, so some always hang on tree. If you see two sizes on same tree, little ones are first year's, big ones are second year's about to fall off. Acorns are bitter, lie around on ground, and slowly disintegrate.

Telling black oaks apart starts you on the path of really seeing trees. All have dark nondescript bark; all have bristle-tipped, sharp-angled leaves; all are good-sized trees. Black oak's inner bark is yellow color; other points of difference between these four are comparative and not so positive. But try it out and catch the feel; you'll have a sense of fresh discovery!

Wood is not so strong, redder in color than white oaks, and markings of grain are not so vivid.

You are most likely to see the following black oaks:

Swamp White Oak

★**Red Oak** is the oak you encounter most often in the Great American Woods. It is the leader of the four horsemen of the Black Oak Group; other three are black, scarlet, and pin.

Note vertical light strips in the bark of red oak, especially on the upper part of the trunk. These are smooth as though someone had ironed them carelessly lengthwise. The whitish appearance is an optical illusion due to reflection of sky light from the semi-glossy surface. Leaves are dull, dark green, and midrib (that's the big vein in the middle) is often red; underside is smooth—not scurfy or hairy like black oak. Quarter-inch buds are reddish-brown, smooth. Twig is likely to be ridged. Red oak acorns lie around on ground. Handsome, one-inch, oblong nut with white meat (bitter to taste) and shallow saucer at base.

Red oak grows fast (a foot or more in height, an inch wide tree ring per year). Wood is so porous you can blow soap bubbles with a stick of it. Boston's parkway system shows what a clean street tree it makes. Around New York this is the commonest oak of the woods.

Quercus borealis

Black Oak is a specific member of the black oak group. This is confusing. Think of it here as *the* black oak. It should be called yellow oak because penknife through black outer bark shows yellow inner bark for quick identification. Lining of acorn cup is bright yellow. Acorn meat is yellow, and so bitter that animals spurn it. Leaves are wider toward top, and broadly pear-shaped compared to its brother red oak whose leaves are wider in middle and outline is oval. Buds are grayish, hairy, and angled. These ridged buds are an interesting point that takes close observation, but easy to see if you look for it.

Beautiful colorful effect is crimson of black oak's unfolding leaves in spring—rich red, soft, hairy, with droplets of sparkling sap. The bright yellow encountered in this tree is valuable tannin—a chemical used for tanning leather.

Quercus velutina (means velvety, refers to gray hairiness of buds)

Pin Oak is the trim, straight shade tree used in suburbs, parks, towns more often than any other oak. One sign of pin oak is the mass of down-turned branches—sometimes touching the ground. However, these may be pruned off by alert park department. It has a staccato accent with sharp, pin-like twig pattern, and deeply cut, angular leaves. Smaller than other oaks—buds are tiny, ⅛ inch, angled and sharp, leaves and acorns little and finely sculptured. Name comes from its tough pin-like twigs used as wooden pegs instead of nails in square timbers of old barns. *Quercus palustris*

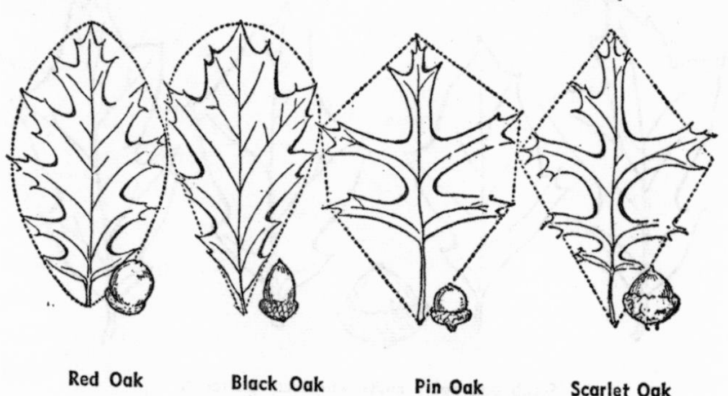

Scarlet Oak can vie with any other tree when it unveils richest red of the fall. Holds its leaves longer than maples, and color is deeper, richer, but not so flaming. Between New York and Atlantic City in October people are dazzled by scarlet oaks. Also seen through Middle West, but not in Appalachian Mountains. Otherwise tree is easily confused with pin oak, having similar deeply cut, angular leaves. Lacks pin-like twigs of pin oak. Leaves, buds are larger. Inner bark is pinkish. *Quercus coccinea*

Scrub Oak is ignored by lumbermen but not by people who enjoy the crooked, picturesque oaks of gravelly, rocky places and hilltops. Leaves come in so many shapes a single tree gives you enough eccentric symmetry to fill your sketch book. In fall these leaves produce a motley of reds and yellows. There's nothing like the leaf whimsies and crooked-twig enchantment of this tree.

Quercus ilicifolia

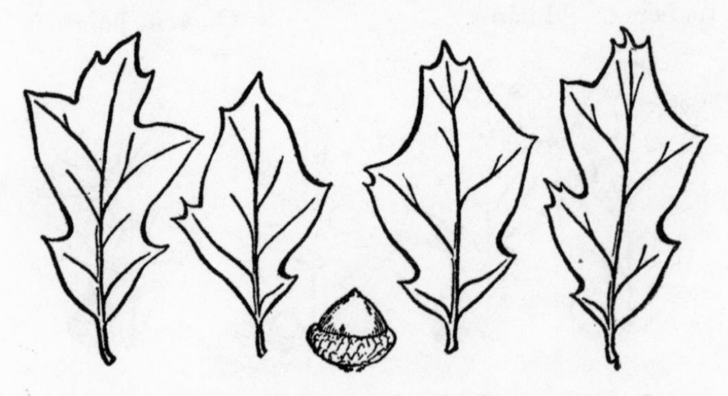

Scrub oak bears many whimsical patterns.

THE MAPLES

If you would see perfection, go look at the maple. It is like truth made into the form of a tree. From over-all proportion to the smallest detail every part fits together in perfect balance. This gives that quality of an organism known as health. Out of air and water the living cell has created seed wings for the maple like those of a soaring bird. It has endowed the wood with whirlings and ripplings like light upon the surface of water. Above all, maples have fitness and strength. This is the quality of our land. Sugar maple is distinctly American; it will not grow in England. It must have pure, fresh air; it is not a city tree. Sugar maple is the insignia of a Vermont hillside, where it blends into the New England scene along with a man-made barn softened by rain and moss. Red maple is the breath of a bog and the frame of a pond, a consonance not so perfect anywhere else in the world.

Know the maples, one from another. In a lifetime you will perhaps see only half a dozen. All bear the family expression in the pattern of their leaves. All have inherited the two-winged seed idea which, like opening scissor blades, takes different angles in the different kinds of maples.

It is symmetrical because every detail grows in duplicate. When it puts forth a bud, this is matched by a twin bud on exactly the opposite side of the twig. This leads to branch opposite branch, leaf opposite leaf. This plan of growth is found also in seed and leaf patterns, where angles and curves of one side seem to be reflected like mirror images on the opposite side.

You will find the three leading American maples—sugar, red, and silver, everywhere from Maine to Texas, and often more numerous than any other hardwood. In suburban parks and along streets maples are the most planted of any kind of tree. These are your trees, enjoy them.

(See also box elder under Middle West).

***Sugar Maple** is most successful tree, and contender for the title of the most beautiful tree in the world. Its wood is bright and polishes attractively to make furniture with an aura all its own. This tree forms a practically perfect oval. Its fruit has the grace and streamlining of the wing of an airplane.

Its fall colors rival the highest color keys of the sunset. Its leaf is a geometric masterpiece.

The Great American Woods is decorated throughout with maple leaves. Two kinds of maple march side by side, sugar and red. Both are so abundant that you can always find the two kinds of leaves within a few steps to hold and compare. The sugar has five lobes that point out, widespreading. Angles between lobes are rounded.

Collecting maple syrup

Now compare that leaf with the red maple. This usually has three lobes that point forward, making the leaf narrower. The edges are not so smooth but have more teeth. The angle between the lobes is sharp. In brief, if the angle forms a U, it's a sugar; if it forms a V, it's a red.

In the early spring when the snow may still be on the ground, and the sun is warm on the bark by day while the nights are below freezing, the sugar maple can be tapped for sugar sap. Boiling it down we get the grand American maple syrup and maple sugar. The pipe that taps the sap is driven into the trunk four feet above the ground, and, by expansion under sunlight and contraction during cold nights, the wood acts as a pump!

Sugar maple is queen of firewoods, doesn't throw out sparks. Keeps burning cheerily and makes fine, clean, white ashes, delightful smell, and flame has pretty play of colors. *Acer saccharum*

★**Red Maple** is the tree to know if you were condemned to know but a single tree. Most red maples are medium

Sugar Maple

Red Maple

sized, intimate—you can reach the branches. Hold the tip of a growing twig (do not tear it off) and see the buds. They are rich, smooth, crimson. The flower buds are bunched around twigs, fat, prominent—their red, gold, orange sparkling with sap when starting to open is a sight you would want to go half way around the world to see. This happens early, same time as pussy willows. Leaves are light green on top, whitish below, making sharp V in the angle between the lobes. The pale undersides give the flash of white over a tree when a sudden breeze turns up the leaves. At all times of year this tree shows red somewhere. Leaf stem is bright red. Fall colors are red and yellow. Flowers in spring are gauzy red, and this when seen against a deep blue sky is a color combination you'll marvel at.

Straight, quick-growing, easy-to-transplant red maple makes a fine street tree where there is moisture. Bark is clean, light gray in upper part of trunk and main limbs—often so smooth and light it can be mistaken for beech. The unique wood grains known as birds-eye maple or curly maple are sometimes hidden in this tree. These are not evident from outward appearances, but who would cut down his red maple to find out? *Acer rubrum*

Silver Maple is well named after the bright silver underside of its leaves. These are fancy, decorative. Lobes are long, sharply toothed, cut in almost to center of leaf. This tree has big, conspicuous clusters of plump flower buds that make twigs in winter look as though something were the matter with them. Silver maples bloom earliest of any tree. Seed wings are big, wide-spread like those of a floating seagull. Trunk divides into long, curving limbs, slightly resembling elm. Many silver maples were sold to last generation by nurserymen who recommended speed of growth; therefore, you see them around older houses. But silver maple is brittle and wind tears them apart through the years. Silver and red maples are known as soft maples.

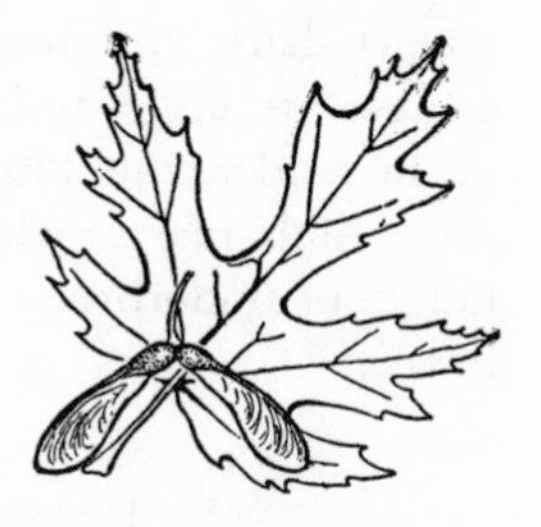

Silver Maple

Acer saccharinum

Black Maple is a version of sugar maple with small, dark leaves suggesting sketches of sugar maple leaves simplified, with clean, straight edges, no fancy teeth. These leaves tend to droop and curl. Often seen around towns in South Dakota and Iowa, and many around Philadelphia.

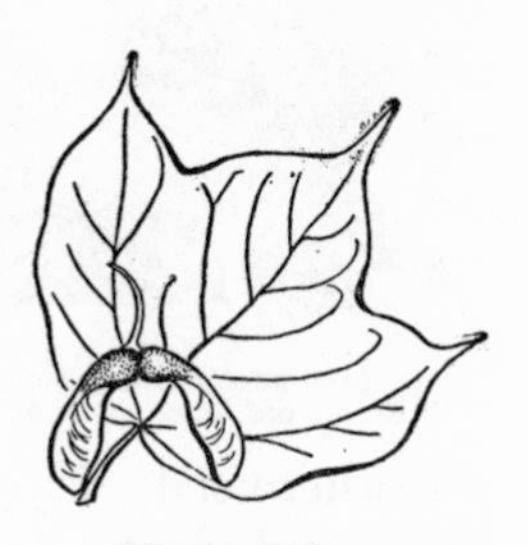

Black Maple

Acer nigrum

★**Moosewood** is a revelation of interesting bark. On twigs and branches this is semi-glossy, exactly the color and texture of a green olive, marked with white lines, as though someone had stroked it with a piece of chalk. This bark is alive, and that fact keeps it satin smooth. Outside bark on most trees is dead, breaks into corky surface when rent by expanding wood, or outer layer of dead skin peals off, as on birches. Moosewood's juicy sugary bark and buds are eaten by deer and moose. Leaves are large, rounded like a deep bowl. This tree is of the wild woods, along mountain streams, in cool, shadowy, high places where you may think there's only a tangle of underbrush. It's worth climbing a wooded hill to see. *Acer pensylvanicum*

Both pheasant and Mountain Maple are found in shady woods.

Mountain Maple is easily taken for a young red maple, but leaves are rougher, darker, rounder. Bark is red-brown, twigs are hairy. Often the dominant tree of the mountain underbrush where ruffed grouse finds cover. Found side by side with moosewood, these two little maples have probably made more mountain hikers in eastern states sopping wet after a rain than any other woodland plant. *Acer spicatum*

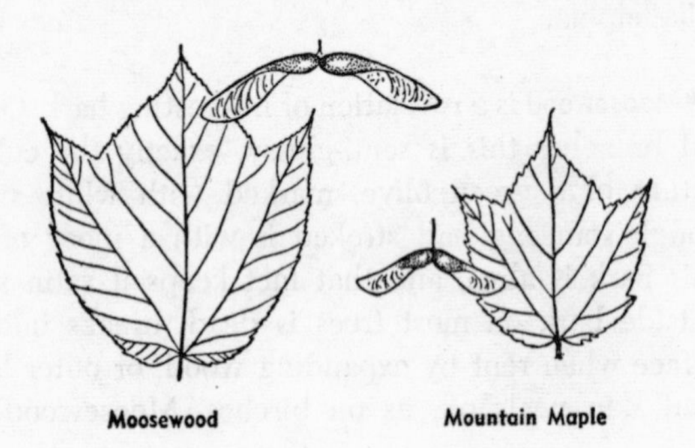

You will often see the following maples on lawns and residential streets:

Norway Maple's leaf is nearly the same shape and size as sugar maple's, and has the same rounded angle between lobes, but underside is dark, glossy green, not dull whitish. Another difference is milky sap in leaf stem. Casts deep shade—it's hard to grow grass under this tree.
Acer platanoides

Schwedler Maple—a version of Norway maple with leaves bronze-red in spring. Popular tree around Minneapolis. Fine row in Brooklyn Botanic Garden.
Acer schwedleri

Sycamore Maple is the sycamore of Europe. Marvelous styling of maple leaf. Just stare at its full-rounded, heavily toothed lobes. *Acer pseudo-platanus*

Japanese Cutleaf Maple is the tiny, wine-red little maple with fancy, deeply cut leaves extended like fingers of a child's hand. *Acer japonicum*

Sycamore Maple

Japanese Maple

THE ELMS

★★★**American Elm** is America's most vivid tree. Here is a superb diagram of the way trees can be fluid fountains. Air and water united by light rush upward out of the dark earth, throwing out branches like a skyrocket sparkling with green leaves against the sky. The most characteristic form of the American elm is that of a column of water mounting with tremendous force. At about one-third of its height the column splits into several branches that arch outward gradually as they mount, until at the crest they dome upward as the thrust is lost to gravity and then pour earthward at the point where the spray vanishes. When man erects a fine fountain at great expense, people come to wonder at it. Nature has distributed these elegant tree fountains all over the eastern half of the United States, and people have not been blind to this either, because elm, purely for its beauty, has been planted along the streets and around the squares of towns more than any other tree. It is the keynote of many New England villages—the tall, steep curves of the branches meeting high above the street as over the nave of a cathedral.

Face under Elm bud (enlarged) is a sleepy one.

Strangely, there are no natural groves purely of elms. They mingle with bushes and other trees in woods and hedgerows. In eastern states elm is the commonest tree seen. It survives better than most trees where man disturbs the countryside. This is partly because its wood is not one of the big demand timbers of the sawmill, and partly because people love the elm as it flourishes in open field, meadow or street as well as in the woods.

American Elm

If calling a tree by name were all there is to knowing it, no more need be said about the elm. But due to its popularity as a tree-fountain, most people overlook details that are unique and fun to see.

Elm leaf is an example of off-center symmetry. It is lopsided at the base, from which the blade curves, forming the segment of a spiral shell. This is the same curve as that of the graceful limbs on which they are borne. Elm leaf has double teeth; it is rough to the touch, and dark blue-green compared to the brighter leaf-green of other trees.

The eccentric swing of the leaf is repeated in the bud. This is tipped to one side, above an oval mark in the twig bark that has the features of a face winking at you. Bud and face look like a rakish fellow wearing a hat.

The twig on which this whimsy is set, although slender and often pendant like a string, is zig-zag. This is because the elm produces no bud squarely at the end of the twig to give it a forward thrust. Therefore, the twig must elongate at an angle—first on one side, then on other side, from successive buds. *Ulmus americana*

The American elm is so much a part of our country's landscape wherever trees are enjoyed east of the Rockies that there is consternation at the possibility of losing them. The Dutch elm disease fungus attacks through a broken or decayed place. Leaves wilt, drop off. Tree should be cut down and burned. This malady, confined for many years to area around New York, is spreading today. More swiftly destructive is bark disease caused by a virus now killing many fine old elms in Middle West and South. Hope that this can be controlled before this tree disappears from our lives like the chestnut is based on recent discovery that virus is spread by leaf-hopping insect.

No other kind of elm has the form and elegance of the American, so, although others may resist the disease, they are not substitutes. Each of the following four elms has individual characteristics that are unusual and interesting to know about.

Slippery Elm can be spotted in winter by twigs and buds with iridescent red hairs. In spring bark slips when you touch it. Inner bark is gummy, good to taste, nutritious. Slippery substance is used in cough drops to soothe the throat. You can't break a twig with a snap because slippery bark is flexible, tough. Leaf is bigger, rougher, than American elm, although tree is smaller. Rub your hand over leaf; it is rough both ways, while American elm leaf is rough one way, smooth the other. *Ulmus fulva*

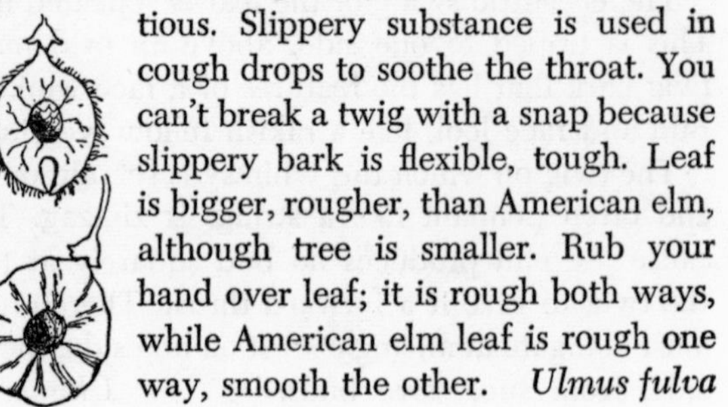
Above—American Elm seed

Below—Slippery Elm seed

Rock Elm (also called cork elm) has form like a hickory with trunk continuous from base to top, contrasted to American elm that divides trunk into several big limbs. Branches are shaggy with thick, irregular corky ridges like those on sweet gum. This tree gets its name from hardness of wood (better wood than other elms). It has interlocking fibers, hard to split, makes mallets and wheel hubs. Seen most in Michigan, Minnesota, and around Great Lakes. *Ulmus thomasi*

English Elm has heavy trunk and limbs that go out at right angles, like an oak in weight and character. This is Europe's common elm. You see it in older parks such as Gramercy Park, New York, and there are some fine ones on Boston Common. *Ulmus campestris*

Siberian Elm (close relative of Chinese elm) is one of the fastest growing trees in the United States. Trunk swells an inch a year, height increases some three feet a year. Small leaves cast gay, mottled shade. Tree's chief defect is brittleness of branches. Provides shade in hot, dry places where other trees are scrawny, and is most widely used street and shade tree in cities and towns along U.S. Highway 81, from Texas to South Dakota. Also main windbreak trees planted by U. S. Forest Service on Great Plains. *Ulmus pumila*

THE NUT TREES

The good wood of our nut trees has been felt by more American hands than any other wood. Rich, chocolate-brown gunstocks are black walnut. Axe handles are hickory. Such wood stands sudden shock with a peculiar twang of elasticity. It never warps or bends from alignment. It is smooth, splinterless, good to feel.

The nut tells its tree as clearly as the acorn tells an oak and the two-winged seed a maple. Both walnut and hickory have the hard-shelled seed encased in a tough husk. The kernel packs food value measured in protein and calories surpassing anything else that grows on wild trees of our woods. Ounce for ounce black walnut has eight times the protein of milk; hickory nuts four times. This delicious food keeps raining down, and the man who keeps his trees reaps their harvests, whereas the man who makes a gunstock or axe handle of his no longer has such crops. But it takes energy and patience to crack nuts and pick out the kernels, and in a packaged food era we miss the healthy fun of nutting that used to be as great a feature of the fall season as gathering pumpkins.

Butternut (left) and Mockernut faces (enlarged)

A small surprise awaits you here. Nut trees have funny faces. These are best seen in winter. Take in hand a twig and look closely below any bud. Impressed in the bark you'll see the tiny face of a horse or camel. On walnuts these faces are clear, neat, with pads of hair like well-clipped forelocks. On hickories the faces are larger, with elongated noses, often lopsided and eccentric. The funny faces tell you what tree it is by their expressions, the way you know people.

***Shagbark Hickory** (also called shellbark) is the tree you have to go out into the country to find. It does not like impure air, and it cannot be hurried, so you seldom find it in the city. In the field or on the hillside it grows slowly, solidly, where it can put roots deep into nutritious soil conditioned naturally by time. It is the companion of white oak, and like that tree it was a sign of a good place for pioneer settlers to build their homes and plant crops.

No other tree has bark like this well-named tree. You'll know a mature shagbark instantly when you see a strong, tall trunk whose bark is loosened so that long, hard, gray

Shagbark Hickory

strips warp out like shingles that have become unnailed on an old house. These strips are all lengths, even up to four feet, and may be loose both top and bottom. Despite its hardness, this peculiar bark is not brittle but elastic. A strip that appears to be on the point of dropping off the tree may hang on for years. If a house were to become loose like this, it would promptly be a shambles, but nature has put no nails or bolts into the shagbark to rust, and this marvelously weatherproof bark builds a picturesque tree that will long outlive the men around it. This feature of a tree whose nuts are so sweet protects its chance for survival. A squirrel, who would not hesitate to strip it clean of nuts, encounters this series of abattis that makes it difficult to run up the trunk.

Elasticity is also a feature of the tough wood; therefore, hickory does not make such good paneling and furniture as maple or pine, which have to be formed, but is used chiefly as axe handles, plows, barrel staves, athletic equipment including baseball bats. You can hear this beautiful wood ring true when you bounce a hickory bat on a rock. Best of all fire logs, shagbark is the king wood for heat. It is long burning, sparkless, with clean ash and beautiful flame.

This tree does not shag its bark until it bears nuts, after forty years. You can tell a young shagbark from the older ones by its leaf with only five leaflets, and its hard gray bark. In winter it has an oval bud of buff suede, and the tree detective will peer closely to see that the scales around this bud have sharp projections at their tips—a sure sign of shagbark. *Carya ovata*

The **Big Shellbark** or **Kingnut** is a version of shagbark found west of the Alleghenies; it is a larger tree with a bigger nut. This tree is so distinctive that by the time it reaches the Middle West it may have leaves almost two feet long and bear huge nuts. *Carya laciniosa*

Pignut is a fine hickory with an unfortunate name. Common in northern states, it escapes attention because bark is not exciting like shagbark. Smooth to touch—smooth leaves and twigs, small round bud on twig tip; even bark is smoothish. Splendid hickory wood; one of three used for scythe and axe handles, baseball bats, and wherever good hickory is used. In order of excellence the best tool handle hickories are shagbark, pignut, and mockernut. Nut is pearshaped, like a little fig; smooth, thin shell, edible but sometimes bitter.

Carya glabra

Pignut Hickory

Mockernut grows in northern states as fine tree with shagbark and pignut. Its wood also makes tool handles. But mockernut has several remarkable points of difference. Big, round bud on twig tip is silky gray suede, has remarkably artistic texture and soft tint. Leaves and twigs are aromatic, delightfully fragrant. Nut is big and inviting. This gives tree its name as shell is mighty and contains slight amount of meat to disentangle; utterly disappointing. Someone with sense of humor named tree. This hickory, stepping down from New England hills, adopts small, scrubby form, becomes part of tangle back of south Atlantic sand dunes with holly and live oak. A strange place to find hickory. *Carya alba*

Bitternut has sulphur yellow bud on twig tips; slender, curved like a scythe blade, sparkling with amber dots. This bud is naked; that is, without covering scales; you can see the tiny folds of the leaf. Bitternut is a stately shade tree, transplants well, grows faster than other hickories. Nuts are so bitter even squirrels spurn them. Wood is poor hickory but good for smoking hams. Often in moist ground in New England, and this is the commonest hickory in Iowa, Kansas, Nebraska. *Carya cordiformis*

Bitternut Hickory

Pecan produces the only million dollar crop from our wild trees. It comes so excellent in nature that man is stimulated to select best trees for breeding, which today goes ahead creating bigger nuts, thinner shells, more delicate flavor. In woods of Georgia, Alabama, Texas, pecan trees soar above 100 feet. Many of them are seen planted in the Middle West and southward, around older plantations. Branches are very long; when not pruned lower ones slope down, giving peculiar reaching-down aspect to tree. Value is in the nut crop; wood is poor but smokes good hams, as does mockernut. *Carya pecan*

BLACK WALNUT

★★★**Black Walnut** is as American as the Indian. But among our big, valuable hardwoods it is the one which surprisingly few people can call by name, because neither bark nor leaf nor outline spell black walnut in bold letters. So this is a good place to discover some not so obvious details that arouse wonder and interest in the reading of a tree.

The surest token is the nut. This can be seen on the tree at the end of summer when black walnut leaves drop off ahead of all other leaves. Then for a couple of weeks black walnut has a peculiar sort of conspicuousness. It stands out stark and leafless when other trees are fully in leaf or turning brilliant colors. The tall dome of branches is studded with the big, round nuts black against the sky.

Leaves are multiple and stand apart on long limbs that reach far out from the main trunk. Sunlight filters through, so that shadows of black walnut have the texture of mottled sunlight, compared to dense shadows cast by maples. The light green of walnut foliage contrasts sharply with the black bark of the long limbs, gives black walnut an accent all its own.

Black Walnut leaf

A sure sign of black walnut is the pith. Slice a twig and see the light brown cross-partitions like ties of a railroad track. Butternut has a similar peculiar pith, but partitions are heavier, closer, and dark brown.

Nuts are unique and frustrating. Husk stains hands brown but is delightfully fragrant. Nut shell has metallic hardness; when shattered with hammer the kernel is found hidden in a labyrinth. But flavor is like no other food in the world, and because it's not lost with cooking, makes good ice cream, candy, cake. Picking out kernels is a home industry in eastern Tennessee where this wild tree-crop is at its best. There's little black walnut to be seen in New England, plenty in the Middle West.

Juglans nigra

★**Butternut** (also called white walnut) has the face of a solemn camel with a downy brow below each bud. An amusing and sure way to know the tree. Butternut grows singly in rich hillside pastures and along roads in New England, central New York State. It's a small version of black walnut, with light, feathery leaves and black branches. An intimate tree compared to the giant black walnut. You can reach its lower branches to see the faces and hairy twigs, and smell leaf fragrance. Nut is small oval with husk covered with red, sticky hairs. Ironbound meat comes out in crumbs, but these are deliciously oily. Too bad butternut kernels are so meager, hard to extract; they have the highest food value of any of our nuts. Name white walnut refers to the clean, white wood.

Juglans cinerea

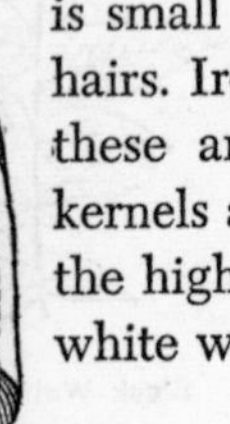

Chambered pith of Butternut twig

English Walnut provides the round, rumpled nuts in your nut bowl. Shells are so thin you can break them with your hands. It should be possible to breed our black walnut with such a shell. The original English walnuts had hard, thick shells, tiny kernels; for centuries men selected best trees in Persia, Spain, Japan—see the resulting walnuts we have today. English walnut picked up its name merely by coming to us via England—it should be called Persian walnut. A fine walnut tree with a nut crop worth millions of dollars. You often see it planted; people are proud of their English walnuts. Big orchards in southern California. See page 222. *Juglans regia*

Chestnut has a long oval leaf with waving scallops tipped with bristles that point forward. It is a masterpiece of rhythm and proportion. The middle vein runs precisely through the center of the leaf, and side veins run parallel from mid-rib to bristles. You'll see lots of chestnut leaves on a walk through hilly Appalachian woods but they do not grow on a tree. They are shoots springing out of a big trunk where one of America's noblest trees used to grow. A bark disease destroyed the chestnuts with their superb wood and burs of good nuts. But they still struggle to live, and perhaps the next generation will see the sucker switches from old roots overcoming the deadly malady and turning into trees again. Meanwhile, enjoy the leaves as a bit of unsurpassed woodland art.

Castanea dentata

Chestnut leaf

***American Beech can always be recognized by its broad bole and strong limbs apparently made of aluminum. The bark is thin and alive so that it stretches as the tree grows, forming silvery smoothness on trunk and branches from top to bottom.

Beech is the brightest of the big trees, for not only does the bark have a silvery glow, but also the leaves are light, glossy green and, held in flat mosaic layers tipped toward the sun, reflect brightness of the sky. In winter these leaves cling on—crisp, shimmering, golden. On a clear winter's day when a bright sun is shining across the snow, beech offers an unforgettable spectacle. If you are an artist at heart, make a note right now not to miss this phenomenal effect of tints: silvery bark against crystal white snow, golden leaves against a blue sky.

Beech buds are unique. No other bud is so long (almost an inch) and so sharp (you can prick your finger). They're like tightly rolled spindles, made of rich tan leather, tooled with a crisscross design. Touch the twig to see these buds, and you discover a bit of the finest tree jewelry.

American Beech

Compare beech with white oak. They are members of the same family, yet bark, buds, and leaves are so different they are never confused. However, both trees tend to hold their leaves all winter, especially younger ones. Both trees are powerfully built—wide trunks in the open, tall pillars in the woods.

It's only a step in evolution from an acorn to a beechnut. Just imagine that beechnut's prickly husk is the cup of an acorn that in this case, encloses the whole unit. Inside this, two nuts are curiously shaped as sharp-angled triangles. These are sweet and edible, deliciously oily as though buttered, but people seldom get a chance to sample this titbit because squirrels, deer, bluejays get to them first.

Beechnut contains two delicious kernels.

The oil throughout a beech is reputed to resist electricity, and therefore a beech is struck by lightning far less often than other trees. *Fagus grandifolia*

Copper Beech, a variation of a European beech, is often seen in city parks. Leaves are glossy, copper-red, and, in reflecting light, give off red flashes in the sun. One of our most beautiful trees.

Fagus sylvatica var. atropunicea

Slender, pointed buds of American Beech

THE ASHES

Ash plays an active part in our everyday lives through tennis rackets, baseball bats, snowshoes, bushel baskets, butter tubs, and oars. Such clean, easily formed wood comes from healthy trees, a pride of our countryside. Because ash is mild and unsensational, it attracts less attention. The multiple leaves are like walnut or hickory. When these come in pairs, with leaf opposite leaf on the branch, it is a sure sign of ash. White ash is the most abundant; chances are that is the one you see, except in prairie states and westward where green ash abounds in the moist ground near streams or springs. Green ash is the State Tree of almost treeless North Dakota. The various kinds of ash have names as though tagged with colored ribbons.

★★★**White Ash** is the most anonymous of the Big Fourteen of the Great American Woods. It does not call out to you loudly as do trees with acorns, maple leaves, birch bark. But though ash speaks quietly, it speaks so clearly that this is the first tree you should discover and recognize beyond the obvious ones.

The parts of ash are so finely wrought that, separated from the tree, each is a thing of beauty in itself. Put together, these artistic details build a tree that wins first prize in tree architecture.

The trunk is utterly simple, lifting the tree upward out of the ground with the harmony of a temple column. This is unmarred by old knots or branches. Around this trunk ridges of bark form a diamond pattern like a woven basket. Ridges are flat on top as though a builder had used a plane to smooth them off a bit. Ash bark is so dark, almost black, in color that you may have to look twice to appreciate its remarkable pattern; it is rough and broken because the outside doesn't stretch but bursts as the trunk expands.

The most stylish of tree buds are more or less inconspicuous because they are not bright and colorful. However, very dark brown or black suede can be elegant, so look carefully. Lay hold of a winter branch, and see how buds grow exactly opposite each other along the twig. This ash twig is heavy and rigid compared to the slender, wiry twigs of the birches or the pendant strings of elm. This sturdy twig has tiny little dark blobs of buds in pairs, opposite each other. Let your fingers run along the smooth, graceful, slightly scalloped twig to the buds at the end. Here are three buds fitted tightly together: two small hemispheres hold in a bowl between them a small dome, capped with an abrupt point. This adornment has a slender crescent like a half-moon underneath, where a leaf stem was attached. The ef-

White Ash

fect is that of a handsome twig finished off at the tip with an architectural design of curves and terraces. Once you are familiar with these big twigs and their end buds, you can always tell an ash by them. Also, make a note to take a look in April just before the buds open and behold their rich suede studded with glistening amber.

Ash leaves are multiple. Leaflets are so large that, seen high up in the tree, they do not appear to be units of multiple leaves, but rather as the standard ovals of other trees such as birch or elm.

Most plants combine stamen and pistil (male and female) in one flower, but ash separates the sexes as do animals so that an individual ash tree produces either male or female flowers. It's like holly and poplar in this respect. Thus only the female trees bear seeds, single winged, compared to maple seeds that have two wings. Winged ash seeds are exquisitely graceful, like tiny canoe paddles. In fact, ash wood is so tough and elastic that it makes the best paddles, as well as tennis rackets, hoe and rake handles, bows and arrows. Ash wood burns while still green because sap is inflammable.

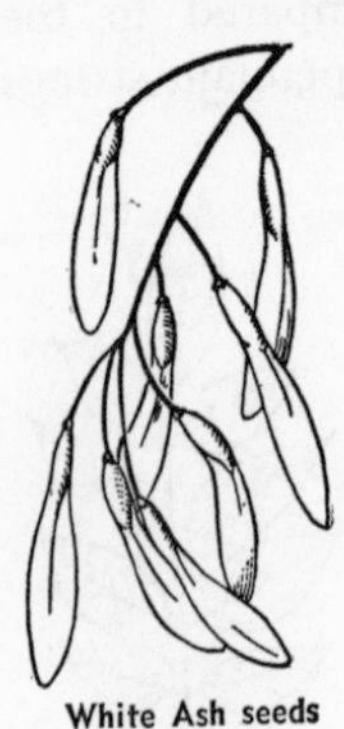
White Ash seeds resemble tiny canoe paddles.

Ash is a member of an aristocratic southern family, the Olives. It marched north with three colorful shrub members of the same family: privet, forsythia, and lilac. *Fraxinus americana*

Red Ash has curious details that give it its name. Buds are covered with dense red-brown velvet; also twigs and undersurfaces of leaves have red hairs. Inner bark of young branches is red. Grows separately in wetter places at the foot of the hills whereas white ash is up on hill-sides and in the upland woods with maple, beech, bass-wood. *Fraxinus pennsylvanica*

Green Ash is the western version of red ash. It differs in not having velvety hairs on buds, twigs, leaves. Under-side of white ash leaf is white; the underside of green ash is green. This is the ash everyone out West knows. It grows in shelter belts on prairies, and in the Far West in stream bottoms and on river banks of dry country. *Fraxinus lanceolata*

Blue Ash has 4-angled twigs. Look for this curiosity made by corky angles of bark. Sap turns blue in water. Tree is common in dry limestone places of Tennessee and Kentucky and around lower Ohio valley. *Fraxinus quadrangulata*

Black Ash is one of the slenderest of woods trees, stretching high with small trunk diameter. Buds are jet black. It is most northern of ashes, abundant in swampy ground in northern New England and New York. Wood is tougher, more elastic than other ashes. After soaking wood, if you bend and pound it, the annual rings sep-arate; make flexible slats for weaving pack basket. *Fraxinus nigra*

SYCAMORE

★★★**Sycamore** (also called plane tree or buttonwood) is the old giant. You know it at a glance by the white, purple, and gray patchwork quilt of its bark. Upper trunk and lower part of limbs may be smooth, bright white all over. This dramatic bark has unforgettable splendor. On a clear winter day, when lighted by brightness from snow, it is like nothing else in treedom. (For colorful, mottled bark see also eucalyptus and madrone.) Sycamore grows only the inner layer of its bark every year. This living bark becomes white on exposure to the sun, and the bark of previous years, not growing and therefore not expanding to fit around the bigger trunk, is forced off the tree in patches. In effect, the tree is bursting its breeches. Varied tints are due to the number of years' exposure of the older layers before they fall off. Sunlight turns bark chemicals gold, brown, and blue-gray.

Sycamore

Sycamore contends with tulip tree for the title of biggest tree of the Great American Woods. In Indiana, headquarters state for sycamore, it comes 150 feet tall, with trunk 10 feet in diameter. Sycamores grow along stream banks in the Ohio River and lower Mississippi valleys in such abundance that seen from an airplane, the courses of streams are marked by lines of white trunks.

When looking at the bark effect in winter, you will notice one-inch balls of its fruit dangling on strings among the upper branches. This gives the tree one of its favorite names, buttonball. The true American sycamore, growing along streams of the countryside, has white patches and single balls. Other kinds, planted in cities, have two or more balls in clusters, and the patches are brown. See London Plane Tree page 89.

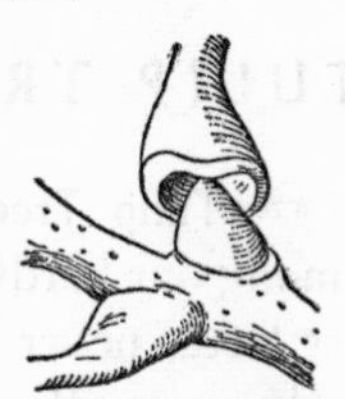

Sycamore leaf-stem fits over bud like candle-snuffer.

Sycamore leaves remind you of maple leaves but are larger and lobes are shallower. Most interesting fact about this leaf is the swollen end of its stem. Pull it off the twig and you'll see that this is a hollow cone that covers the winter bud as an old-fashioned snuffer covers a candle flame. This bud does not have overlapping scales like most buds; it's like a smooth, red-brown tam-o'-shanter. All the way round the base of the bud the twig is terraced where the leaf stem was attached.

Despite its greatness, sycamore does not grow symmetrically. To make its appearance even more ragged, this patriarch is torn by a fungus disease. It is the first of our hardwoods to grow on earth, having survived millions of years to attract us with its bark and balls. Zigzag branches are irregular and angular as though striking out from the huge trunk. The wood is hard to split, and it's clean, white, odorless and tasteless—fine for butchers' blocks. *Platanus occidentalis*

"Button ball" of Sycamore tree

TULIP TREE

★★★**Tulip Tree** is supreme for bigness and harmony among our hardwoods. Tulip tree grows among other forest trees, never forming pure cathedral-like groves that make sequoia so awesome. Thus people of eastern United States don't realize that they won't have to travel to the Pacific Coast to see one of the world's finest forest trees. Its trunk pours straight upward, uninterrupted by limbs, to a great height. Passing motorists can enjoy some of the biggest, spared by the axe, as features of parkways in eastern and middle western cities. In upper Manhattan are some old tulip trees occupying 100 square feet of the world's most expensive real estate.

In winter, tips of bare branches hold up broad champagne goblets, silhouetted high against the sky. Twigs curve deftly to hold these upright. They are the winter remains of the "tulips" which bloomed on the tree in June.

These tulips, which give the tree its name, are actually magnolia flowers. But since the petals are light green on the outside and grow high among the leaves, not many people have discovered them. If you can find a flower on the ground you will see that a tree famous for its trunk and not its flower has as harmonious and elegant a blossom as a water lily. Note the deep orange splashes on inside of petals.

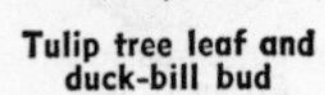

Tulip tree leaf and duck-bill bud

Tulip tree leaf is broad and clean, and

flutters in the wind as do leaves of trembling aspen. This superficial resemblance has given tree the name of yellow poplar, although it is really a magnolia. The leaf is a masterpiece of design. Because it has a squared-off summit, it suggests the primitive simplicity of Inca architecture as contrasted with the Gothic style of the maple leaf. There are no sharp angles. The truncated leaf is not harshly square like the belfry of a country church, but the top line is drawn as the curve of a saddle.

Tulip tree "cone." Each "petal" bears a seed.

In every part tulip tree is fluent. It holds its immensity on tiptoe, standing lightly on its feet. The wood is light weight; the trunk is so tall it has slender proportions; the leaves dance to the slightest breeze; the roots are tender and fleshy and do not lay hold of rocky land with iron-bound power as roots of white oak and hickory do.

Another expression of this smooth, fluid nature is the winter bud. Instead of overlapping scales there are two outer scales, flat and broad like the bill of a duck. These make a valve, in the same way a clam shell makes a valve. When there is pressure inside, the two scales open like a mouth, and out come spring leaves.

The charm of the tree is ingrained. Its wood takes a high polish, and because it is white, easy to work, and comes in wide boards, it makes wonderful paneling or veneer. This is the wood used for hat blocks as it doesn't absorb moisture under steaming process.

Harmonious tulip tree has a scientific name that is a musical one to hear yourself say.

Liriodendron tulipifera

BASSWOOD

★★★**Basswood** (also called linden) is fun to know because of its remarkable bag of tricks. People who think all Chinamen look alike might confuse this tree with elm—tall trunk, shallow-fissured bark of no distinction, long limbs reaching up at steep angles. The bark is lighter gray than elm, and basswood leans while elm grows straight up.

The surest sign of basswood is the unique flower-fruit apparatus. In early summer, weeks after other trees have flowered, basswood breaks out, a harvest of light yellow, star-shaped, half inch flowers. These dangle in clusters of six or so from a stem that comes out of the center of a peculiar, special leaf, resembling a 4-inch length of stiff green ribbon.

These flowers, fairly dripping with nectar, have such honeyed fragrance you can smell a basswood nearby. Bees are so intoxicated with joy over basswood flowers that, with all their buzzing, you may even hear a basswood as well as smell it. If there's a hollow in the tree, it's a prime place for a beehive. The flowers turn into round, hard nuts the size of small peas, that dangle from the center of the ribbon-leaf, which becomes a sail for the fruit in October. The contrivance is nicely balanced, with heavy little seeds swinging below the leaf. You can find these hard, green-gray little "peas" on the ground any time of the year. They decay slowly and may take several years to sprout a baby basswood.

The tree's name has nothing to do with gamey sea fish.

It is derived from bast, fibers that are used to weave mats or ropes or to wind around split handle of a hoe or rake. This bast, or inner bark, encloses the trunk of the tree like a tough, stringy shirt, and is also used for weaving into chair-bottoms and baskets.

Basswood buds are rich red or a deep red and green combination; a colorful tone-blend to capture in drapery or wallpaper. Only two scales show, and you can instantly spot a basswood by the way one of these bulges out, making the bud lopsided. This eccentricity carries over into the leaf, which also bulges out on one side becoming lopsided, but with a fluid curve as though the whole leaf were gracefully turning to one side.

More people have probably touched natural basswood (without knowing it) than any other unfinished wood. It is clean, white, odorless, unsplintery; it glues well and steams and bends easily. It is good for small things your hand often touches, such as toy airplanes, strawberry baskets, yardsticks, wooden partitions of honeycombs, Venetian blinds. Smooth, compact straight-graining makes good artists' charcoal.

Tilia americana

Basswood leaf (above) and special sail-leaf with fruit (below)

Common Linden, seen in city parks, is smaller than basswood; has round, pretty head, round leaves. These are heart-shaped and lopsided at base like American basswood. This is Europe's common linden that gave the name to Berlin's Unter den Linden. *Tilia vulgaris*

BLACK LOCUST

★★★**Black Locust** is our most eccentric tree. It plays dead most of the year because its leaves come out much later and fall off long before those of other trees. The leafless black locust is tall, gaunt with a battlefield look as though a vulture should be leering from a broken limb. In fact the tree is easily identified by its stark silhouette.

When black locust finally puts forth leaves, they seem to sprout, not from buds, but mysteriously from inside the tree. The absence of visible buds, the callous place in the bark of a twig, and a pair of short, wicked prickles are clear identification of this tree.

The multiple leaves are ten inches long. Small egg-shaped leaflets are arranged in pairs. In the rain or at night leaflets fold up like a book, the leaf stem droops, and thus in gloomy weather the tree looks forlorn. But when young leaves are fully exposed in the sunlight, the foliage of black locust is the most beautiful green of our hardwoods. The latest leaflets to unfurl at the tips are bright yellow-green; those which have been exposed to the light for a week are darker blue-green. This gives the foliage a rich duotone, especially effective in copses of young black locusts often seen along country roads.

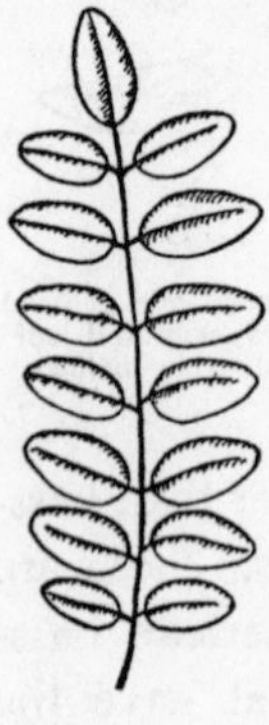

Black Locust

The bark of an old black locust is deeply furrowed, contributing to the rugged aspect. Heavy, disorganized ridges are a vivid point of identification. This trunk with its chaotic sculpturing is a mighty vault for wood that is among the hardest of our trees. Black locust wood is so tough that it almost never is used in sawed lumber, but is grabbed for fence posts, hubs of wheels, and railroad ties. To get a full-sized tie takes 45 years of growing. Our ancestors made wooden nails for ships and colonial houses of black locust. Today we make pins to hold the glass insulators of telephone wires, one of today's great uses for wood that can withstand weather and friction. As firewood, black locust is beautiful and unusual, although hard to start. Burns like coal, with bright-blue, concentrated flame almost like acetylene torch.

The flowers, like the leaves, are another contradiction of this scarred and heavy-wooded tree. In early summer black locust produces quantities of white sweet peas, with a delicate fragrance that permeates the air. The tree belongs to the same family as the sweet pea, and produces pods which may be seen hanging on the tree all winter. These are flat, 3 inches long, rich leathery brown, almost black. Open one, see the glistening white inside.

Black locust was almost blotted out by the Ice Age; the tree survived on earth only in a narrow oval in the southern Appalachian valleys. In our time it spreads with almost weed-like vitality, and you can see it in every state east of the Mississippi except Florida. Much of this is due to early settlers planting the tree for the beauty of its foliage and flowers, which make their remarkable contribution to the glory of the landscape after the tree has stood long months as an ungainly skeleton.

Robinia Pseudo-Acacia

Curling pods of Honey Locust

Honey Locust is one of the most remarkable trees of our land. Leaves are double multiple with small leaflets that give a tropical airy-fairy lightness to the foliage. Bark has a rough-smooth aspect, as though very rough bark had been smoothed with a trowel. Tree is detected quickly by long 10 inch pods. These are artfully twisted so they roll when tossed off the tree in a wind, providing a peculiar kind of seed dissemination. A jelly substance around the seeds in the beans is sweet, good to eat like honey. Even when pod is dry, the seeds can be sucked for the sweetness.

Honey locust has terrifying thorns in fantastic clusters. These are formed as single 4-inch needles and also as three-pronged daggers. These thorns are actually branches emerging from their own buds, as contrasted with tree thorns that are superficial prickles on the bark. A thornless variety is often planted in city parks. Biggest honey locusts are in southern Illinois, but tree extends all over West, flourishes in hot, sunny, dry ground. Much seen in South Dakota.

Gleditsia triacanthos

Honey Locust

THE BIRCHES

★★★**Paper Birch** is so unlike any other tree that everyone knows it. It's the picture-book tree. The graceful white trunk beside blue waters, the bright green leaves have been seen in paintings and photographs by far more people than have ever seen the tree itself. It is a northern tree, not even getting as far down as New York City, except on mountains. In New England the paper birch is common in the hills, and graceful clumps lean beside the shores of lakes. It's usually part of the picture where people are skiing.

Paper birch is well named because bark can be peeled off in sheets of foolscap on which you can write. This sheet is chalky-white outside and golden-brown on the under surface. Where it has been peeled you see the orange inner bark, and white bark never grows again on that spot. Although soft and smooth to the touch, this is one of the most durable of plant substances. One birch log was buried so long in Siberia that the wood turned to stone, while the fossil log still wore its birch bark unchanged through centuries. Thoroughly waterproof, birchbark ca-

Paper Birch
leaves and tassels

noes made the American Indian famous.

If the artists hadn't claimed paper birch first, the engineers would have discovered it. Wearing this extraordinary bark, paper birch braves the blizzards right up to the Arctic Circle. Here is a fine example of cork insulation: a laminated (thin layer upon layer) skin of cork is built upon the tree. The cells have air spaces which give protection against sun and frost. Whiteness turns away the over-bright sun (most thin barked trees are very sensitive to intense light), and the corky, air-filled layers insulate the living cells just beneath the bark from the fierce deep-freeze of the North. Moreover, the slenderness of the trunk offers slight interference to high winds, and birch wood is springy. The tree will bow over and whip around, but recover serenely when the punishment is finished. It is this tough, elastic quality that makes birch ideal as a whipping rod—one way in which pioneer boys learned to know the name of the tree. Smooth and soft, this wood doesn't chafe fingers of symphony conductors who like their batons made of birch.

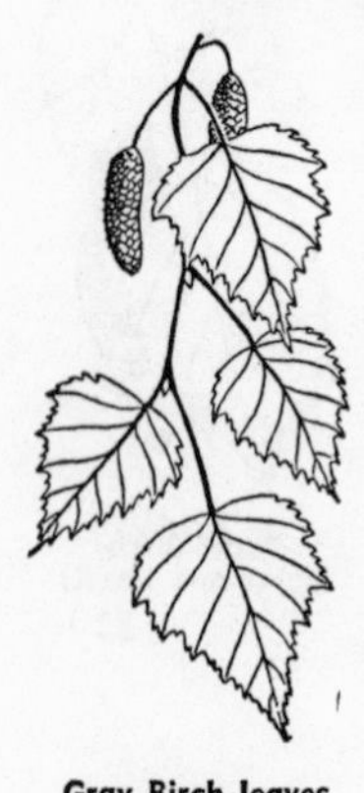

Gray Birch leaves and tassels

There are two white-barked birches, paper and gray. Both are important and distinctive, both are loosely called white birch. *Betula papyrifera*

Gray Birch grows like a weed around cities. It is one of the commonest trees in greater New York. Southward it grows on unfertile land around Washington, Baltimore, and Philadelphia. Under these conditions, where most people catch sight of it, the bark is gray-white, often yellowish or dull. It bears many black marks, especially the conspicuous black triangles where old limbs broke off.

But also, gray birch goes northward where its bark is whiter, and it sets up an imitation of paper birch. To tell these two vivid trees apart, note how gray birch bark is silvery, not snowy white; also it is tighter and does not peel off in wide strips. If you're still not sure, look at the leaves; find them on the ground in winter. The gray birch leaf is a triangle with double teeth. The sides of the triangle tend to curve inward, narrowing the leaf and giving it a long, sharp point. The paper birch leaf is less angular, broader, and with a more rounded base.

Betula populifolia

★**Yellow Birch** has gold-and-silver curls all over its bark. These are thin, translucent, glistening with highlights. Best time to see this effect is in winter when the trunk is lighted by sunlight or snow. Take a curl of yellow birch bark in your hand, see how it shimmers silvery or golden. Yellow birch is a woods tree, it needs the moisture of shadows. In Appalachian and New England hills it is abundant around ravines with hemlock and moosewood. Bark curls are inflammable, make good tinder for starting a campfire even on a rainy day (be cautious!). Big, visible roots of yellow birch lay hold of rocky hillside like monstrous claws, or flow down from an old stump where a yellow birch seedling sprouted, then along the ground like serpents until

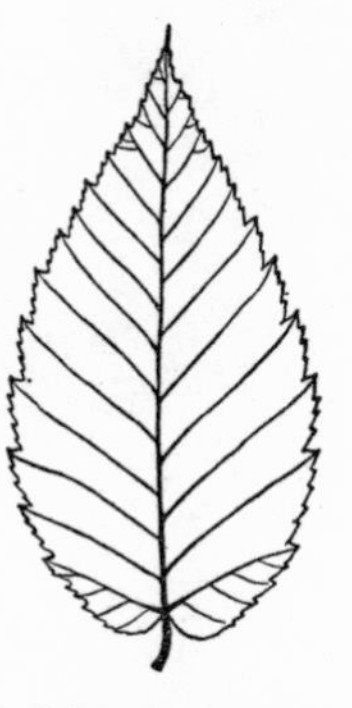

Yellow Birch and Sweet Birch leaves are similar.

they plunge into a pocket of soft humus. Twigs have mild wintergreen flavor not as strong as sweet birch. This is a rewarding tree to see on a hike or ride through the hills.

Betula lutea

Sweet Birch (also called black birch, cherry birch) is the wintergreen tree. On young trees, smooth, glossy, dark brown bark is peppered with white dashes. You might mistake it for a cherry tree until you taste the strong wintergreen flavor of twigs or buds. This is a commercial source of wintergreen oil. Sweet birch, as well as yellow birch, holds its seed tassels all winter, scattering tiny winged seeds conspicuously on the snow where they are important food for birds. The March wind litters the snow with these birch seeds in maple sugar season in northern New England woods. Sweet birch heartwood is brown with red tinge, takes fine polish, and is often used as imitation mahogany in furniture and boat trim.

Betula lenta

THE POPLARS

Poplars are fast-growing, gay trees with leaves that quiver. As a national asset they start rebuilding the woods fast after a fire. Poplar seeds germinate with alacrity in a burned place; little poplar trees make a cool, moist shadow for sprouting seeds of hemlock, oak, beech.

Poplar wood is soft and weak for construction. But its rate of growth keeps a good supply of wood coming for excelsior, match sticks, book paper. Also poplar wood holds nails firmly and offers clean, smooth surface for stenciling and labeling, making good crates and shipping boxes.

The name poplar brackets two other names—aspen and cottonwood. You can see the difference in these two kinds of poplars in the smooth, light green or whitish bark of aspen, compared to the deeply furrowed gray bark of cottonwood.

★★★**Trembling Aspen** is a bright tree—bark is smooth, light olive green and foliage lighter green than the trees around. Leaves quiver like sparkling water, twinkling with the highlights of the sun and their lighter undersides. This is the only tree which can be identified by the way it moves. Other trees may wait for your close inspection, but the wonderful trembling aspen attracts the eye with its fluttering hello.

This is the only transcontinental broadleaf tree; no other grows naturally from Maine to California. It takes its stand in conspicuous places, at the front of the woods in full sunlight. It likes hillsides. This is the common aspen of the northland. You see it around cabins and lakes of canoe country. The straight trunk of young aspen with smooth olive-green bark is a color note as vivid as birch. An Indian name for it, "noisy leaf," translates the shimmering motion from the eyes to the ears.

Trembling aspen also has eye-filling details. Buds are a polished red-brown, sharply pointed, twisted like a small cornucopia that lies snugly against the twig. Other trees have more formal or decorative buds, but poplar buds have flair and vitality with a feeling of freedom and energy that's good to share.

Trembling aspen leaf is small, almost round. Look well at its stem; this is the most characteristic detail of the tree. Whereas most leaf stems are merely stiff attachments, this one is soft, flexible, and flat. The leaf dangles on a ribbon set at right angles to the leaf blade. This makes the whole thing wiggle in the slightest breeze.

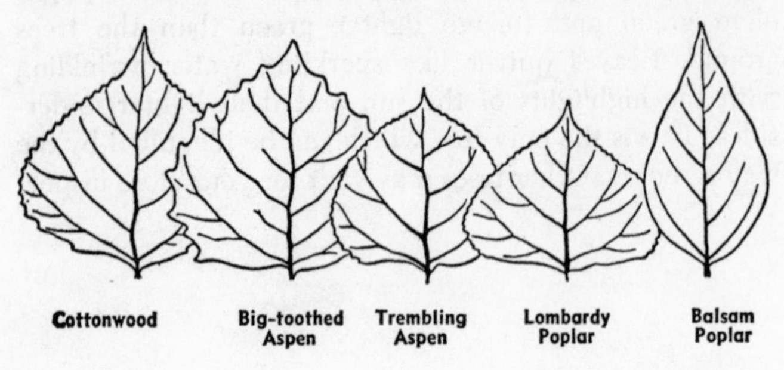

The tassels poured forth by this tree in April have given it the name of necklace tree in some places. These are the flowers (catkins). Aspen separates the sexes, as do ash and holly; thus one trembling aspen produces tassels with gorgeous deep-red stamens, while another one bears cottony tassels with seeds. Both kinds, cast off, cover the ground under their trees in spring, and are a sight to behold. *Populus tremuloides*

Bigtooth Aspen has a bit of leaf magic. At first leaves are like flannel, and densely white and woolly on under sides. Later they turn thin, green, and flutter like other poplar leaves. They have irregular, unusual scallops. Always you can tell the bigtooth by the big teeth on leaf edges. Otherwise it's hard to tell this tree from trembling aspen, except for an over-all feel. It grows in a lower, moister place, while trembling aspen usually stands on the hill. It is a larger tree, and young branches are brighter gray or yellow while trembling aspen's are red-brown. Plenty of both these trees around, compare these two common aspens and you'll find yourself reading trees. *Populus grandidentata*

Balsam Poplar (also wrongly called balm of Gilead) has the exception to the flat, flexible leaf stems of poplars. Stem is round; egg-shaped leaf does not flutter. This common poplar of Alaska, Labrador, North Canada, crosses our border into Maine and grows transcontinentally in Minnesota, North Dakota, and the northern Rocky Mountains. Buds in winter resist big freeze with heavy, glistening coating of resin, delightfully fragrant, sticky. *Populus Tacamahacca*

White Poplar

★**Cottonwood** is as familiar as the family dog. It is the usual, often the only tree over more space across these United States than any other one in our book. It takes in stride searing winds, drought, blazing sun, sudden sub-zero nights—and cheerily bobs up as the fastest-growing tree in the place. Cottonwood leaf with broad base is the outline of the pyramids of Egypt; right-angled teeth the stone steps.

Leaves begin dropping in mid-summer on top of the cotton tassels that whiten the ground. Thus cottonwood lays a soft rug where it's often too dry to grow grass.

This is the common tree in the 25 thousand miles of prairie shelter belts that airplane travelers see. Like willow, it can be grown from a fresh, green twig thrust in moist ground. *Populus deltoides*

Lombardy Poplar is the sharply narrow oval pointing to the sky like a church steeple. It is famous in pictures of roads of France. With a form so striking we forget to look at the leaves, but you'll find a geometric figure of a broad triangle with baseline at right angles to the stem. Planted from Maine to Oregon. *Populus nigra var. italica*

White Poplar is the peculiar tree with leaves snow-white and woolly below and dark green above, planted so much in parks and cemeteries. The "black and white" leaves vary in shape but suggest small maple leaves. The astonishing white wool creeps onto twigs and buds but rubs off nicely if you want to polish them up. *Populus alba*

Most Poplar leaves join ribbon-stem at right angles.

THE WILLOWS

★★★**Black Willow** is the wide, ragged tree of the countryside. You see its heavy trunk, often two or more together, leaning over water from the bank of a stream or pond. It grows in rows along wet banks. Twigs spray out in large numbers from angles or knots in the trunk.

The bark of an old willow is heavily treaded and is often swirled and distorted, giving it a rugged grandeur all its own. However, this trunk is willow's only pretense at being a monarch. The wood is soft and almost useless for timber. Its twigs, called osiers, are woven into baskets and wicker furniture. Buds are smooth and dainty without overlapping scales, resembling bits of red sealing wax pressed between thumb and finger to flatten them against the twig. The mighty trunk supports a crown that is surprisingly light and delicate. Twigs are long and brittle, often so weak and flexible that they dangle, and from them swing leaves that are only 1½ inch wide and 5 inches long. These strangely narrow leaves taper sharply and have small, sharp teeth along the edge, like those of a fine saw. Two little sickle-shaped leaves circle the stem below the main leaf. These twin circular leaves are one of those surprising details you discover when you explore a tree.

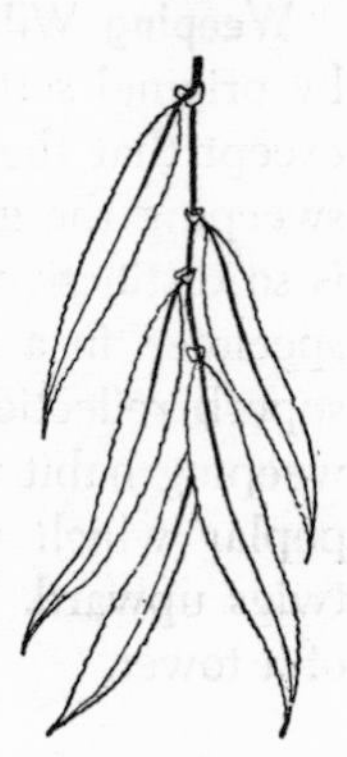
Black Willow

Next to the fact that willow grows in wet places, its most conspicuous feature is the yellowness of the twigs. In winter these polished twigs catch the sun's rays and hold them with colorful effect of yellow against blue sky. The only tree which rivals willow with the winter color of its twigs is the poplar. However, poplar twigs are a dull, deep orange color, compared to the gold of willow. These twigs are not only the most conspicuous but also the most animated part of a willow. They behave like seeds in the way they reproduce the tree. Put a live willow twig into a glass of water and in a few days roots will grow out of one end and leaves out of the other. All it takes to plant a willow tree is to thrust one of these twigs into moist ground. The tree casts off its twigs the way other trees cast off their fruits.

The reason there are so many willows along so many streams in every part of our country is that one will lean over the water and drop twigs; these ride on the water and take root where they lodge in moist earth.

Salix nigra

Weeping Willow (who doesn't know it?) was planted by original settlers from Europe. It is like black willow except that the twigs are longer and dangle downward, sweeping the ground beneath the tree. Weeping willow is so distinctive that it is a landscape feature as a single specimen in a moist meadow, in a cemetery, or with a superb reflection in a park lake. Compare this willow's weeping habit with another planted tree—the Lombardy poplar which grows exactly to the contrary, shooting twigs upward. This willow makes a tree shower instead of a tower. *Salix babylonica*

For willow and cottonwood of the West see pages 191-192.

THE UNDERSTORY TREES

It is a healthy sign when you see little trees under big trees. The next generation is growing up. They offer you the best chance to reach out and touch leaves and buds, and you compare the roughness of elm leaf with the softness of walnut, the broad, black ash bud with the needle-sharp beech. Once you have held and stared at the crimson red maple bud, you will never again feel indifferent to buds. In addition, hidden in the camouflage of the understory are trees most people don't know. They usually have slender trunks that bend and run out toward the nearest space with the most light. Formless, according to the standard idea of what a tree should look like, these little trees of the shadows have marvelous art in their details, and extraordinary fruits:

★**Sassafras** is famous for its three shapes of leaf on the same branch. This trick starts off tree exploring with a bang. If you have an artist's eye, you will be even more delighted with the green tone of the leaf. Its richness is enhanced because there are no highlights. This tree

Blue Sassafras fruits sit on coral stems.

grows in mottled shadows which mellow the beautiful suede green. If you could reproduce this wonderful green in home decorating, it would be deeply satisfying.

A positive check on sassafras is the flavor of its twigs. Twigs are bright green near their tips and turn up gracefully. Chew this —you taste spicy, aromatic oil not to be described in words. Sweet birch twig is wintergreen, cherry is bitter, spice bush is cinnamon, sassafras is sassafras. For a totally different flavor than the one used for sassafras tea (made from the roots) and gumdrops, the leaves are dried and powdered and a few spoonfuls added at the last minute to a kettle of gumbo soup for excellent flavor and thickening. Only the South's Creoles make the real thing.

Typically American, sassafras grows nowhere else in the world except southeast Asia. All over our eastern states it's common both as an understory tree and also in dry, sandy spots along roadsides. Southward, it achieves 50 feet, with deeply furrowed bark that creates an illusion of great age.

Yellow-green flowers in early spring are conspicuous. More thrilling is the huge caterpillar that fills his body with translucent green fluid from the sassafras leaf where he feeds. A black spot looks like a fierce cyclops' eye at the tip of his nose. He's harmless and will turn into one of our most beautiful butterflies—

Sassafras leaves come in three shapes.

the swallowtail.

Sassafras variifolium

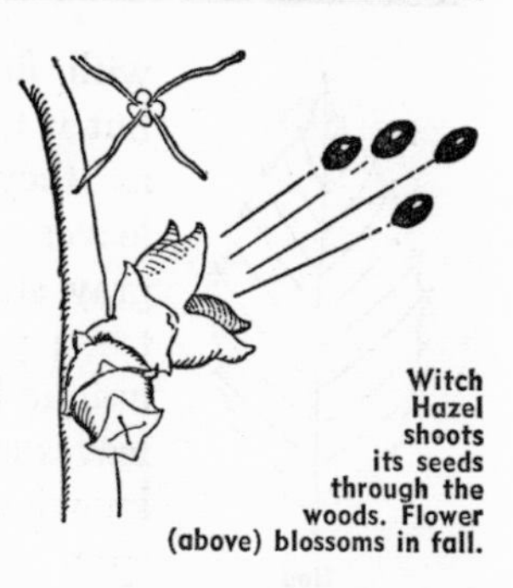
Witch Hazel shoots its seeds through the woods. Flower (above) blossoms in fall.

★**Witch Hazel,** unlike other trees, flowers in the fall when tiny yellow ribbons dangle all over it. Often these petals curl and hang on all winter. In New England witch hazel is a large shrub, becoming a tree in the Carolina and Tennessee mountains. The leaf has eccentric charm. Margins ripple smoothly while the whole leaf is thrown off-center as though by a steady breeze blowing across it.

Witch hazel packs its biggest surprise in the pop guns scattered over its twigs. These are tough, powerful seedcases, each holding two tiny black footballs. When cold dries this contraption in the fall, it opens like a bird's mouth and shoots out the seeds some 10 feet into the woods. Witch hazel bark, distilled, makes a solution that smells delicious, feels so clean you find it on drugstore shelves—try it for mosquito bites. *Hamamelis virginiana*

Hop Hornbeam (also called ironwood) growing slowly in the shadows builds such hard wood it burns like anthracite. This makes a good mallet handle, or rake teeth, but it's hard to whittle. The best identification is the fruit. These resemble oval paper bags, each of which contains one seed; unusual, for most fruits have numbers of seeds. These paper bags overlap and dangle in a loose cone-like cluster. Leaves are flannel soft,

Witch Hazel

with fine sharp teeth—really exquisite, but it takes scrutiny to appreciate them, as they superficially look like birch leaves. Bark is shredded with narrow gray strips. Easily confused with other trees; you know it first by spotting the unique fruit, then fitting it together with leaves and bark—hop hornbeam is worth knowing. Grows in dry woodsy places from Maine to Texas. *Ostrya virginiana*

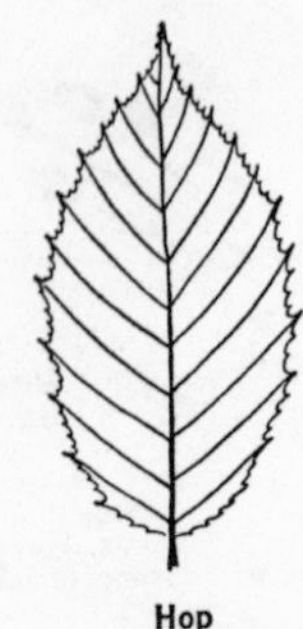
Hop Hornbeam

Cluster of Hop Hornbeams paper-bag fruits

Blue Beech (also called American hornbeam) has a trunk with muscular ridges like a man's forearm when he clenches his fist. Bark is smooth, blue-gray. Wood is hard like hop-hornbeam, but trunk is too slender to be useful. This tough little tree dangles clusters of nuts, each fixed to an ornate wing, shaped like a narrow maple leaf. Blue beech is said to be "shapeless;" actually it is dynamically formed, shaped by light, its muscular trunk and wiry twigs reaching for the sun. You find it along woodland streams, and in wet places from Maine to Texas. *Carpinus caroliniana*

Blue Beech seed attached to graceful wing

THE BIG FLOWERING TREES

What is your power of observation? If good, then you can enjoy many kinds of beautiful flowers on trees, such as elm which bears a crown of dark purple gauze in early spring before leaves are out. Red maple flowers are rich red, conspicuous against blue sky. Norway maple has bright yellow-green flowers. Sassafras has compact bunches of yellow flowers. Basswood, after the leaves are out, is loaded with cream-white flowers.

A few large trees have flowers so vivid that when they are out, they arrest attention even when you aren't looking for them. Flowers are their best identification.

See also black locust, magnolia, tulip, sorrel, black cherry, horse chestnut.

Catalpa (also called Indian-bean) is the front page tree. Everything about it is interesting. Any time of year, find the nearest catalpa and it gives you something you can't forget. In late June flowers pile up all over the tree in ten-inch mounds. Petals are scalloped and ruffled, mostly white, but with brown or purple spots and two

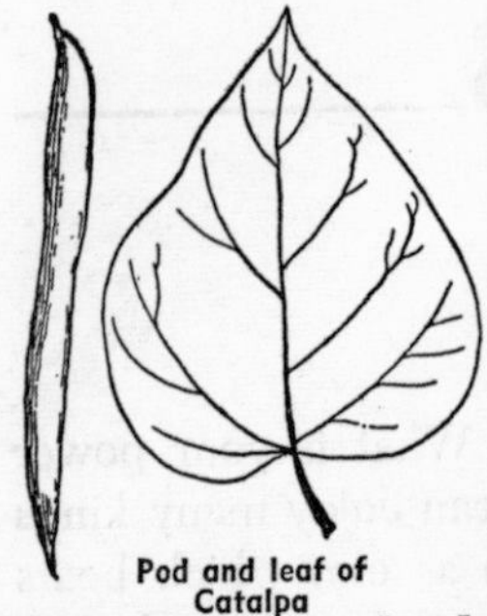

Pod and leaf of Catalpa

gold stripes. These lines point toward the nectar well, so that a bumblebee knows the way.

Leaves are big hearts. They have a basic simplicity the way a child might draw them with broad strokes. Compare these with the round, gay little heart-leaves of redbud. Catalpa leaves, strangely, secrete nectar, as do flowers. Notice the nectar glands at the base of stem.

Pods stream down in large numbers, hanging on most of the winter. Although from a little distance they resemble giant string beans, these are not true beans, but long, tough seed cases, round and slender as a panatella cigar. Catalpa seeds released the following spring are equally strange—out of its string bean pod come papery flakes an inch long with silver fringe at each end.

In winter, the tree is stiff, dead looking. But the awkward branches have marks on them by which you can identify catalpa instantly. They are oval scars on raised bases. They go round the stem in whorls of three, one little scar and two big ones. As they mark the places where leaves fell off, it follows that catalpa leaves grow in whorls of three around a branch.

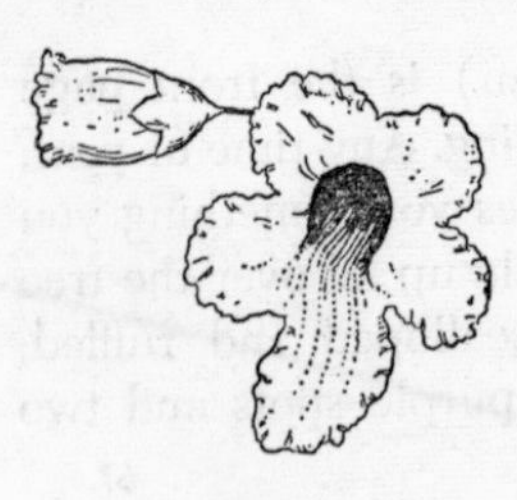

Catalpa flowers

For a tree that grows so fast that it can add an inch wide ring to its wood in a year, the wood is surprisingly durable. Railroads make ties of catalpa.

Catalpa bignonioides

Paulownia (also called empress tree) is the fastest growing commercial wood tree in America. In a single year a seedling may rise 20 feet. Ailanthus and sumac compete in speed of elongating, but these are weed trees with pithy wood, while paulownia's wood has commercial value.

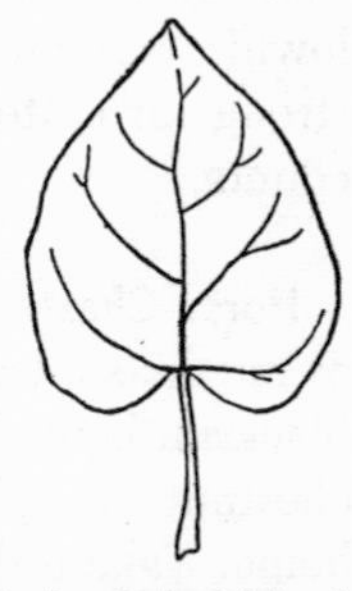

Paulownia leaf (above) is less pointed at tip, has bigger stem than Catalpa.

Paulownia is a medium-sized, beautiful shade tree with enormous leaves, often seen in parks, on streets, college grounds in eastern United States, especially around Philadelphia, Baltimore, Washington. This is one of the American settler trees, brought from the Orient during the past century, which escaped from cultivation and became part of our land. Others are ailanthus, mulberry, weeping willow, ginkgo.

People who know the big, light green leaves of catalpa often mistake paulownia for that tree. But paulownia flowers are light purple—catalpa, white. When leaves are off, paulownia arouses curiosity by conspicuous fruits unlike any other tree's. People say, "What is that tree with the large clusters of grapes?"

These fruits are oval, the size of a healthy pecan nut. They are startling in their reproductive power—each contains 2 thousand little winged seeds. If you count the fruits on a lusty paulownia, you can figure that a single tree produces 21 million seeds. No wonder foresters are eyeing this tree. It grows in almost any soil—in Washington, D. C., one achieved three feet from a seed

Paulownia pods

that landed in mortar between bricks of a wall. Paulownia can build sawlogs fast. Extra light weight but strong for crates and boxes in air express, where weight counts. *Paulownia tomentosa*

Horse-Chestnut from the Balkans is at home in America as much as a tree can be. Ever since Longfellow's village blacksmith made his anvil clang under this "spreading chestnut," people in eastern states have planted it around home. Take a drive in late May and someone in the car is sure to cry out about the tall, heavily leafed dome with candelabra of white flowers scattered all over it. These have yellow and red spots, and long yellow stamens that protrude far out of the flower tube.

There's no excuse to think this a catalpa because of the flowers. It blooms a month earlier, but glance at the leaves. Five, sometimes seven, big, wedge-shaped leaflets fan out like the fingers of your hand. Leaf opens like an umbrella. At first the leaflets are turned down, then in a single day they lift, broaden out, and the tree seems covered with countless little whirling helicopters.

Lower branches curve up and down and up again like a roller coaster. At twig tip is a huge bud. Look for this; it glistens with resin as though just varnished.

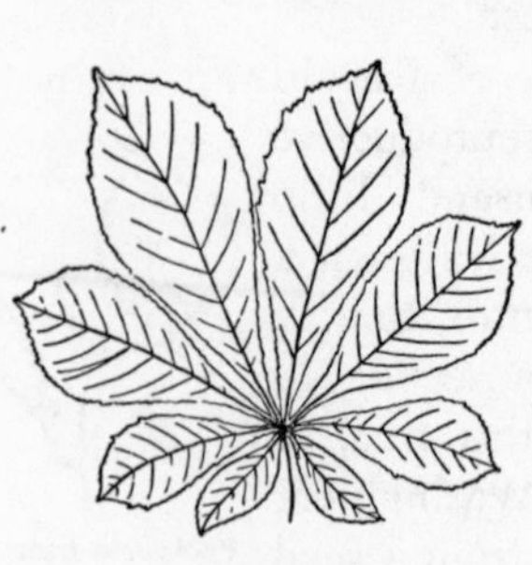
Horse Chestnut

Horse-chestnut is elaborate but mussy. Flowers fall off, litter the lawn. Fruits keep dropping. They are exceedingly prickly; nobody goes barefoot under a horse-chestnut. When leaves fall, they come all apart so that leaflets and stems flutter down separately. The seed is a beautiful brown leather ball with a gray eye. It's bitter, narcotic, only fit for horses they used to say, and that's how the tree gets its name. *Aesculus hippocastanum*

Buckeye is scattered around the Middle West. * Comments on horse-chestnut apply to this tree. Differences are incidental but clear, and of interest to tree detectives: flowers are pale yellow, instead of white. Leaflets are narrower, smaller. Big bud is dull, smooth, not glistening with varnish. Crushed leaves and bark have a rank odor to sniff for identification, otherwise to shun. Buckeye wood is light, springy, hard to split, is used for artificial limbs. *Aesculus glabra*

*Ohio's tree-conscious, strong-arm settlers, carving out their homeland with gun and axe, admired the flowers and leaves of this tree, built their homes beside it. They coined its lusty name which rolls so smoothly off the tongue that Ohio is proud to be called the Buckeye State.

THE LITTLE FLOWERING TREES

These are like playthings compared to the big trees, and are often no taller than the ceiling of your room. The trunks are usually slender, inconspicuous, and lean a little in support of compact, round heads, which flare in springtime as though bright white or purple-pink parasols had opened suddenly in the sunlight. Many people see these trees who ordinarily pay little heed to trees. But in May, when people rush out into the country, dogwood, cherry, redbud, shadblow are startlingly vivid. Moreover, you see little flowering trees: magnolia, crab-apple, cherry, hawthorn, cultivated for their flowers in city parks, yards, and gardens. Certain little flowering trees are ideal for streets and corners of big, modern cities; they fit into small space, producing blooms even in light reflected from walls of buildings. As the big shade trees of the horse and buggy era vanish from downtown streets and squares, the little flowering trees can bring back a value lost from the heart of the city.

★**Redbud** (also called Judas tree) is the only wild American tree with bright purple-red flowers. Riding in

Redbud pods

mid-spring (same as dogwood time) in Pennsylvania, Ohio, and southward, you'll see redbud with hackberry, oak, walnut, hemlock in hilly places, and often only a single tree blazing on a hill-side pasture. In peach-tree land (Georgia, Alabama, the Carolinas) redbud, at a distance, could be mistaken for a peach tree in bloom, or a purple flowering crab. But these fruit trees are cultivated, while redbud is the colorful doll of our hardwood forest. Its bright, garish purple does not look well with blue sky, but redbud is effective because it is small and usually overtopped by other broadleaf trees, evergreens, and shadows.

Flowers cover the tree, springing out from twigs, main branches and even from the trunk, whereas most tree flowers bloom from the tips of twigs. Redbud flowers are like sweet-peas, and whirling around their stems they resemble little dancing shoes.

If redbud didn't put on such a brilliant show of flowers it might be famous for its leaves. These are round hearts; press some for Valentine's Day. Pods also are a feature. Shaped like ordinary pea pods, these are rose colored. Buds are purple-red, as the name of the tree implies, but they're only ⅛ inch and hard to see. It's an exciting little tree. *Cercis canadensis*

Redbud leaf is a perfect heart.

★**Flowering Dogwood** is America's most decorative tree and enjoys among trees the same reputation as the robin among birds. Dogwood chooses the week in the year when it will be most conspicuous before leaves come out on surrounding trees to unroll broad white blossoms in the sunlight. Each is a masterpiece of design, like an ivory Maltese cross. All the flowers on the tree unroll at the same time and are extended in layers with shadowy spaces between the blossoms that accentuate this effect. This makes a mosaic that people strive to reproduce on draperies and wallpaper. Examine the twigs that support this mosaic and you will see how gracefully they curve to form the planes. Each flower is held at right angles to the direction of brightest light, giving it maximum exposure. Thus in the open the dogwood covers itself with an umbrella of flowers shaped by the dome of sky. On the edge of the woods it will hold its mosaic toward the parkway, where the motorist catches the effect even at fifty miles an hour.

The dogwood is a small tree, so that in the woods it is part of the understory, along with cherry, shadblow and redbud that bloom about the same time. In the midst of the woods the dogwood marquee is spread low among the tall, sunlit tree trunks. This is one of the most unusual effects of the spring woods, but you have to get out of the city to see it.

Dogwood

To understand this tree, mark it when the flowers are out so as to find it in the winter when it seems to have disappeared. You'll see the flower buds held up at the twig tips as though the tree were offering a toast to the woods with a thousand tiny silver goblets. Peer closely, note the four bud divisions. The sealing material between them will melt, the four segments will lift and re-

Silvery Dogwood bud can be seen in fall and winter.

volve outward, exposing their white inner surfaces. Each part elongates from the base, as fingernails grow, and not the tips. What were bud scales now turn into what look like broad white petals. On most trees bud scales fall off when buds open, but the flowering dogwood converts them into the most conspicuous part of the flower.

In the northern part of its range, New York and New England, the flowers are white as snow; they turn to waxy white and light greenish white as they move southward. Near Lancaster, Ohio, grows a dogwood that produces pink blossoms which provides nurserymen with grafts to raise "red flowering dogwood".

Red chemicals are hidden in this tree. Its berries are shiny red footballs ½ inch long, Its fall foliage, too, is deep red.

Flowering dogwood is hard but doesn't weather well, so no mill thirsts for it. Once upon a time spear shafts were made of it, and recently shafts of golf clubs.

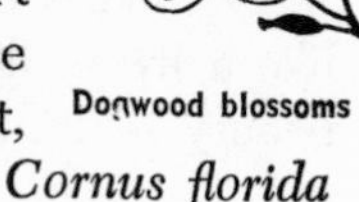
Dogwood blossoms

Cornus florida

Shadblow (also called serviceberry) is like a puff of white steam in the early spring woods. The white flowers may appear at the top of a slender trunk that reaches high, for a little tree, but gets up only to the mezzanine of a tall woods. Shadblow is often a shrub, in New England,* where you see it on the edge of the woods or scattered around pastures. The very earliness of its

*Between Boston and Providence low pastures are white with it in April. But the typical place is the high, hilly woods.

puffing out among leafless trees where sunlight fills the woods makes shadblow conspicuous. Shadblow petals are narrow white ribbons. Fresh out of the bud, they stand wide apart forming little five-bladed propellers.

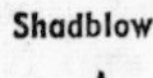

Shadblow

Shadblow

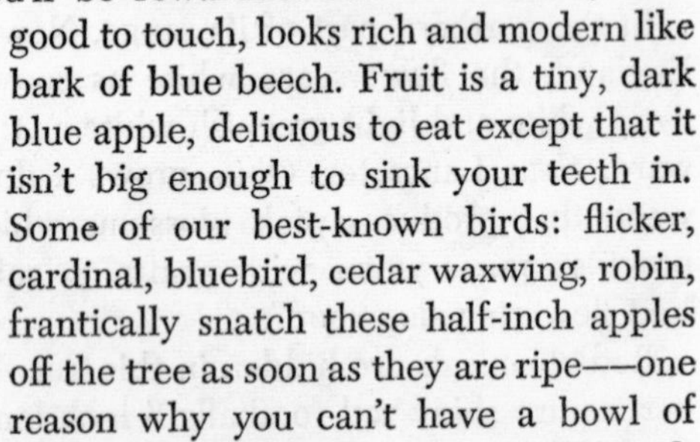

When leaves come out, shadblow vanishes. But mark it for further watching; you'll be rewarded. Bark is smooth, feels good to touch, looks rich and modern like bark of blue beech. Fruit is a tiny, dark blue apple, delicious to eat except that it isn't big enough to sink your teeth in. Some of our best-known birds: flicker, cardinal, bluebird, cedar waxwing, robin, frantically snatch these half-inch apples off the tree as soon as they are ripe——one reason why you can't have a bowl of them on your table. The shadblow bud has long, red-brown scales edged with silver hairs that tend to twist like a living flame at the tip of the twig. Its flare and beauty is unsurpassed in tree buds.

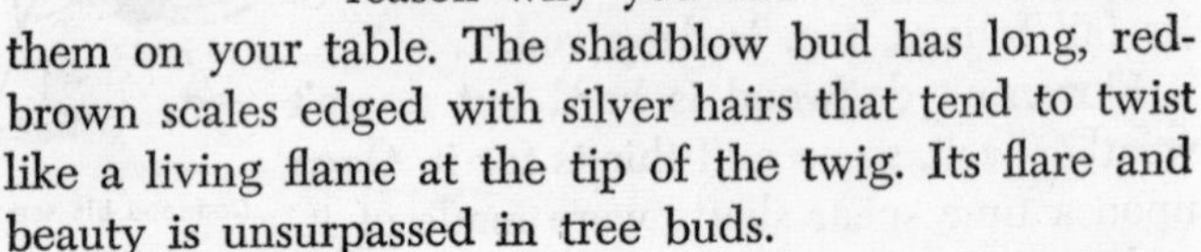

Amelanchier canadensis

Hawthorn is eccentric in both appearance and behavior. Zigzag branches stab out horizontally. Leaves have sharp, irregular teeth. Hawthorn bears white roses in June and in the fall tiny red apples that hang on all winter. Rose, apple, and hawthorn all belong to the same family.

Hawthorn is encountered in rough, rocky fields or near brooks, and is known by its long, straight, exceedingly sharp thorns in the impenetrable tangle of branches. Honey locust and osage orange also bear vicious thorns but are so different in form, leaves and fruit that there is no confusion with hawthorn. This is the only heavily thorned tree with sharply toothed, single leaves.

When men cleared the land and laid the axe to forest trees, hawthorn woke up and evolved so many new species even experts can't keep track of them. Gray's Manual lists 180 kinds. They invade pastures and are a pesky nuisance to the farmer, although picturesque to the artist. A slow-growing tree with tough wood and roses for flowers can hardly be termed a weed. Moreover, birds love to build their nests in hawthorn for the armor gives protection from cats, children, squirrels, hawks. Hawthorns are citadels for goldfinch, cardinal, cedar waxwing, robin. Here are the hawthorns you are most likely to see:

1. Cockspur Thorn, long daggers up to 8 inches shoot out from above little oblong leaves. *Crataegus crus-galli*

2. White Thorn, frequent in old pasture fields. Small, so you can look right over the top. Intricate branches conceal song sparrow nests. Almost thornless compared to the others. *Crataegus intricata*

Cockspur Thorn

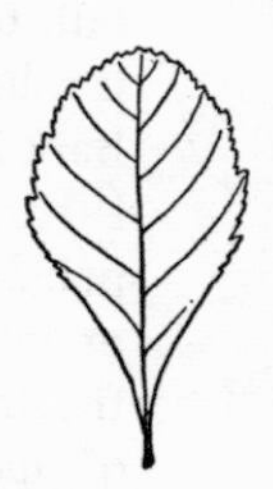

English Hawthorn

3. Washington Thorn, taller, southerly, but common around Washington D. C. Superabundance of flowers, and bright red fruits attract the eye all winter. Filled with slender exceedingly sharp 2 inch thorns.
Crataegus Phaenopyrum

4. English Hawthorn, best-known park and garden kind. Varieties with white, pink or red double flowers. Leaves fancy with three lobes. Strong 1 inch thorns. All over England in hedges that have made literature.
Crataegus Oxyacantha

Yellowwood (also called virgilia) is so interesting you should ask your park commissioner or botanical garden where you can see it. Discovered on limestone cliffs in Kentucky and Tennessee, this tree is now planted as far north as Boston, and Cleveland is raising a great number for street trees. Leaves are silver velvet in spring and turn clear yellow in fall. Fragrant white flowers of a large sweetpea type spout out from the ends of twigs in early summer, bending them over with their weight so that clusters dangle like wisteria and the tree buzzes with bees. These flowers are a special event because they may skip a year or two, but, even without flowers, yellowwood is a healthy tree with attractive foliage. Bark is silvery smooth like beech. Wood is hard, bright yellow, takes a beautiful polish, but is seldom used for furniture or interior trim due to the rareness of the tree in forests and the slenderness of its trunk. The name "virgilia" is pleasant to remember. *Cladrastis lutea*

Yellowwood

Mountain Ash takes first prize for producing the most brilliant fruit of any of our trees. This little tree of rocky places, where cold spring water moistens the roots, is laden in fall with massive clusters of orange-red fruits. They are like tiny pears and so bitter no one eats them. Even birds turn away, eating them only as emergency rations. The eye appeal is so great that if you travel in northern places—hilltops in New England, cool shores of Lake Superior and Huron, you will be thrilled by the sight of this tree. White flowers in flat-topped clusters festoon it in early summer, but these flowers get scant attention because the intense fruits steal the show. Don't miss the leaves; they are like ferns up to ten inches long with artistic saw-edged leaflets.

Not a relative of the true ash, mountain ash is akin to the apple tree, but resembles nothing but itself.

Sorbus americana

European Mountain Ash is from the highlands of Scotland, has similar leaves but is weighted with even larger fruits. Planted in parks and yards. *Sorbus aucuparia*

Hercules' Club (also called devil's walking stick) has the biggest multiple leaves of any tree in the U.S.A.: 3 feet long, 2 wide. These are compounded of a double series of small leaflets so you get no impression of big leaves at first glance. Hercules' club looks like nothing else in our treedom. Trunk is a pole six inches thick, rising 20 feet or so unbranched, often with several poles growing in a clump. The big leaves gush out from peak of pole, falling by their weight into form of broad umbrella. Skin-tearing prickles are scattered over bark so boys never shinny up this pole. Effect is that of a small royal palm; foliage has tropical luxuriance. Unfolding leaves are bronze colored and turn bronze-red mottled with yellow in fall.

Creamy white flower clusters mount like geysers four feet above leaf tops. Berries resemble little white ivory billiard balls, ripening to blue, devoured by bluebirds and blue jays.

This peculiar tree grows in warm nooks at edge of woods from Pennsylvania to Missouri, southward. In the South it grows up to 50 feet. *Aralia spinosa*

If you explore the mountains of Tennessee and North Carolina, you may discover two little trees loaded with white flowers as though a landscape gardener had gone

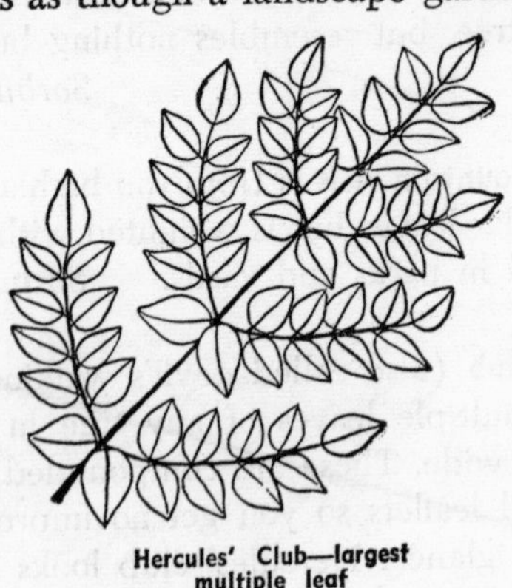

Hercules' Club—largest multiple leaf

into a ravine to plant them. But you may see them more easily in parks, gardens and lawns up north. Both trees are slender with plain oval leaves. Only the flowers stop you; otherwise you may as well skip these trees:

Silverbell Tree has elegant snow-white bells pendant all over tree appearing same time dogwood and redbud are in bloom. Each is shaped like a snowdrop flower of a late winter lawn.

Halesia carolina

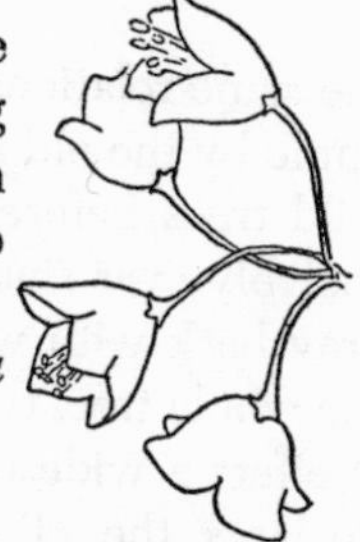
Silverbell blossoms

Fringe Tree gives gay, fringy effect with delicate buff-white clusters of flowers. Oval leaves are in pairs, have smooth edges. It flowers in early summer after lilacs are through. An old-fashioned tree decoration that goes with southern colonial homes. Fruit is like small purple plum. *Chionanthus virginicus*

Fringe tree flowers

THE FRUIT TREES

★**Apple** tree stands in the same relationship to man as the dog. There leans the apple by the old American homestead. It was tamed from wild trees before written history and has lived with us sociably ever since. It has a short, muscular trunk, steel-gray bark with wide, round ridges that spiral as though the whole tree, twisted by wind, had spun around a little. It offers a wide umbrella for cool shade on a hot day. It declares the climax of spring with its white fragrant flowers. It sends a boy back to school in the fall with a mouthful of crackling, juicy fruit.

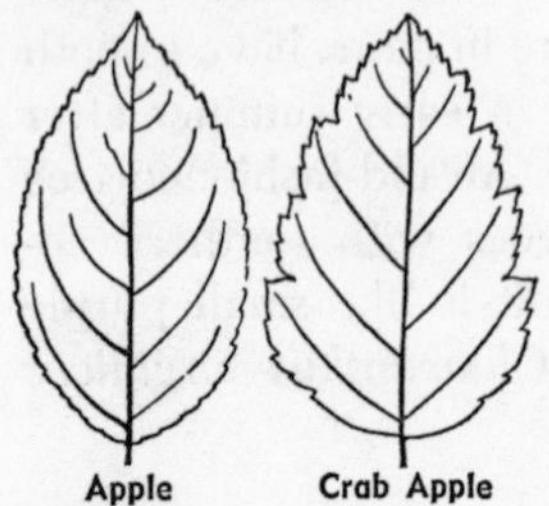

Flowers and fruit are so diverting we forget to see the apple tree closely. Many twigs fail to shoot out in length—they are stubby, thick, like a short segment of a compressed screen door spring. Each lumpy segment, a fraction of an inch in length, is a year's growth. There is singular fitness in this. A good apple is heavy, it is a beautiful porous ball 85 per cent water. If apples were carried on ordinary long slender twigs, they might bang together and be bruised in a high wind. The strong rigid spurs bear the load with safety and economy.

Good eating apples have names such as Baldwin, McIntosh, Delicious, Northern Spy, Pippin, Rhode Island Greening. Plant their seeds and you'll have a tree bearing small, sour apples. This mysterious fact shows how quickly a tame apple tree reverts to the wild state. Apples are held true to type through the equally mysterious fact that the fruit is constant in quality only if it is bred through wood instead of through seed. The original Baldwin tree was discovered in a fence corner at Lowell, Massachusetts, in 1793 by Mr. Baldwin. Since then, through grafting, millions of trees have produced Baldwin apples, all of them borne on the same stream of wood unbroken from that single, original tree. McIntosh, an Ontario farmer, over a century ago was alert enough to recognize good apples on a wild tree that started another stream of wood bearing the McIntosh apple down to us. Saw handles are made from apple wood, and it's excellent for whittling. *Malus pumila*

Crab Apple is the little, stiff, crooked tree in the hedgerow or old pasture. It shows that animals are active and happy thereabouts; white-tailed deer, raccoon, skunk, fox go for the small acid apples and scatter the seeds. If people get there first, the result is clear, orange-red crabapple jelly. The small apples (1 inch in diameter) feel waxy to the touch, indicating lots of jelly-making substance in the skin.

With its low, wide top and crooked branches, often shrubby with several trunks, it looks like a crab walking across an old field, if you feel imaginative.

Crab flowers are pinker, more fragrant than the eating apple tree. Nurserymen sell imported types just for their showy flowers. The flowering apple tree you see in the park is apt to be a Siberian crab. *Malus coronaria*

★**Black Cherry** is on the first team with the American hardwoods—growing all over eastern U. S. with elm, oak, maple, birch. It has so little outward distinction that few people recognize our only valuable cherry tree. Branches are often broken, dishevelled, and favorite pastures for tent caterpillars. Buds are inconspicuous; dark red, shiny. Leaves are stereotyped ovals. The bark of an old trunk is almost black, made of small broken pieces of the original smooth surface. But run your eye up to the top of trunk and limbs—you may see there the glossy, dark red cherry bark peppered with short horizontal lines.

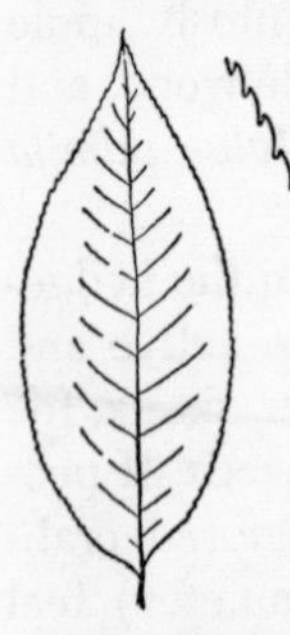

Black Cherry leaf has incurving teeth.

The lines are breathing pores (lenticels) to let air inside the tree where the shoe-polished bark is air-proof. White flowers droop in clusters the size of your longest finger. Dark purple cherries, two months later, are seldom seen because some 70 kinds of birds go after them.

For sure identification chew the end of a twig, taste the peculiar cherrystone bitterness. Another detail to check is the unusual incurving of the teeth along leaf edge.

Early settlers cut big cherry trees for paneling and furniture, rivaling black walnut in beauty. Cherry wood grows richer, darker with age. They also made cherry bounce from fruits, though we wonder how the crop was picked before the birds took it. With scarcity of big trees, cherry wood today is used for small things where smooth perfection of wood with no warping is needed: spirit levels, saw handles, blocks for electrotypes. In a tough, scrubby form, black cherry is one of the commonest trees in woods around New York City.

Prunus serotina

Fruit of Black Cherry

Sweet Cherry is better recognized as cherry because the trunk keeps smooth, glossy, red-brown bark. Horizontal lines in the bark turn yellow and callous but they are vivid, decorative. Sweet cherry leaves have irregular teeth as contrasted with the even saw-teeth of black cherry. Old homestead property often has this cherry, and it escapes to the edge of the woods. It bears so many good eating cherries that people as well as birds can have some to eat.

Prunus avium

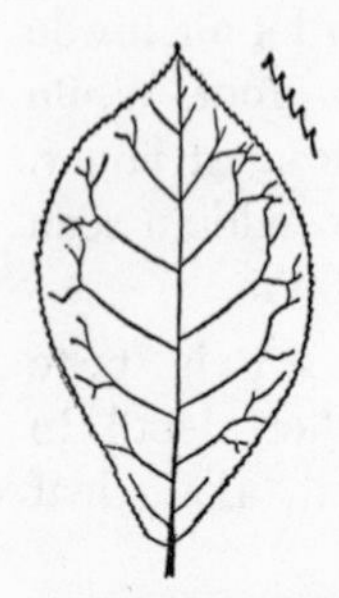

Chokecherry has tiny jagged teeth.

Chokecherry is a scraggly version of the wild black cherry. Its red-purple fruit puckers your mouth, but makes good pie. The fame of this tree is in the way it attracts birds. Twittering in the thickets is often caused by excitement over it. Dangling white fingers of flowers make this small rough tree with black bark conspicuous in the spring. Teeth of leaves point out, compared with incurved teeth of black cherry, twigs are as bitter to taste. One of the most widely distributed trees in North America. *Prunus virginiana*

Wild Red Cherry (also called bird, pin, or fire cherry) has bright translucent red cherries on long stems, a few together in clumps instead of finger-like clusters. The red-brown bark is smooth and peels off. Grows in burnt-over places with aspen and gray birch.

Prunus pensylvanica

Peach is the first fruit tree to bloom in the spring. Rose-pink blossoms flare while rest of landscape is still drab. You can't miss this tree while motoring in March-April through Virginia and southward. Cherry, apple, and pear have white flowers. In size and color peach flowers look like redbud, but the latter blooms later, in the woodland, while peach is planted by a house or in an open field.

Prunus Persica

Other fruit trees planted for flowers in gardens and parks are oriental cherries (finest rose-colored, double-flowered display in America in Brooklyn Botanic Garden), plum, almond, prune, apricot.

CITY TREES

City people used to live with trees as easily as country people. They simply moved in elm, maple, linden, and so on. For a generation cities like Columbus, Ohio, would hardly be recognized without its elms—in that city four rows of elms stood along downtown Broad Street. The inexorable pressure of big buildings, crowds, automobiles has pushed trees out of the cities—except in parks. But a blank was left in people's lives—green is easy on the eyes, shade is comforting, buds are reassuring when they open in the spring. People have missed them and yearn for them.

Today city planners are searching for trees from a fresh viewpoint. The traditional shade trees are not coming back. How to make a tree grow in an intolerable situation? The problem: polluted air; desert aridity of pavements; salt used to melt snow and ice; visits of male dogs.

Certain trees resist city conditions better than others, for example, pin oak, catalpa, poplar, Norway maple will do business in crowded suburbs. Cleveland is experimenting with small flowering trees. In big downtown industrial cities the following three trees have supreme fortitude.

Ginkgo leaf

Ginkgo (also called maidenhair tree) should be exciting as a crocodile on a big city street. Yet millions in Washington, New York, Cincinnati, and other cities pass by without a glance because ginkgo seems like an ordinary tree. But its leaves are fern leaves, from the Age of Reptiles. A weird fact is that the pollen of this tree is unlike that of other trees of our day, but swims like fern sperms wriggling through rain or dew instead of being blown or transferred by insects. Science once tried to relate ginkgo to yew, a member of pine family, with berry-like fruit. Now a class of tree has been set up by botanists for the ginkgo alone. There is no other tree like it, delivered, as it were, by parcel post from the age of dinosaurs into the heart of our teeming cities.

See the little leaf fans with wavy edges and a slice like a thin piece of pie cut out. Fruits like tiny buff plums dangle on stems. Outer husk has foul smell; nut inside is shelled by pinching its thin coat, out pops silver-white kernel; nourishing, but tastes like rancid butter. Don't expect to find these fruits often. It takes 30 years to produce them. Most ginkgos are too young or else are male trees that have no berries.

Somehow ginkgo's peculiar leaves resist fumes and soot; somehow a tree evolved in a bygone age can take our ruthless cities, creating trunk, leaf and fruit from miserable dirt below the scorching pavements.

Ginkgo biloba

Ailanthus (also called tree of heaven) is the luxurious backyard tree you see over the city fence. Or if there is a square foot of soil facing a hot dirty street, ailanthus will grow as though in a cool, moist garden. City rubbish seems to make satisfactory fertilizer for a tree that has more virility than most weeds. Pith of twig is huge, bright orange, bark is decorated with big shield-shaped scars where branches used to be attached. Leaves are tropical ferns in aspect, spouting up gay, fresh green, but if you crush one, the odor is rank. Seeds are airplane propellers, two blades twisted, spinning the seed through the air when it lets go. *Ailanthus altissima*

Ailanthus

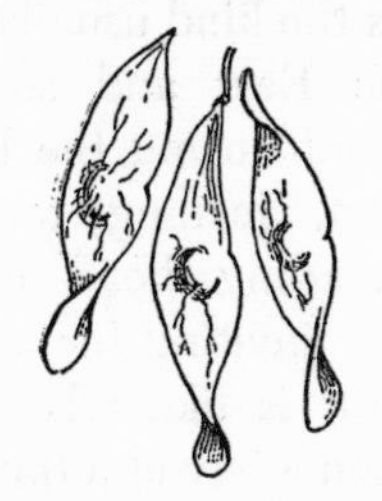

Ailanthus seeds

London Plane Tree is like a sycamore with patches of yellow and brown on trunk, instead of white patches. Fruit balls dangle in twos from branches. This tree was bred by crossing two kinds of sycamores. It prospers downtown better than any other standard shade tree. New York City has many in midtown streets, as in front of Rockefeller Plaza, and it is doing a good job providing cool shade for bench-sitters in little park back of Public Library in heart of Manhattan. *Platanus acerifolia*

THE MULBERRIES

Mulberry is an exciting little tree. The leaves suggest that evolution of the ages is going on before our eyes, but has not yet settled on a fixed mulberry leaf form. Although all leaves have sharp, irregular teeth with vivid veins sunk into them, some are oval, others have an eccentric lobe or two, like your thumb, or merely a lump. Others may have a number of lobes and turn into fancy designs. Sassafras leaves also come in a variety of shapes but have smooth edges.

White Mulberry is the kind usually seen planted around older towns of the East and sometimes along New England roads settled during the last century. It has a short, leaning trunk and low, wide-spreading head casting dense shade; very inviting for a picnic on a hot day. Fruit is like white blackberries. These ripen a few at a time during several summer months instead of ripening and falling together like most tree fruits. People don't enjoy the taste but mulberries are a great attraction for birds, and good for fattening poultry.

White Mulberry

This is the silkworm tree. American settlers, including George Washington and Benjamin Franklin, planted mulberry freely, hoping to start a silk industry. But, for Americans, it was too much work to pick and feed leaves to silkworms at just the right moment. The fastidious worm will only eat them slightly wilted, rejecting a fresh leaf or one that is badly wilted. It takes a ton of leaves to make a few pounds of raw silk. Cut a twig when sun is hot and see the milky sap ooze out, and you will see the chemical which is turned to silk threads by the worm. *Morus alba*

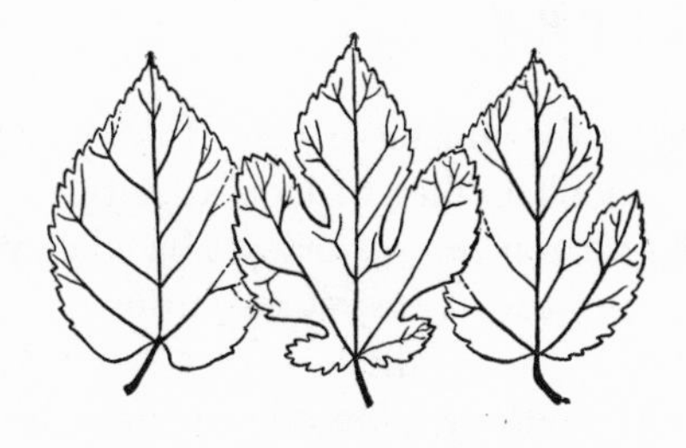

Three kinds of White Mulberry leaves

Paper Mulberry is a true colonial landscape feature. Thousands of visitors marvel at this tree in Williamsburg, Jamestown, and the old Virginia estates. It's fairly common throughout the South. The characteristic that stops you is the trunk contorted with huge convolutions that seem to speak of great age. This is an abnormal growth common to this tree. Where the bark is normal it is smooth and yellowish, with dim lines interlacing like etching on a ground glass surface. *Broussonetia papyrifera*

Red Mulberry is our native American tree that grows tall and straight in the southern Appalachian woods. You're not likely to see it. Middle Western and Southern farms seek it out for fence posts, for the wood is hard, tough, and doesn't decay on contact with soil.

This mulberry makes good shade tree to plant beside chicken yard where it drops fattening food all summer long that poultry love. Like all mulberries, sap is milky. This is family relative to tropical fig and rubber trees. Milky sap of the latter is latex for natural rubber.

Morus rubra

HACKBERRY

Hackberry is the unknown tree. Taking it for an elm, most people don't bother to look at it twice. In Middle West and South you can see many a hackberry with a tall, wide sweeping head that arouses curiosity in the way it reaches skyward so royally.

Around old southern plantation houses and campuses (for example, Hampton Institute, Virginia) the light gray bark catches the eye with its corky lumps.

Another peculiar way to spot hackberry is by dark clumps of twigs, called witches' brooms, high in the tree. A fungus disease stimulates these clumps. This mars the appearance of a fine tree, but it usually doesn't hurt its health, and makes a point of identification that can be seen from afar, especially in winter. Witches' brooms on hackberry can be confused with mistletoe, but the latter has evergreen leaves, while the witches' brooms are all twigs when the leaves are off.

Without corky lumps on the trunk and witches' brooms aloft (hackberry may lack these abnormalities), look for a peculiar detail seen when you split a twig lengthwise with a sharp pocket knife. The pith of most tree twigs is whitish or yellow in the center. Hackberry pith has a row of tiny white wax paper partitions close together but with air spaces between.

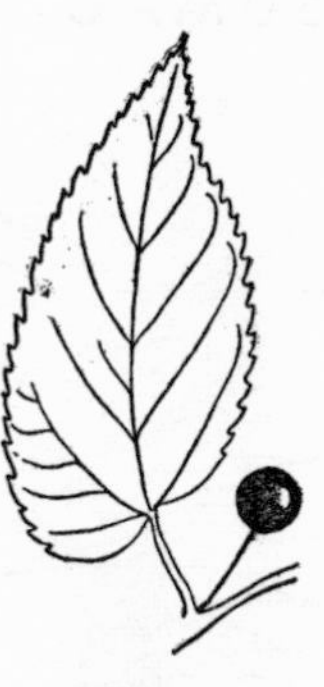

Hackberry leaf and seed

When leaves are out, you see wonderfully graceful leaf designs. One side has a wider sweep, making it lopsided like elm and basswood leaves. Hackberry, however, tapers exquisitely, forming a curve that is a segment of the dynamic spiral described by a clam shell, or a sandy beach curved by water currents, or an airplane in a sweeping turn.

This tree produces berries the size of peas dangling singly along a twig. When ripe, they are dark purple and sweet to eat. But birds usually get them first, and anyway the flesh is so thin you chew mostly on a hard seed.

Celtis occidentalis

Sugarberry, a southern hackberry, has narrower leaves, smaller berries, more warts on trunk, and is often used for a shady street tree, especially in New Orleans.

Celtis laevigata

SUMAC

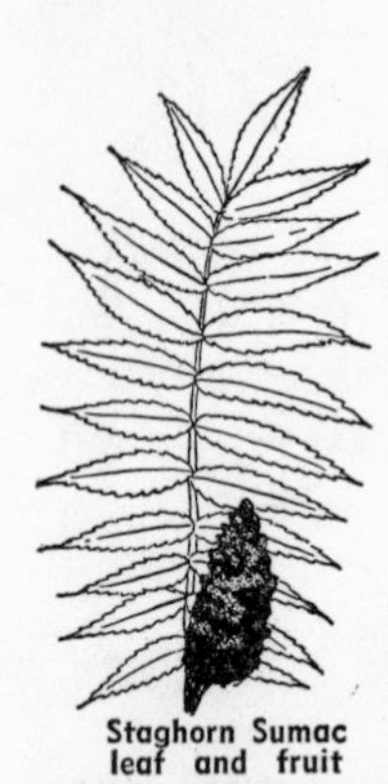
Staghorn Sumac leaf and fruit

Staghorn Sumac is the small, rank tree that grows in clumps along roadsides and on rocky, sterile spots. Tropical, fern-like foliage is surmounted by crimson plush berries in dense rough pyramids. Clump is lemony to taste, helps quench thirst, makes good lemonade. Lush and colorful, and with red fall foliage, sumac is one of the features of our eastern landscapes. You'll know staghorn by dense, sticky hairs on berries and twigs. In winter, dark branches; angular, awkward, blunt, suggest hairy antlers of young stag. Wood is soft, milky, useless—but if you push out big orange pith you have a tube to blow through to make fire burn better. *Rhus typhina*

Poison Sumac is more vicious than poison ivy. Know it to avoid. Signs are smooth-edged, graceful leaves on slender treelet in swampy place. October leaves are gorgeous flame color—look out—don't take any home! Berries dangle in loose cluster, waxy white, while berries of harmless sumac are red. Remember danger sign: white berries on pretty little tree in swampy place. *Rhus vernix*

Dwarf Sumac is commonest of this group. It grows on dry uplands and roadsides from Canada to Texas. Leaf stem has wings between pairs of leaflets. Berries are red, and plant is not poisonous. Usually a shrub.

Rhus copallina

THE EVERGREENS

The day you walk up to an evergreen and say that it is a pine or spruce, or hemlock, and so on—that day you'll discover trees in a way that brings pleasure wherever you go. Evergreens are to be seen almost everywhere.

The needle is as true a leaf as a maple leaf, even though it is exceedingly long and narrow. The cone is a peculiar kind of fruit. Instead of juicy flesh or husk or seeds encased in various kinds of containers, the cone consists of wooden discs on which seeds lie naked upon their upper surfaces. The discs are folded up tight while their seeds are ripening. Finally they swing wide open and winged seeds fly away in the wind. The cone is, indeed, a silent, efficient mechanism.

You can instantly tell six kinds of evergreen trees as follows:

Pine: Long, flexible needles in a bunch, clasped by a papery sheath where they are attached to twig. Number of needles per bunch is 2, 3, or 5 depending on the sort of pine it is.

Spruce: Short, stiff needles, angular in cross-section like a shoemaker's awl, set singly, not in bunches, around a twig. Each needle is attached to a curved peg. Sure sign of spruce is to remove needle and see its peg fixed to twig. Also note roughness of the older twigs with pegs left where needles fell. You can tell spruce in the dark simply by feeling twig.

Hemlock: Short, flat needles in horizontal plane along twig. Undersides have two white lines. Note tiny upside-down needles lying along top of twig between outspreading rows of needles.

Fir: Short, flat needles like hemlock, but longer, lighter green. When needle is removed, no projection is left on twig as with spruce; instead a smooth round mark with dot in center. Another point is that cones stand up on fir, while on other evergreens they usually turn down.

Larch: Short flexible needles spout from ends of heavy spurs on branch. Needles are cast off in winter leaving twigs bare, and spurs give branches lumpy, coarse appearance.

Cedar: Two kinds of needles spell red cedar. Some are tightly fitting, overlapping scales that do not stick out but fit tightly around twig, and others are short, sharp needles that flare haphazardly. White cedar has only one kind of needle: smooth, rounded overlapping scales that make the twig light green, polished, decorative.

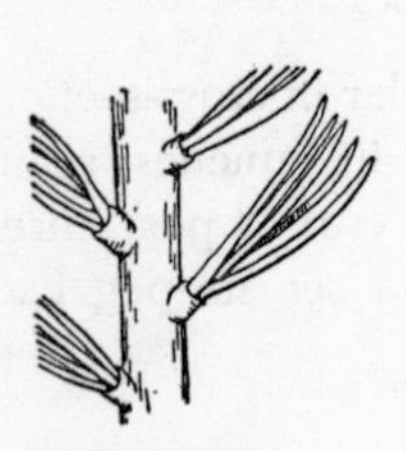

Pine needles grow in clusters.

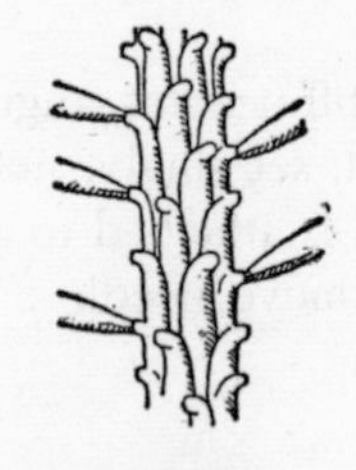

Spruce needles are on tiny pegs.

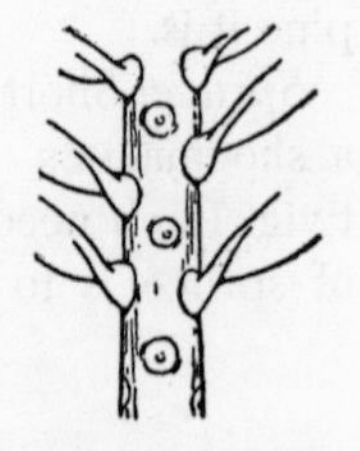

Fir needles leave small circle with dot in it.

THE PINES

★★★**White Pine** is the rugged, giant pine tree of northeast United States. You often see it as a solitary, massive survivor of white pine forests that have vanished into lumber. Heavy limbs stab out at right angles from the trunk. The angular dark masses of foliage show bright light of sky between. Twigs tend to grow upward above their branches so that the needle masses are underscored by horizontal black line of limb on which they grow. The general effect of an old white pine is that of a broad, eccentric triangle.

On the ground under a white pine you'll find artistic cones, some up to six inches long. These are gracefully curved. Their plates are wide open, showing how the seeds have been discharged. These hard, tough cones make a crackling, cheery fire, with bright bursts from the incandescent resin with which they are heavily sugared. White pine cones with tassels of needles are the State Flower of Maine. This pine cone makes an attractive indoor decoration. Cones on the ground fell after their seeds were gone. Overhead in the branches, mostly near the top of the tree, grow younger cones, with their ripening seeds sealed in tightly beneath smooth green plates.

Note the way pine needles grow in bunches. Count them. White pine has 5 needles clasped together. They have the feel of flexible, springy wires 4 inches long. Straight rows of tiny white dots are the breathing pores of the needle. Peer closely and see how the edges are

Cone of White Pine

saw-toothed. Such perfection of details reveals the precision that goes into the making of a tree.

White pine branches spring out in whorls around the trunk at the rate of one whorl a year. You can tell the age of a white pine by counting these whorls from base to top. Add three for the first years when the seedling did not produce regular side branches. This age token is inaccurate for old specimens when bark has obliterated the marks left by whorls of early years.

White pine has vitality. The seeds from a single tree can people an undisturbed meadow with young white pines in a year or two. Youthful pines may grow 4 feet in height and an inch in diameter in one year.

The tree is named after the clean, white wood. This was the timber of the tall masts and spars of New England clipper ships. Pine panels, fragrant with age, are a prize feature of colonial houses. Widths of upwards of 3 feet testify to the size of trees in the vanished white pine forests of New England. *Pinus strobus*

Red Pine (also called Norway pine) is the other big, valuable pine tree. It is more northerly than white pine. Wood is as good, and is usually sold as white pine. Red pine is tall and straight with red bark. Healthy, grows fast, is excellent for reforestation. Be on lookout for one of best pines of our Northeast. Needles are extra long, clasped together in 2's. *Pinus resinosa*

Red Pine cone

Pitch Pine is the small pine tree you encounter in large numbers along New England's coast. In New Jersey pitch pine covers hundreds of sandy square miles, make an unusual and famous type of forest known as the New Jersey pine barrens. This is also the pine of rocky hilltops where it invites your camera for a windblown picture. Cones hang on after discharging seeds; they are dynamic, broad, wide open, add much to the artistry of the branches. You can't miss this tree—needles (in 3's) are sharp, stiff; stand out at right angles. It's a fighter. *Pinus rigida*

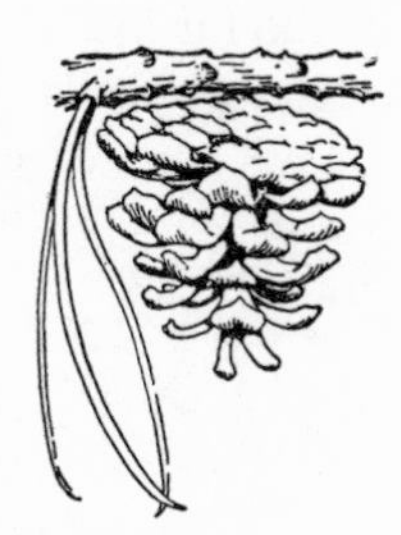

Pitch Pine cone

Scotch Pine is a bent, leaning tree often planted in poor, dry soil. Perhaps seen more often than others by city people, as it has been much used for gravelly spots in parks, and in large numbers around reservoirs. Foliage is light-colored with needles in 2's. You can call out the name of Scotch pine when you see orange bark, especially bright orange toward upper part of trunk and on branches. *Pinus sylvestris*

Scotch Pine cone

Jack Pine has shortest needles in 2's. They twist and separate with a flare that gives tree light, airy aspect. Cones are small, narrow, hard; they are curved, hug the bark tightly closed. Like the counterpart of this tree, lodgepole pine

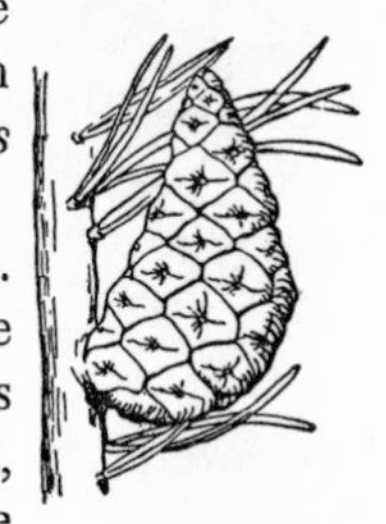

Jack Pine cone

of the far West, it takes a fire to crack cones open and discharge seeds. Jack pine is most northern of the eastern pines. Common around Great Lakes, in dry sandy places. *Pinus banksiana*

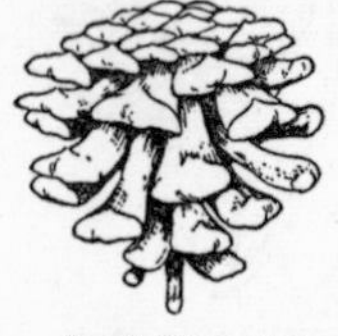
Scrub Pine cone

Scrub Pine has 2 short needles that stick out at angles. Looks like jack pine. Makes broad, picturesque, scrubby patches in southern New Jersey and Virginia. *Pinus virginiana*

THE SPRUCES

Norway Spruce points skyward, high and sharp as a church steeple. Bottom branches, instead of dropping off like most spruces, sweep out close to ground with a low curve, giving a broad formal base to a towering tent. You always see it beside square Victorian houses, in cemeteries, older parks, on University campuses such as University of Vermont, Burlington. Easy to recognize by its twigs that dangle on older trees instead of poking out stiffly. Bears longest of spruce cones. Look for these handsome ovals; rhythmic, with lights and shadows spiralling across the evenly spaced surfaces of their many scales. This big spruce is an out-of-date tree from the lace curtain era. *Picea abies*

Norway Spruce cone

Blue Spruce is styled for decoration. Stiff branches are horizontal. Bottom branches hold on vigorously, making a healthy, dense pyramid that conceals its own trunk. You know it by the light, gray-blue color of needles. Blue spruce is native in Colorado where it acquired the ability to grow in a dry place. Next to Norway, it is the most commonly planted spruce in eastern states, a staple of the nursery industry. See also page 179. *Picea pungens*

Three spruces are left to know: red, white and black. They all look alike, compact, acute arrow heads pointing skyward from the mountains and bogs up north. They are the trees of places least disturbed by man until recently. Dark and timeless spruce settles in cold north woods humus to create the wilderness home of beaver, bear, and deer. Spruce is constructed to hold deep, white burdens of snow on its stiff branches. Their quivering wood is so resonant it makes sounding boards for violin and piano. Today more and more people are seeing spruce, as these are the trees of the land of the skiers. But spruce forests have been invaded in another way. The streams of northern United States and Canada carry not only the canoes of fishermen and hunters but some are jammed with logs crunching and jerking their way to the pulp mill, to turn up at your newsstand. It takes the annual growth of a stand of 252 acres of spruce forest for an average Sunday edition of the New York Daily News. Paper companies are developing forest management to protect the supply of this valuable tree.

Red Spruce is the spruce tree seen all over the Adirondacks, Green and White Mountains. It is the spruce of Bear Mountain, highest mountain in Connecticut, and

Greylock, highest in Massachusetts. Red spruce fronts the ocean on the Maine coast, looks picturesque through the spray above the rocks. Look for the small red cones. These lovely, broad ovals lie on the ground under the tree which sheds them every year. The amber gum oozing from the trunk is good chewing. *Picea rubra*

White Spruce is the tall lumber of the north woods. Its needles have a whitish tint which labels the tree from a distance, gives it the name. White is taller, with longer cones than other spruces. Cones are cylindrical, smooth, tan-colored, about two inches long. Resin on trunk and branches turns white when it dries. Superb and valuable as it is, white spruce is identified by the bad odor of its young twigs and needles. Crush them and take a whiff. This is the chief tree of the Canadian forest, and supplies most of the pulp for newsprint. *Picea glauca*

Black Spruce is the courageous, rugged tree for your drawing pad. It makes a sharp arrow head when young, but top becomes tortured by its struggle with the severe climate of the cold northern bog where it grows. Dwarfed

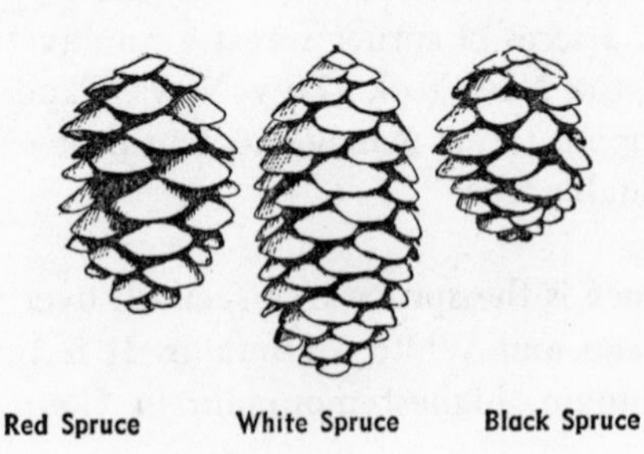

Red Spruce White Spruce Black Spruce

by subzero temperatures, black spruce only a few feet high may be 50 years old. This is the tree of the famous floating bogs of northern Minnesota. Sometimes a lower branch reaching out and down penetrates the sphagnum mosses and takes root. Older black spruce is loaded with countless little purple cones that hang on for years. Next to white spruce, this is Canada's most important source of paper pulp. *Picea mariana*

HEMLOCK

Hemlock is music in the form of a tree. It is a tall, graceful spiral like a Christmas card evergreen, but with sweeping, curved lines, instead of the stiff staccato of spruce. Hemlock needles are flattened and rounded at the tips while spruce are 4-angled and sharp. The top surface of hemlock needle is polished and curved, reflecting blue highlights of the sky that shimmer through its foliage. Such trilling blue light is peculiar to this tree—don't miss seeing it. Little red-brown cones dangle from the tips of flexible wiry twigs, vibrating up and down.

Needles are attached spirally around their twig, but their stalks bend so as to hold them in a horizontal plane forming two rows on each side of twig. Underside of needle has two white lines, and a sure token of hemlock is the row of upside-down needles flat along upper side of twig.

Hemlock cone

This is one of the decorative trees of our woods. Growing farther south, or lower on mountain sides, than spruce and fir, you see it often mingling with maple, beech, elm, and hickory. Its place must be damp, and hemlock is at its best in shadowy ravines. New York Botanical Garden has fine old hemlock grove.

Hemlock wood is second-rate which may be why we can still see many of these stately and beautiful trees. It splinters, warps, is filled with knots as hard as rocks, and makes dangerous firewood that throws out sparks.

Tsuga canadensis

BALSAM FIR

Balsam Fir holds title as the north woods' most popular tree, with delicious fragrance released by the needles after they dry. Confusion between kinds of evergreens reaches a climax when balsam fir pillows are labeled a breath from the "pines." Because needles are fragrant and hang on longer in the house, this is better Christmas tree than spruce. When you buy, test for fir by removing a needle, see if twig is left smooth with tiny round mark and dot in its center. (This test does not apply to Douglas fir, the leading Christmas tree out west.) Needles are flat with whitish underside; longer, lighter green than spruce and hemlock.

Balsam Fir cone stands upright on twig.

Balsam fir bark has little blisters containing clear reservoirs of resin. This is so pure it is used for cementing microscope lenses and mounting microscopic specimens. Every laboratory worker knows "Canada balsam."

Cones stand erect like candles on

fir tree boughs. On other evergreens they dangle or are turned down. The big cylinders three inches long and an inch thick look too heavy for the twigs. However, every camper who has made his bed with springy balsam boughs knows how easily and gaily they carry weight.

Abies balsamea

LARCH

Larch (also called tamarack) sheds its needles in the fall, and grows a complete set of fresh needles in the spring like a broadleaf tree. Yet, when needles are out, larch looks like any normal evergreen and bears small, tan cones resembling hemlock's. This extraordinary behavior of a cone-bearing tree is also a feature of bald cypress. Both larch and bald cypress grow in swamps, and it is interesting to speculate whether roots in water may have influenced these two cone-bearing trees to become leaf droppers.

Another claim to fame is the appearance of larch in its far north bogs—always straight, clean, serene, while its companions, black spruce and balsam fir, are usually wind-twisted, look like fierce fighters of the elements. These three trees grow northward to the treeline tundra above the Arctic Circle.

Needles, like seasonal leaves, are soft, moist, compared to the crisp, woody needles on other cone-bearing trees. They are less than an inch long, and radiate from the tips of wooden knobs, a bunch of some 18 spraying out at wide angles. They are blue-

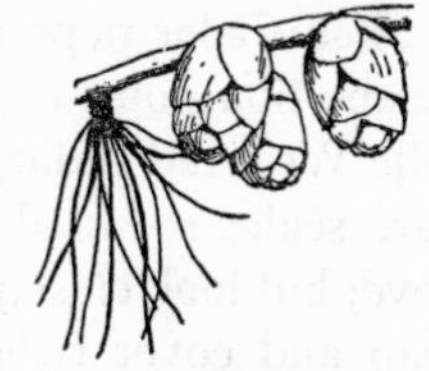

Larch cones

green; foliage is feathery and light-tinted. New twigs of the season, before woody knobs are formed, put forth needles scattered along singly. One feature not so easily seen is the system of long, tough root fibers that may drop twenty feet through a bog to get a firm bottom. These root strings are as heavy as waxed thread used by a shoemaker. Indians used them to sew together birch bark canoes. *Larix laricina*

THE CEDARS

Entirely different in style from all other trees of our landscape, cedars can be instantly recognized. Among trees that are tall, loose, and reaching, cedar looks clipped formal, geometric. Foliage is compact and dark. Density is increased by myriads of tiny twigs concealed by overlapping needles so that a cedar may appear as having no branches, but built out of a mass of green shaped into a pyramid or oval.

Three kinds of cedar of eastern states are easily recognized with a little practice. But you seldom see all three growing near each other. The different cedars herd together in different places, and the first way to identify one is by the place where you see it.

Red Cedar peppers New England hillsides like an exclamation point turned upside down. In South and Middle West red cedar takes a wider, explosive form. Leaves are scales so small you can barely see them with naked eye; but look closely and admire how perfectly they overlap and cover twig on four sides, making twig appear square in cross-section. Young twigs have needles sharp and long, entirely different from the scale needles. Best check on red cedar is the small, sky blue berries. These are "cones" whose scales have turned waxy and blue and become welded together. Heartwood is beautiful red with aroma fragrant to our nostrils but hated by moths. This is the wood for lining closets and cedar chests. *Juniperus virginiana*

Red Cedar has two kinds of needles.

Arbor Vitae (also called northern white cedar) is the marvelous yellow-green column in the coldest parts of New England and Lake states. You can plant cuttings of fresh twigs in sand and grow them easily for planting around your home. Nurserymen offer tailor-made specimens. Twig is covered by overlapping scales as tightly fitting as a snake's skin. Branching twigs form flat, polished frond, one of the most artistic designs discovered on the twigs of any tree in the world. Wood resists decay, makes good shingles and fence posts. *Thuja occidentalis*

Arbor Vitae

Southern White Cedar is a dark swamp tree that hugs the Atlantic coast. This is the tree of the cedar bogs, feature of the famous New Jersey pine barrens. Trunks buried in New Jersey swamp mud were dredged up, untouched by rot, turned into tough PT boats in Second World War. Resonant wood makes good pipe organs. *Chamaecyparis thyoides*

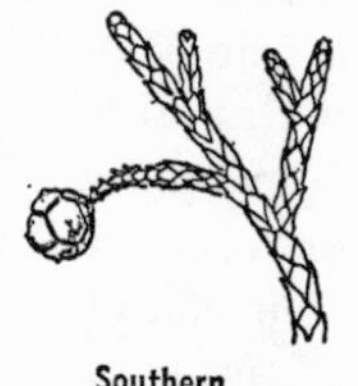
Southern White Cedar

THE MIDDLE WEST

Trees pour into the Middle West from four points of the compass, so people there cannot boast of many of their own kinds of trees. Trees seen in New England cross the Appalachians, spread out over most of the Middle West. Everywhere are big standard trees—elm, white oak, hickory, trembling aspen, sycamore, beech, tulip, willow, maple, cherry, and the understory witch hazel, sassafras, hop hornbeam.

Nevertheless, the mixing in of southern and prairie trees, the dropping out of northern ones like paper birch, changes the emphasis, gives Middle West trees a distinctive aspect. Many more black walnut, sweetgum, hackberry, persimmon, hawthorn, honey locust appear on every hand. Black cherry grows larger. Shagbark hickory becomes shellbark. Sugar maple is called hard or rock maple. White and gray birch disappear, and abundant river birches line the waterways. Cottonwood joins with trembling aspen. Bur oak becomes the Middle West's greatest oak, abundant in Kansas and Nebraska. This is a true Middle West tree. It contests possession of land with prairie grasses, pushing forest fingers into the wide open spaces. These groves with no understory of trees or shrubs, but with carpets of clean grass are famous as "bur oak openings."

Between the Corn Belt of Kansas and Iowa and the Appalachians are nine states that form a huge mixing bowl of trees. This holds the greatest number of species and the most broadleaf trees of any forest of America. The northern part of this tree domain has millions of acres of evergreens. Indeed, white pine, which was the backbone of New England's shipbuilding a century ago, today has its best stands in Minnesota, Wisconsin, and Michigan.

Most of the original forest has been replaced by farmland, but from the Tennessee mountains and from farm woodlands we get a large quantity of the best-grade hardwood lumber.

The Middle West might well claim to be headquarters of the Great American Woods. People traveling back and forth between the nine states of the central forest and eastern states meet no great surprises nor puzzling styles of trees as they would when traveling south or far west. The Appalachians oppose no barrier to interchanging our best-known trees. Certain trees that are especially characteristic of the Middle West are as follows:

★**Bur Oak** (also called mossycup oak) is king of the White Oak Group in the Middle West. Its massive black trunk and big horizontal limbs make impressive silhouette in the murk around Chicago. Patriarchal aspect is heightened by deep furrowed

Bur Oak Acorn

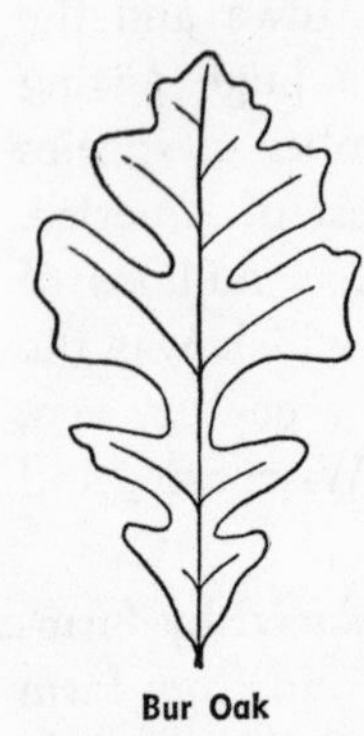
Bur Oak

bark. This is so fire-resistant that it explains the survival of many giant bur oaks, especially in woods of Indiana and Illinois. Westward where wooded country shades off to prairie, bur oak forms open groves, contesting the land with the grasses. Small bur oaks bridge the Great Plains and turn up in the foothills of the Rockies. Two peculiar details tell the bur oak: leaf is almost cut in two where the opposite sinuses try to meet. Acorn cup is extra deep, covering half the nut, and it is shaggy, with heavy spines on rim.

Quercus macrocarpa

★**Box Elder** (also called ash-leaved maple) is the tree you see everywhere in the Middle West. Double-winged seeds always tag a maple—just as acorns always identify an oak. Box elder's winged seeds make a sharp angle like closing scissors. They hang on most of the winter. Leaf is multiple with 3-leaflets (sometimes 5)—the only maple with an un-maple-like leaf. But the over-all outline of 3 leaflets together suggests maple leaf form. Perhaps this is a diagram of evolution going on before our eyes showing how a standard maple leaf can evolve from 3 leaflets.

Box Elder leaf is only a step away from conventional Maple leaf.

Twigs are pastel red, purple, or bright green coated with soft white bloom. Coating rubs off with finger, revealing a glossy twig, and giving inner satisfaction as does rubbing off silver polish to see the shine.

Branches are brittle, scattered over ground by wind. But tree is planted far and wide along streets. You see it in Chicago, Denver, and Dallas. It's America's most agreeable tree, doing well in high or low places, sunlight or shade, moist or dry places. East of the Alleghanies you seldom see it, and people from New England might take the leaves for poison ivy. It branches out this way and that spontaneously with no clear shape. Wood is soft and used to make cheap furniture, easily broken toys. *Acer negundo*

Box Elder seeds

Osage Orange was an industry before the invention of barbed wire. Western settlers used it for fencing to keep out cattle. Touching it carelessly gives you shock from 1-inch thorns sharp as needles. Remnants of old hedges remain with "oranges" hanging among barby branches or rolling down onto the road where they often squash and make mess with seeds and pulp. This peculiar fruit on the ground signals to passerby that osage orange is near. It is like a big green orange, but stippling is coarser, its rounded bumps and ridges vaguely suggesting a brain. Milky sap from fruit and broken twigs has pungent fragrance of oriental lacquer, sticks to hands, quickly turns black. Fruit is inedible, but small boys use it to play catch.

This healthy, dangerous tree has wonderful wood. Heartwood is yellow streaked with red, enclosed in white sapwood, and takes a luxurious polish. Elastic, so Indians made bows of it; and we make policemen's clubs.

Osage Orange

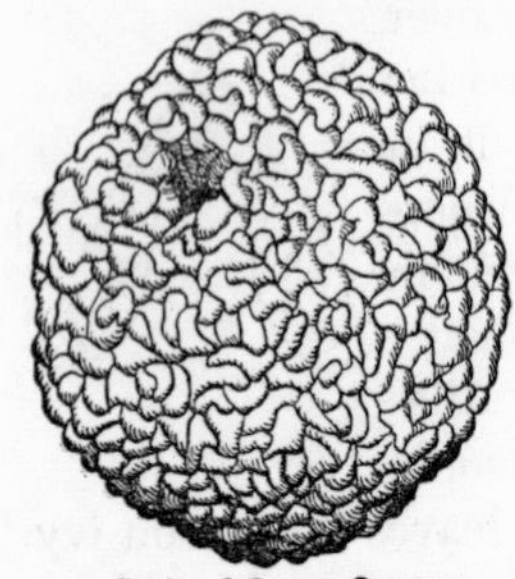
Fruit of Osage Orange

Leaves are smooth, curly and gay—catching highlights in a striking way. Bark is yellow (bark on roots is surprisingly bright orange), and deeply furrowed like black locust.

Osage orange is a museum piece from the settlement of our western prairies. First settlers in St. Louis got it from Oklahoma and Texas Indians; later, men profited by selling osage orange for use as barbed wire fences that need no repairing, came rigged up with fence posts. *Maclura pomifera*

Sorrel Tree (also called sour wood) is the mystery tree of the hills from Ohio southward. It peppers the woods where oak, maple, hickory, and such well-known trees grow. The tree is inconspicuous, middle-sized. Bark is nondescript like sour gum; leaf is unexciting, glossy, oval like peach tree. Nobody notices sorrel tree until something happens.

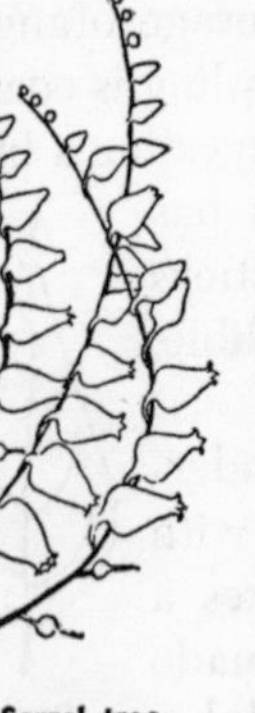
Sorrel tree flowers

The first event occurs in mid-summer when other tree flowers are gone and forgotten. Then this straight, clean tree holds out clusters of thousands of white flowers like lilies-of-the-valley. They dangle in rows on curving stems 7 inches long. Each flower is an exquisite white bell. These are fragrant, and a source of good honey, making one of the world's best bee trees. Each flower turns into a seedcase, a gray urn shaped like the white flower, that is a remarkable bit of tree jewelry. The second event is the fall color of sorrel tree. Leaves are sour, taste one, as this is a point of identification; the lemony tang is pleasant. Acid in the sap turns leaves bright red when frostbitten. The pinky red of sorrel tree is one of the fine sights of the woods around Chattanooga and southward. Its foliage can compete with sugar maple on this score. *Oxydendrum arboreum*

Sorrel tree

Kentucky Coffee Tree shows how eccentric a tree can be. Branches are bare until late in spring; leaves fall before all others. Translation of its scientific name "Gymnocladus" describes it well; first part means "naked," as in gymnasium where you strip for exercise, and "cladus" means branch. The twigs are fat, crooked and appear coated with old whitewash that has turned gray and is flaking off. See the colorful, salmon-pink pith in their center.

Double multiple leaves (compare honey locust and Hercules'-club) are enormous, up to 3 feet long. These appear magically out of tiny winter buds that are almost invisible. Leaves are so open they cast little shade, but filter the sunlight. Big broad pods seem made of tough old leather, dark red, blackened with age. Half a dozen hard seeds rattle in these pods. First settlers in Kentucky, cut off from coffee, ground up these seeds, made a good substitute. They thought their coffee tree was a wonderful

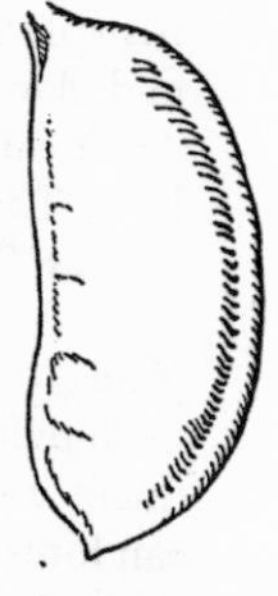

Seed-pod of Kentucky Coffee tree

discovery that would make them rich, but imported coffee won out. Eccentric twigs and big leaves make a picturesque lawn tree. Planted as such especially in South Dakota. *Gymnocladus dioica*

Kentucky Coffee tree

"We think the typical American trees and flowers are those described in our own tree and flower guides —elm, oak, maple; witch hazel, sassafras, shadblow; alder, blueberry, hazelnut; violet, marsh marigold, iris—these are typical big trees, little trees, shrubs, and flowers of our hardwood forest. These are as American as baseball. Yet they did not always grow here. They were not even created on our hills and valleys. They came from the south, where they fled from the Big Ice and then radiated north over the glacial delta. They were returning to where they had been before the Ice came. While this part of the continent was being rebuilt by the Big Ice, our American forest was crowded down along the slopes of the southern Alleghenies."

from OUR FLOWERING WORLD

Wafer Ash (also called hop tree) hangs beautiful bunches of circles all over itself. Each circle resembles modern plastic. It has two seeds in a compressed box surrounded by a translucent creamy-green diaphragm an inch across. These exquisite circles show how nature has been way ahead of us in creating plastics, efficiently, simply, out of sap and sunshine.

Smooth-edged leaves in multiples of 3 leaflets, shiny, could be mistaken for poison ivy. Wafer ash grows on edges of woods in shade, especially on rocky slopes in the Mississippi valley. For closer acquaintance, taste and smell the bitter bark. *Ptelea trifoliata*

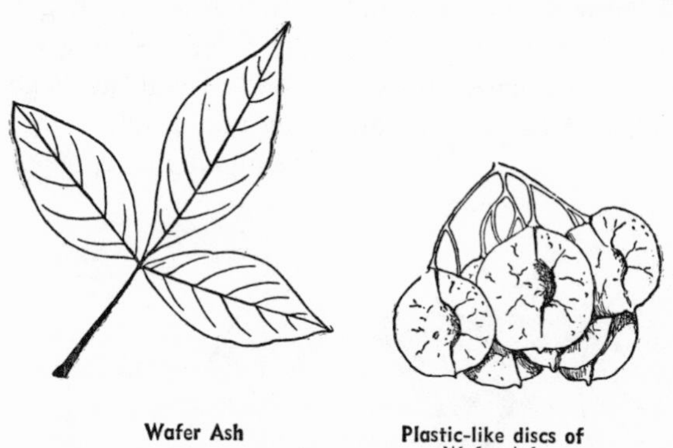

Wafer Ash

Plastic-like discs of Wafer Ash

Pawpaw looks tropical. Big 12-inch leaves spout from the tips of upturned branches, and then droop with their weight, making a pattern of green umbrellas. In April triangular flowers bloom, the color of well-done beefsteak. Bees and insects like their odor, but it's disagreeable to us. These dark peculiar flowers are inconspicuous in shadows, but their fruit is famous; a fat, short banana, overripe, with dark brown, loose skins, containing an insipid yellow custard. If we didn't have regular bananas, there might be a market for pawpaw fruit. Seeds look like lima beans. This is northern version of tropical custard apple. Pawpaw grows biggest in southern Indiana and Tennessee near streams flowing into Ohio River. Middle Westerners find it in bottom-land thickets.

Asimina triloba

Wahoo (also called burning bush) is the little tree of Arkansas that has four-lobed, flame-red fruit. In most of the Middle West it's a bush with equally startling fruit in fall. New Englanders match the display with garden shrubs related to this tree or with their climbing bittersweet. Indians made arrows of wood; if you say "wahoo" with vigor, it sounds like an arrow taking off.

Euonymus atropurpureus

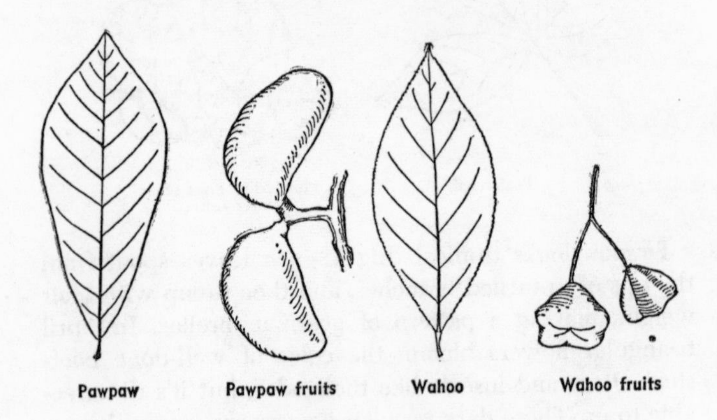

Pawpaw Pawpaw fruits Wahoo Wahoo fruits

THE SOUTH

Many trees you see in New England are growing down south: elm, oak, walnut, maple, sycamore, poplar, willow, tulip, locust, dogwood, ash. Even typically northern trees as sugar maple, shagbark hickory, red oak, and basswood have traveled to Alabama on the Appalachian ridges but that doesn't make them southern trees. In reverse, sweet gum, honey locust, hackberry, sassafras move north.

However, as you drive south, it's thrilling to see trees change. Certain kinds have the flavor of the South, and, if you're a northerner, give you the feeling of being away. No one who travels through our south Atlantic and Gulf states should miss southern magnolia, holly, live oak, bald cypress. In addition, hackberry, persimmon, sweet gum, black gum, honey locust are larger and more numerous.

South of Washington, D. C., you drive through mile after mile of tall, straight pines. This is part of the biggest pine forest in the world. It occupies much of the coastal plain, a broad band 100 to 300 miles wide to Florida and then westward around the Gulf of Mexico into Texas. Loblolly, shortleaf, longleaf, and slash (all four called southern yellow pine by lumbermen) are the big four. In the midst of this vast, sandy kingdom are swamps and bayous where grows the only bald cypress in the world.

Not characteristic of our South, but with peculiar interest, the southern part of Florida holds the only subtropical trees in the U. S. A. This is so despite the post card concept of palmetto and moss-draped live oak as being tropical vegetation. They are southern, and picturesque, of course, but not tropical.

If you live in the North, eight oaks of the South are surprising. The first five have plain oval leaves, unlike typical oak leaves. The next three have whimsical leaves to delight your eye.

****Live Oak** is the South's post card tree. It has an ample, easy-going contour, with comfortable horizontal limbs from which silvery Florida moss swings lazily. This festoonery is not a true moss but a queer member of the pineapple family that lives on air, uses trees and telegraph wires for support. You begin to see live oaks on south side of Chesapeake Bay; they follow the coast to Texas, are fine street trees in Savannah, New Orleans, and are features of the famous deep South gardens.

Massive limbs, bigger than most tree trunks, travel far out horizontally—one of the wonders of wood. Your arm straight out cannot support great weight. Consider what strength bears the tonnage of these limbs against the leverage applied where they join their trunk. Wood is even harder than the mighty white oak and was used for shipbuilding until steel took its place.

Leaves are small, smooth-margined ovals, whitish beneath, dark glossy green on top. The notion that trees stripped of leaves in winter are dead gives name to live oak—it has evergreen leaves.

Look for graceful acorns. Slender, one-inch, rich chestnut-brown, tapering at both ends. This landmark of plantations is also common in scrubby form on sand dunes.
Quercus virginiana

Water Oak is seen much along streams, and as a street tree in coastal towns. Leaves oval, but often broader near tip forming pear-shape; hang on until Christmas.
Quercus nigra

Willow Oak is a fine shade tree around southern homes, and is often seen on low hills and near swamps and streams. Leathery, narrow leaves are pointed at both ends. *Quercus phellos*

Laurel Oak is tall with glistening, almost evergreen leaves and black bark. A common street tree in Far South towns, a big tree in eastern Florida. Leaves have bristle at tip, stems are yellow with interesting groove.
Quercus laurifolia

Shingle Oak has large shiny oval leaves with wavy margins. Note bowl-shaped acorns. Handsome park tree. Southern mountains and uplands, abundant in Missouri. Wood is fine for clapboards and shingles, hence its name.
Quercus imbricaria

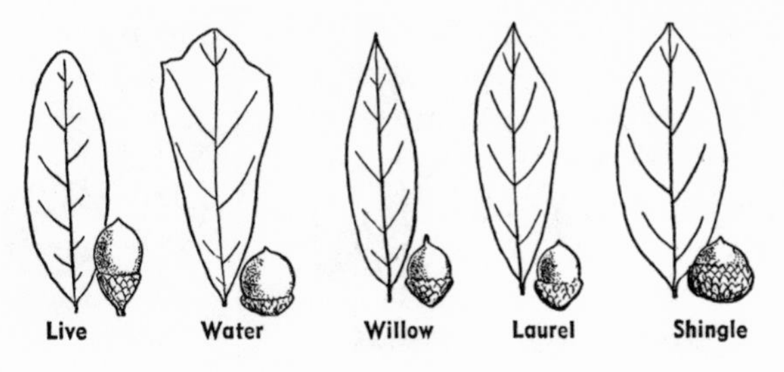

When traveling through the South, don't overlook whimsical leaf patterns on the following three oaks:

Spanish Oak has fluid leaves with slender lobes that curve like scimitars. They are utterly gay, freely drawn, a real delight if you have an eye for informal design. This lovely shade tree is common on dry uplands; and often makes acres of woods in sandy soil in Virginia and southward. *Quercus falcata*

Black Jack Oak is the common, scrubby, crooked oak that decorates poor sandy places all over the South (and as far north as New Jersey). Instead of passing it by for cooler, shadier places, pause and see the leaves. They round out with three lobes at top, have the outline of a boy's kite, or, turned around, they suggest broad bells. *Quercus marilandica*

Overcup Oak has a curious leaf with wide lobes at the top, narrow at the bottom, as though leaves from two kinds of oak had been cut in half and fitted together. A large tree beside coastal rivers and in deep swamps. You know it instantly if you find acorns with rough cup that all but encloses and hides the nut part. *Quercus lyrata*

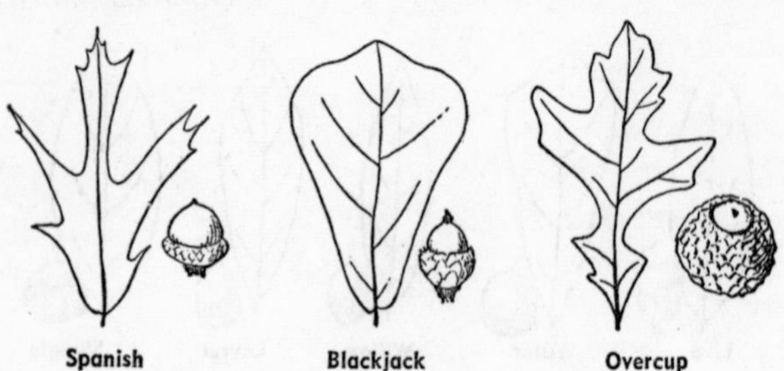

BALD CYPRESS

★★**Bald Cypress** is as great a feature of the South as live oak. To see only these two trees gives you a lifelong memory of what our South looks like. From Chesapeake Bay southward highways run through swampy areas where standing water shimmers. Unlike scrubby tangle and stunted trees in northern bogs, a stately forest rises out of the water and muck. This is headquarters of bald cypress—the only region in the world where it grows. The farther south you go the more this forest is draped with swaying Florida moss—it all looks and feels like a tropical jungle of awesome stillness, and with cathedral-like twilight. This peculiar soft glow contrasts with the black shadows of northern needle-tree forests. Cypress needles are pale green and wide open in the form of delicate feathers that filter sky brightness, and let diffused light permeate the forest. This is softened again by silvery festoons, and around the tree bases eerie brightness is reflected from mirrors of still water.

Notice the engineering of a bald cypress. The superb trunk tapers gradually from a wide, flaring base, formed like the shoulder of a bottle. This is fluted and buttressed. Thus, the center of gravity is lowered to help balance a tonnage of wood held straight

Fluted trunk and "knees" of Bald Cypress

and slender a hundred feet into the sky, though anchored in unstable water and mud.

You may see things that look like small stumps, or knots of roots around the base. These are the famous cypress knees. Often they make fantastic shapes—wood sculpturing at its most imaginative. The knee is a unique invention of bald cypress to get more air into the tree's system, prevent drowning of the roots. Ordinary trees get enough air from spaces between soil particles, but steps have to be taken to get more air when tree roots are under still water. Knees are just the right height to hold their tops above the average water level in that place.

Cones are round, an inch across. Strangely, this cone-bearing needle tree drops its needles and also twigs to which they're attached. This makes it look dead, and when fresh, feathery needles come out in the spring, they tint the soft glow of a cypress swamp with iridescent bluish-green.

Cypress wood is almost decay-proof—excellent for gutters, coffins, and shingles. *Taxodium distichum*

Pond Cypress

Pond Cypress is a smaller version of bald cypress, seen farther south, along Tamiami Trail and lower Everglades. Needles are pressed along twig instead of stretched out in form of feather. *Taxodium ascendens*

PALMETTO

★★**Palmetto** captures the imagination as a South Sea Island symbol of Florida's climate. It grows all over Florida, forms dense groves on Everglade hammocks, and palmetto finds pockets of warm sun as far north as South Carolina. You know it from other palms because its leaves are huge fans that stick out like pins in a pincushion ball at the top of the trunk. This is the leaf much used by churches on Palm Sunday. Palmetto is all trunk and leaves, no branches. The trunk is heavy, equal in diameter all the way up. Often it is enclosed in a loose basket made by the crisscross of old leaf stems. Sometimes leaves, instead of falling off, turn down and form a straw skirt. The fibers of leaf stems are used to make whisk brooms. Older palmettos have smooth gray trunks like cement. It's almost as durable; therefore palmetto trunks make good piling for wharves.

On the trunk top sits a single huge bud, the size and style of an artichoke. This is delicious to eat when cooked like a cabbage. (Local people call the tree cabbage palm.) But the removal of the bud ends the tree's life, and who would destroy fifty years of tree building for a single dish?

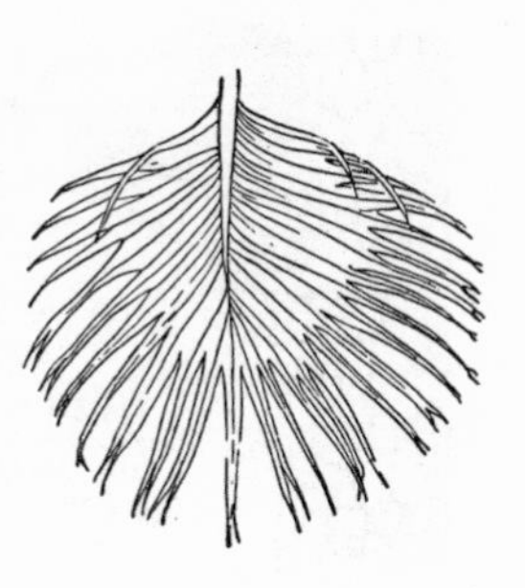

Palmetto leaf

Just look at the palmetto and consider that this tree, with nothing about it such as wood, bark, bud, or leaf like ordinary trees, is from the Age of Reptiles.

Sabal palmetto

PERSIMMON

Persimmon is the possum tree. The furry little animal gorges himself on the fruit, falls asleep hanging by his tail. Lacking the possum, there are other ways of recognizing persimmon.

This is mostly a southern tree, common in the woods, but left in fields and along roads by people who cleared the forest because they liked its fruit—and also wanted to catch possum. Thus you'll see plenty of persimmon when driving through, for example, North Carolina.

Persimmon arrests the eye, especially with leaves off. You'll say, "What are those trees with the crooked branches?" The trunk is graceful and straight, but the branches spring out above like mad snakes.

In the fall, after the leaves have dropped, the persimmon fruits look like little, tired, yellow apples; but when they look the most spoiled and wrinkled, they taste their best. An unripe persimmon is filled with tannic acid, a powerful astringent. If eaten then, it shrivels your mouth painfully so that you'd rather be stung by a wasp. This tree is a member of the Ebony Family, the hard, black wood from tropical jungles. Persimmon wood is only streaked with black. Harder than oak, it is used for spinning shuttles and for wooden golf club heads.

Possum in Persimmon tree. Notice chunky bark.

Diospyros virginiana

THE GUM TREES

★**Sweet Gum** rewards you with more peculiar surprises than any other tree of our land. Leaves offer instant identification—clear, well-made stars, the size of maple leaves. Five points are spaced as a six-pointed star, one omitted where the stem is attached. These star-leaves have a high gloss, making the whole tree twinkle in the sun. If you have a sweet gum near your home, make a note to look at it in the rain, for when wet, leaves are stars of glass with silver dripping from their points. As for fall color, no note is needed, for the deep wine-red of these leaves will stop you with their beauty.

Leaves and buds of sweet gum crushed between your fingers have a woodsy, resin odor. The deep, corky bark oozes with chewy sweet resin gum—also fragrant, one of the real natural perfumes, simply waiting to be enjoyed. It offers good chewing gum for the taking. Drug manufacturers make tincture of benzoin of it.

Sweet Gum

Through the mid-South this is one of the commonest large trees

Thorny ball of Sweet Gum

seen. This clean, straight tree is often used as a shade tree in many towns of the Ohio River Valley; for example, Cincinnati and Louisville. People who walk along streets with their noses down will see one-inch thorny balls on the ground where their shoes crunch them, balls so hard they lie around all winter, and they are tough on auto tires. These peculiar castoff balls, the shells of sweet gum fruits, tag the tree for many people.

Less conspicuous, because they are often high on the tree, are the twigs which bear another surprise. Cork is manufactured at a high rate on them. The bark-making mechanism with an abundance of the fragrant gum ingredient seems to overproduce along the twigs where only a thin bark would be needed. This results in eccentric corky ridges being built up. Cork on twigs is one of the best tags of a sweet gum in winter.

Sweet gum is a leading furniture wood, and, next to black walnut, the greatest for veneers—not in its own name but as an imitator! The fine grain has no character of its own but stains to look not only like walnut, but mahogany, maple, or birch. Your television and radio cabinets may be sweet gum.

Corky ridges of Sweet Gum

Danbury, Connecticut, has the farthest north sweet gum, but it is not common north of New Jersey except as street or park trees. Let the scientific name roll off your tongue: "Liquidambar"—a perfect name for a tree that oozes golden balsam. *Liquidambar styraciflua*

★**Black Gum** (also called sour gum and tupelo) is a sudden exclamation with its short, crooked branches that stab out horizontally from a straight, sharp trunk that is continuous from base to top. Lower branches may slant downward, but the main effect is nearly horizontal. Black gum's zig-zag branch holds leaves, clustered near the end, in a flat mosaic. Each leaf is a smooth oval with no teeth or lobes. Although the simple oval might seem conventional as a leaf form, actually so many trees have compounded their leaves or conjured up fanciful geometric designs that plain oval leaves on trees in the woods and fields of northeastern United States are rare, except on black gum and dogwood. The South, however, has many trees with smooth, oval leaves. The black gum leaf is thickened around the margin, as though it had a rim to give it strength and finish.

This tree exclamation point is more vivid in fall, when the leaves turn intense, deep red. Black gum is one of four medium-sized trees that turn so marvelously rich red that people who are not thinking about individual trees at all are stopped in their tracks; these are black gum, sweet gum, sassafras, and dogwood.

In the South black gum grows to greater size, and is common, often found in damp ground with red maple. Occasionally an old black gum in an open field in the mid-South develops with heavy, widely reaching limbs that remind a traveler from New England of white oak until he looks at the leaves.

Nyssa sylvatica

Black Gum

Water Tupelo, another gum of the South, grows in swamps with bald cypress. Like black gum in most ways, it distinguishes itself by standing in water and unstable muck, and has a remarkable, swollen base to give it a low center of gravity and keep it from toppling over.

The wood of both black gum and tupelo is peculiar in the way it is reinforced with tough, crooked fibres that interlock the grain. This makes it hard to split—fine for hubs, wooden wheels on roller skates, rollers for wire cables to pull coal cars in anthracite mines.

Nyssa biflora

Bulging base helps Water Tupelo stand upright in unstable muck.

Sunlight on paper birch traces the brightest tree etching of the winter woods.

TOP: Tall crowns of scattered pines against clouds is a pageant of the South.
BOTTOM: American elms accent the colonial atmosphere of Williamsburg, Va.

TOP: Trees and flowers make New England roadsides the gayest of our country.

BOTTOM: Contrasting forms of red cedar and elm combine with a Pennsylvania cottage to design a winter picture.

Black walnut's long limbs reach far out. (The New York Botanical Garden)

Pin oak's finespun branches plunge down. (near Richmond, Va.)

Apple blossoms flash below a stately elm at Lime Rock, Conn.

The swaying of weeping willow's flexible branches is a remarkable tree motion. (The James River at Berkeley Manor, Va.)

Elms and maples give New England towns the settlers' touch.
(Salisbury, Conn.)

Sugar maple, a distinctly American tree, is a masterpiece of art in every detail. (Hotchkiss School, Lakeville, Conn.)

Massive arching branches of live oaks, festooned with Florida moss, give picturesque atmosphere to the deep South.

Pitch pine is picturesque tree of rocky and sandy places. (Photograph shows Connecticut's highest tree, atop Bear Mt.)

A native Washington palm towers above lush planting at Sequoia High School, Redwood City, California.

Ponderosa pine is the tree feature of the scenery of Rocky Mountain National Park, near Denver. Col.

Branch pattern of white oak vibrates with its strength and vitality.

Sweet gum quietly opens its leaf stars on the rim of the tragic Crater at Petersburg, Va.

Underwater roots of bald cypress breathe through their peculiar knees. This tree of our South is unique in all the world.

Just before leaves cast shade, the Great American Woods gets a brilliant carpet of spring flowers.

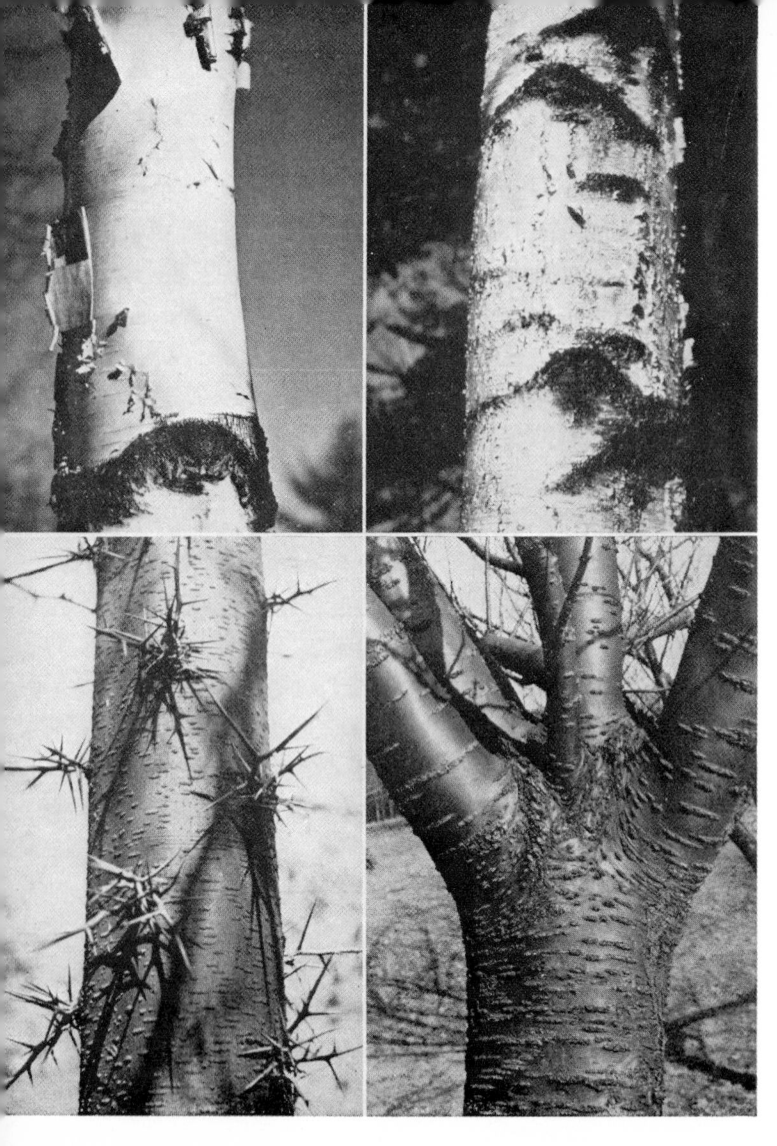

TOP LEFT: Peeling paper birch. RIGHT: Silvery gray birch. BOTTOM LEFT: Thorny honey locust. (Morton Arboretum, Lisle, Ill.) RIGHT: Satiny cherry. (Brooklyn Botanic Garden)

TOP LEFT: Stringy eucalyptus.
BOTTOM LEFT: Smooth beech.

RIGHT: Mottled sycamore.
RIGHT: Chestnut oak.

Weeping spruce, one of our country's rare trees, in the Siskiyou Mountains on the Oregon-California border.

Colorado blue spruce in all its splendor at home in the Rocky Mountains west of Denver.

Sharp straight spires march up steep ravines in the Northwest. Photograph shows firs in Annie's Creek section of Crater Lake National Park, Oregon.

Anchored under massive rock a mile high, mountain hemlock is incredibly straight and tall. (Crater Lake National Park, Ore.)

Coming down from Alaska, sitka spruce is the most exposed tree of the Oregon coast.

The massive base of sequoia casts the shadow of timeless eternity. (Stout Grove, California)

Lodgepole pine, abundant in Yellowstone Park, surprisingly also grows as a beach pine in white sand dunes of the Pacific.

Aspen, with almost white bark, has Engelmann spruce as a companion in the Rocky Mountains.

Tree buds and their astonishing styles are best seen in winter.

LEFT TO RIGHT: Red maple, butternut

ash, elm

poplar, bitternut hickory

TWO ECCENTRIC TREES

LEFT: Paper mulberry is usually contorted with burls.

Gumbo limbo waves like a fire hose. (Key West, Fla.)

Chestnut leaves are long ovals, sharp at each end, beautifully scalloped along the edges.

Southern magnolia has broad oval leaves, very dark green but brilliant with highlights.

Slash pine, the commonest tree of Florida's sand prairies, is formed by the winds with infinite variety.

THE MAGNOLIAS

Three types of this decorative family look entirely different. Most people know the evergreen magnolia with dark, shiny leaves (like the old-fashioned rubber plant in hotel lobbies). Two other magnolias, old original members of the ancient Appalachian forest, shed their leaves in winter. When leafless, they resemble other broadleaf trees, and few people realize they are magnolias that will have gorgeous flowers. These are the cucumber tree and the umbrella tree.

Then there are the oriental magnolias with dusty, smooth bark and gorgeous red, rose, and white flowers breaking out in very early spring before the leaves. These magnolias are planted much around parks and streets, staging a wonderful show, in April. Boston and Rochester are especially proud of their oriental magnolias.

★**Southern Magnolia** is the elegant aristocrat of American trees. When you travel from New England southward, this deep-toned, round-topped tree is your beacon of a warmer climate. It is so heavily leafed that it forms a tower of leaves, and the trunk is hardly seen.

Flower of Southern Magnolia

No tree of our land has leaves more aristocratic and simple. These symmetrical ovals have the texture of leather. Rich green, they are so dark that in a thunderstorm or sunset light they appear black. The polished upper surfaces flash in the sun. Turn one over and look at the underside; it is rusty red suede—a surprising contrast to the deep-toned, shiny topside.

Flowers burst out over a period of time through late spring and early summer. They are like water lilies, creamy white; a magnificent accent among the big leaves. They are so fragrant that a still day near this magnolia has a heavy redolence as in a greenhouse with the windows closed. Flowers are released from mammoth buds at the tips of branches. They do not have scales like conventional buds, but instead each is covered with a well-tailored coat of seamless brown fur.

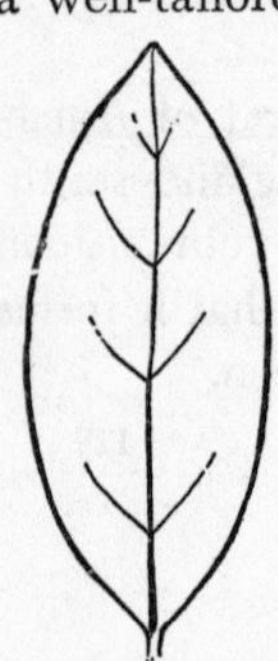
Southern Magnolia

You see this magnolia around Washington and often in Virginia, where it is planted for its elegance. Farther south, it grows naturally, especially near lakes, thriving in moist air. Plenty of southern magnolia in Louisiana; its flower is the State Flower.

This sumptuous tree is one of the few that Californians who have so many highly decorative trees of their own, have demanded from the East. It is planted extensively in moist coast towns, especially along the streets of Pasadena. *Magnolia grandiflora*

Cucumber Tree is a fine-looking member of the forest, but you're not apt to see it unless motoring through West Virginia, Kentucky, Tennessee, where it's abundant around the bases of the mountains. The leaves are big and broad, and come to an abruptly sharp point. When leaves are off the tree, buds are conspicuous, ending every branch like a sparkling silver spearhead. The flowers are as large as a tulip, but greenish-yellow, the same color as the leaves, so they are hidden from sight. The fruit is a cone that looks like a small cucumber.

Have you noticed the soft, light wood used in the bottom and sides of cheap bureau drawers? It's apt to be cucumber wood that is soft and easy to nail.

Cucumber tree blossom

Magnolia acuminata

A version called **Large-leafed Cucumber Tree** has the largest single leaves of any tree in the world. They measure up to 30 inches long—and flowers are in proportion, 12 inches across. The enormous leaves have two little ears at the bottom, as though the tree had a passing thought to evolve some lobes. This tree is interesting to know about, even though common only in limestone valleys of North Carolina. To preserve the tearing of its huge, sail-like leaves, it must avoid windy places.

Magnolia macrophylla

Umbrella Tree is often planted as far north as Boston. It has enormous leaves and flowers—24 inches and 10 inches respectively. Not quite as big as the preceding tree. The name comes from the way these great leaves

radiate like open umbrellas from the ends of branches.
Magnolia tripetala

Sweet Bay is a miniature of the southern magnolia. It copies that tree's dark, glossy leaves, except its oval is narrower, and undersides are silvery-white, with smooth and silky sheen. The small, exquisite white flowers are fragrant, giving the name to the tree. Everyone who goes south should look for sweet bay or have it pointed out to them. There's plenty of it around marshy places of the coastal plain. Its wood is chosen for dam building—by beavers. *Magnolia virginiana*

Holly is the unique American tree. The rich, glossy green of its leaves with the pure red of its berries has set such a pace for Christmas that outside its range lots of people hardly realize that this is a common member of our native woods—and not a florist's invention. The opportunity to make gay more homes than any other tree lies not only in the colors but also in the extraordinary fact that leaves and berries cling on. And even when dry, they keep their colors.

You can't miss holly when you drive from Washington, D. C., southward through Virginia. It's the common understory tree of the tall woods. When other trees are bare of leaves, its green is conspicuous everywhere. Often you spot a fine triangular spire, but most mature holly trees have been taken, and you usually see along the highways decapitated, maltreated remains, vigorously trying to recover tree form after being attacked.

Beautiful holly trees grow around big southern plantation houses and in historic towns; for example, Williamsburg. Even these do not always have berries because holly divides its sexes. Some are female with berries, others are male with almost unseen pollen flowers.

Holly bark is smooth, light gray (compare this with beech). Often it is yellow, due to the simplest green plant in the world, a single microscopic cell called an alga, that likes the dampness under the cool shade of holly and develops such dense colonies that they give the bark a yellow hue. This hospitality to algae does no harm. Holly is remarkably clean; its wood is white; its glossy leaves are so leathery insects turn elsewhere, and so prickly they frustrate chewing animals.

Birds are undeterred by prickles and help plant holly trees by eating the berries, evacuating the four hard seeds which each berry contains. Holly attracts some of our favorite birds, bluebird, kingbird, orchard oriole, hermit thrush. *Ilex opaca*

Holly leaves and berries

THE SOUTHERN PINES

In one respect the South has a simple tree pattern. A New Englander used to his broadleaf woods, colorful hills, green meadows, and varieties of skyline might find the wide plains and low rolling piedmont of the South monotonous. In Virginia the straight highway is cut through mile after mile of pine forest; farther south sandy plains are covered with tall pine trees spaced out over far horizons. In northern Florida the sand is flat, and yet again wherever you look, straight pine trees with wind-blown crowns are silhouetted against the sky. The limitless pines stretch westward through the Gulf States into Texas. This region of pines contains vast cypress swamps, and is interspersed with broadleaf trees. Near the coast are monarch live oaks, and the hinterland is checkered with cotton plantations, but, measured in sheer square miles, the South is predominantly a pine landscape.

The straightness and height of the pines catches the eye. Note the smoothness and remarkable red and orange colors of bark. These are called **"yellow pine"** by the lumber industry—a name which is used for four kinds of pine. Why not recognize each of the four and enjoy your trip that much more?

Southern yellow pines are fast-growing trees. They are

an important source of pulp for paper. Paper companies are alert to the need for keeping their supply of raw material growing and energetic conservation projects are bringing results in insuring the survival and increase of the pine forests. The creative forestry program of leading paper companies is based on growing trees as a crop. One company sends foresters to work with landowners, distributes seedlings, and has set up a modern system of fire detection and control.

★★**Longleaf Pine** has longest needles of any pine in the world—up to 18 inches. These remarkable, flexible needles, in clusters of 3, radiate from ends of branches in dark green plumes. You can't miss this; it's arresting. Cones are up to 10 inches long. Bark has orange tinge on thin smooth plates. Fine straight-grained timber gives wood great value but has tragically reduced numbers of longleaf pines, as they are the first choice of the screaming saw. The mighty timber of this tree is used in heavy construction such as bridges, railroad cars, ships. Fire through scrubby ground cover doesn't hurt the almost

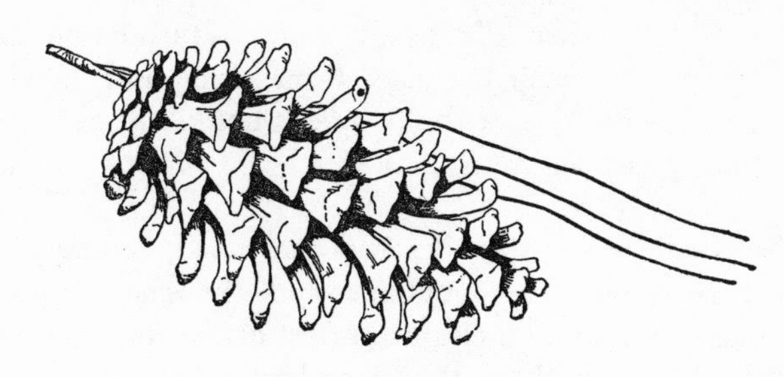

Longleaf needle cluster and cone

fireproof bark of mature longleaf pine; in fact fire may help it to survive by clearing ground of grass that would smother the seedlings. Thus controlled fire is helpful in the reforestation of longleaf pine. Longleaf also has the ability to grow in dry, poor and gravelly ground. One of the world's great trees. *Pinus palustris*

Slash Pine's tall, wind-blown crown competes with the clouds to give the sandy spaces of northern Florida a fresh outdoor feeling. It grows in open stands across the sand prairies and is the dominant tree on the sand hills around Lake Wales. The straight trunk is free of branches to the crown, where abruptly angled branches have a gay, free aspect.

Slash has 10-inch needles, not quite as long as longleaf. They do not flare out to form wide plumes but tend to lie together along the branch. They are bundled in clusters of 2's and 3's. Bark is orange-tinged; smooth plates are longer, narrower than longleaf.

Slash Pine cone

You see big scars on the trunk where slash pine is tapped. The bulk of the world's naval stores (turpentine and resin) comes from slash and longleaf forests. The gashing of the tree does not kill it, but slows its vitality and shortens its life. *Pinus caribaea*

Shortleaf Pine is spread across the broad, rolling piedmont between the mountains and the coastal plain. Needles (in 2's and 3's) are shortest of the four southern yellow pines; bark is the smoothest with light-tinted, red-brown plates; cones are the smallest (about 2 inches). Shortleaf has light, 2-winged seeds that blow like dust. These have planted shortleaf from Pennsylvania to Florida to Texas. Mile after mile of it in western part of Virginia and the Carolinas, enjoying the bright warm sunlight of the South. Its lumber is good but not compared to the heavy timber of the superb longleaf. Much used for paper pulp, boxes, crates, excelsior. *Pinus echinata*

Shortleaf Pine cone

Loblolly Pine (also called old field pine) is a tall dark dome, a feature of the landscape around Richmond, Williamsburg, and southward near coast. Has a tendency to move into abandoned fields; all over the South the handsome pine with rounded dome top that stands alone in the old field is loblolly. Cinnamon-red flat ridges of bark are separated by deep furrows. Long needles are in 3's. Loblolly is tallest of the southern yellows, builds its dark billowy head 150 feet or higher into the sky. Its wood is comparatively weak, brittle. Makes kraft paper, splintery boxes and crates. Latin name *taeda* means torch because resinous heartwood burns vigorously. *Pinus taeda*

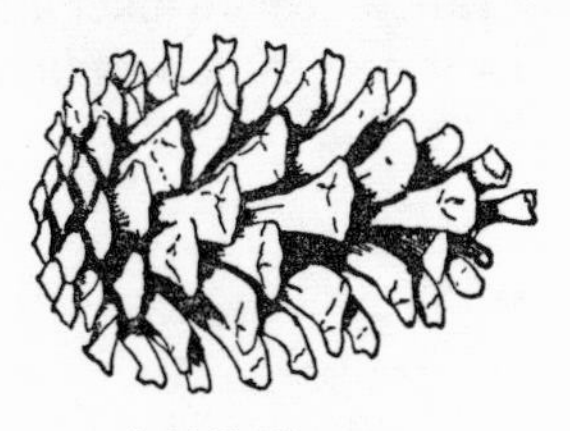
Loblolly Pine cone

UNUSUALLY INTERESTING SMALL TREES OF THE SOUTH

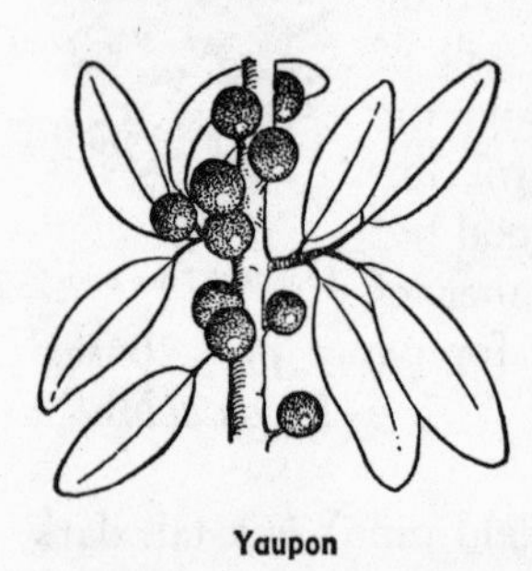
Yaupon

Yaupon is a holly with red berries and 1-inch evergreen leaves, wavy-edged, not prickly like our Christmas holly. Conspicuous back of sand dunes from Virginia south and along the Gulf coast. In southeastern Texas it's a tree up to 25 feet tall. Yaupon leaves make a brisk tea. This tree is kin to South American maté. Scrubby, contorted versions of live oak and mockernut hickory grow with yaupon in sand dune thickets. *Ilex vomitoria*

Toothache Tree (also called sting-tongue and pepperwood) grows around margins of swamps over the sandy coastal plain. East Texas people know it well. Bumps on bark look like barnacles topped by sharp prickles. Bark is hot to taste, like pepper, and is chewed for toothache. This weird tree forms thickets in Arkansas where it is also called tear-blanket and wait-a-bit. *Xanthoxylum Clava-Herculis*

Bark of Toothache tree

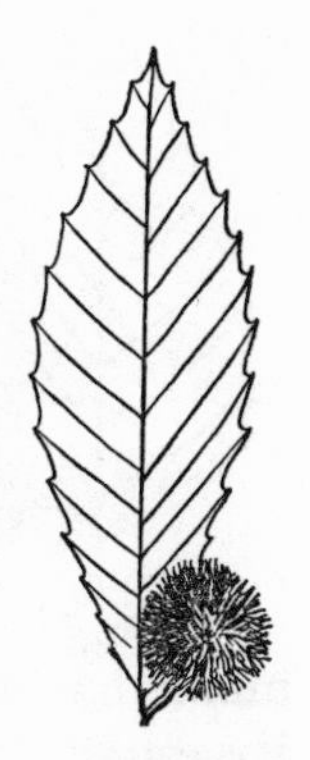
Chinquapin leaf and nut

Chinquapin is the little brother survivor of the mighty American chestnut. When the latter was destroyed by a blight, the chinquapin continued to grow in Arkansas and Texas, and, as a little tree or shrub, in undisturbed upland woods eastward to North Carolina. Leaves are the same slender oval with scalloped teeth as the chestnut; burs are the same. Each contains a shiny chestnut-brown nut with delicious sweet meat. The catch is that there isn't enough of it to get a good mouthful. This nut is shaped like a toy top. You can spot this little tree (usually a shrub east of Mississippi) by bright yellow-green leaves, shiny on up-side, silvery, hairy underneath. It's a fine discovery. *Castanea pumila*

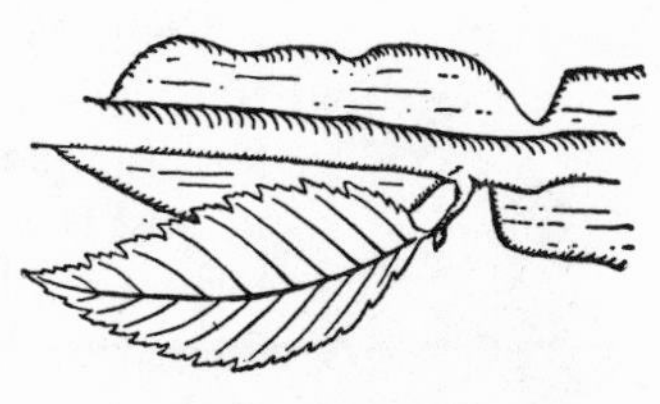
Corky "wings" along twig of Winged Elm

Winged Elm (also called wahoo) is the smallest of our elms. It has 1½-inch elm leaves. You find it on dry gravelly hillsides from Virginia to Texas. Look for rows of thin corky ridges along the twigs—these are remarkable and give the tree its name. Sweet gum also has corky ridges on twigs, but they are heavier, more irregular. Seeds of winged elm are red, compared to light green seeds of American elm, and give the tree a delicate red tint. This is the commonest elm of the piedmont of the South. *Ulmus alata*

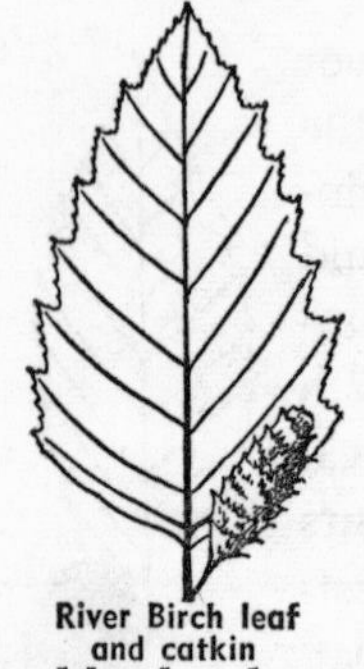
River Birch leaf and catkin

River Birch is in the race for America's most graceful tree. It divides near base and two long slender trunks soar as high as 90 feet. Bark is colorful as anything in tree bark. The overall effect is cinnamon-red, but look closely at the translucent golden red of the loose paper outer layers and how they curl back showing pink-brown tints of inner bark. This is the South's only real birch, and unlike birches up north, it prefers wet ground, reaches largest size in bayous of Louisiana where it stands in water for part of year. River birch makes a good binder for loose river banks. May be seen in warm wet places as far north as Ohio and Illinois. The Kankakee and Tippecanoe Rivers in Indiana have river birch curving over their picturesque waters. *Betula nigra*

Crape Myrtle flower cluster

Crape Myrtle is the big shrub or little tree you see all over the South, a feature, for example, in Williamsburg. The commonest tree decoration in Florida—counterpart of lilac up north. Blooms all summer with lush 1½-inch flowers, white, pink, or purple. Six petals are crinkled like crepe paper. *Lagerstroemia indica*

SOUTHERN FLORIDA

Florida is like a finger partly thrust into the Caribbean warm water bowl from which the Gulf Stream flows. The tip segment has no frost the year round. Thus, trees that hopped over from the West Indies, Yucatan, and South America can dress up the only natural tropic scenery in the United States. All this is interesting to romantic and artistic people and to botanists; but the person familiar with ordinary American trees finds little to recognize in this unrelated province.

The pattern is even more confused because men have hauled in trees from far-away places. Some of these have prospered so well they are features of the landscape—royal poinciana from Madagascar, beefwood from Australia, silk tree from Persia.

Except for parks and plantings around hotels, the region may disappoint you if you are seeking a tropical paradise. Fragments of tropical jungle can be seen at Royal Palm Hammock, 40 miles south of Fort Myers, and Matheson Hammock, 2 miles from Coral Gables. The Keys are monotonous, and have been ravaged by hurricanes. Poison ivy and suffocating honeysuckle are invading. Most of the famous colorful tree-snails have been collected. But there's still much to thrill the tree explorer.

The most conspicuous change in the trees from temperate to tropical is the disappearance of the pines with the dominance of broadleaf trees which now become evergreen, with smooth bark, milky sap. Here are some of the trees you are most apt to see:

★**Royal Palm** is the tall palm you see around hotels and along streets of southern Florida. No tree in the world is more stately and decorative. You tell it from palmetto by the leaves which are enormous feathers instead of fans, and it is much taller. The amazing cement-like column bulges in the center and flares at the base, giving it striking balance and form. You can see this tree in a tropical jungle setting at Royal Palm Hammock, a state park of southern Florida. *Roystonea regia*

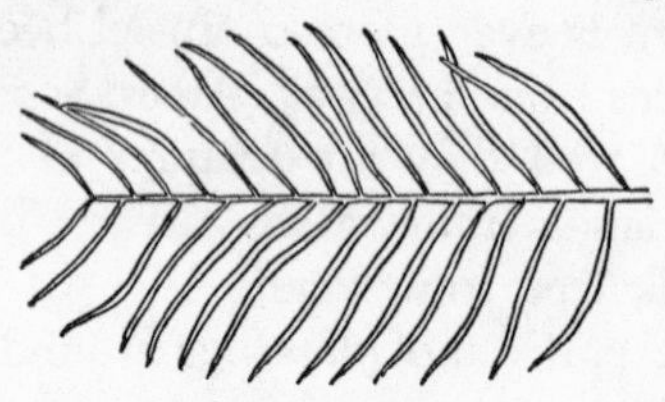

Leaf of Royal Palm

Coconut Palm is the tall slender palm with a spray of fern leaves at the top. You see it leaning over the water of Biscayne Bay at Miami, Florida, and southward along the beaches of the Keys. It looks informal, windswept, often seen in pictures of hurricanes.

This tropical tree came to the warm fingertip of the United States by floating its seeds across the seas. The coconut is the biggest seed in the world, with its embryo bathed in oil and sugar, sealed inside a buoyant shell resistant to salt water. Coconut has three soft spots (where the tree can sprout through the hard case), which suggest a monkey's face. "Cocos" is the Portuguese word for monkey. *Cocos nucifera*

Date Palm has huge fern leaves that shoot upward from a fairly short trunk and then arch outward. This decorative formal tree is planted around parks and hotel grounds of southern Florida. It takes dry, hot desert climate to ripen fruit. Over in Coachella Valley of California, they get crops of dates for the market, but it's only a majestic decoration in Florida. *Phoenix dactylifera*

Mangrove is a crooked little tree that builds shorelines, protects property. Stands in brackish marshes on west coast of Florida as far north as Clearwater and in shallow water along the shores of the Keys. In southern sector it makes extensive low "forest" suggesting looking down from an airplane on a tropical rain forest. Mangrove is a big bush or small tree some 40 feet high. Instant identification is the platform of arching air roots on which the tree is held above tidewater. Leaves are plain ovals—dark, leathery. Look for seeds sprouting while still hanging on tree. You can see the root coming out of the fruit. When seed grows too heavy, it falls off, plunks into the mud, plants another mangrove. Sea birds, especially long-legged waders, often seen in mangrove swamps. *Rhizophora mangle*

Beefwood (also called Australian pine) is finest feature along coast facing the Gulf of Mexico. Points long branches at the clouds. Tall, feathery, it waves slowly

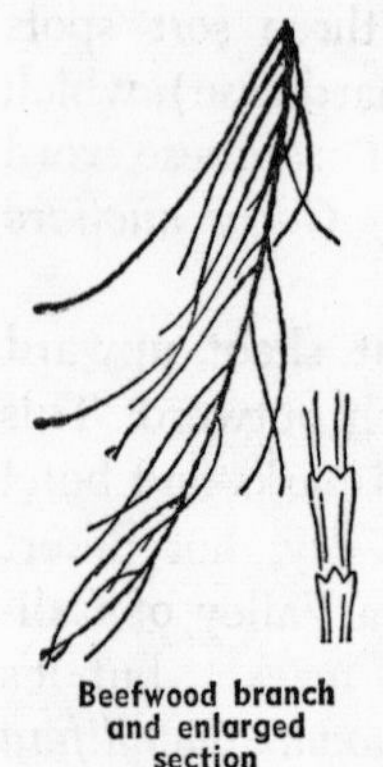
Beefwood branch and enlarged section

back and forth in the breeze. Often mistaken for pine tree with long, soft, pendulous needles. Peer closely, instead of a pine needle you see a green stem curiously jointed with whorls of minute scales. A person from the North instantly is reminded of the curious horsetail plant. Grows rapidly in sand. Makes windbreak for orange groves. A useful, unusual tree of both Florida and California. *Casuarina equisetifolia*

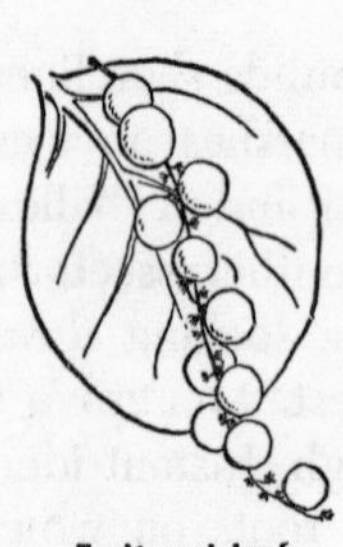
Fruit and leaf of Sea Grape

Sea Grape will stir your curiosity by its round leaves, 8 inches across with marvelous red veins, abundant in sandy places bordering beaches along the Keys, often seen under a picturesque coconut tree. Big clusters of purple fruits from huge crooked branches are quite a sight and make good jelly.
Coccoloba uvifera

Certain trees, even when there are only isolated specimens, are so spectacular that they catch the eye, and you like to write home about them. Here are five such trees:

Royal Poinciana is the showiest tree in the world. The sweet-pea family has achieved this forty-foot tree with its feathery leaves, among which are draped enormous clusters of flame-red flowers. Each flower's flamboyancy is increased by a color mixture of four scarlet petals and one white one with orange spots. It blooms in June and July—too late for most Miami visitors. Over on Puerto Rico this is much planted; blooms in May. *Delonix regia*

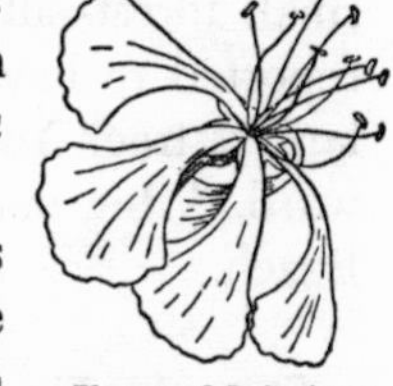

Flower of Poinciana

Kapok is the colossus of the tropics with so much engineering at its base you marvel at what the dividing cell can build. Vertical buttresses stand five feet high and spread across ground in a hundred-foot circle. Fruit is round, leathery, a little larger than a baseball, packed with seeds embedded in silky hairs good for stuffing pillows and life preservers. *Ceiba pentandra*

Sausage Tree is seen by more people in proportion to least number of trees of any tree in the U. S. You will stop your car on highway a few miles south of Coral Gables to ponder 2-foot sausages (as many as 40 of them) swaying from ropes. Another sausage tree is seen at McKee Jungle Garden, Vero Beach, and there are a few more. You never fail to recognize sausage tree because it bears the world's easiest-to-remember tree name. Sausages are fruits, tough as gourds, not edible. Though you would never guess it, this is a close relative of our common catalpa. *Kigelia pinnata*

Fruit of Sausage tree weighs up to twelve pounds.

Banyan is the massive tree that drops roots from its branches. These scramble along the ground like snakes, or a large one may penetrate the ground and form another trunk. Eventually the multitude of trunks makes a small forest—all just one tree. One banyan in India is reported to have 3 thousand trunks. Is this the world's largest tree? You see banyan in Fort Myers and southward. A big one shelters a filling station in West Palm Beach. *Ficus benghalensis*

Strangler Fig expresses the law of the jungle. It starts as a vine on any tree at hand to hold it up. The vine flattens out so that it looks as though light gray lava is flowing around the trunk of the holding tree. In time this forms a hollow trunk. Meanwhile fig leaves are sprouting above. These overtop the victim tree which, with its bark encased and its leaves in shade, dies. This leaves a big fig tree standing. You can stare in awe at strangler fig in Matheson Hammock, and there's a great deal of it on the road to Cape Sable and along the Keys. *Ficus aurea*

In addition, many other South Florida trees are arresting and interesting. Let local people point them out to you. These include:

Orange, semi-tropical, it lives farther north than truly tropical trees. The largest orchards are in central Florida. Radiant deep-green leaves with oranges are one of finest color combinations among trees. This feature too often overlooked because tree is so common and its crop so valuable. *Citrus sinensis*

Grapefruit looks like orange tree, grows in same localities. *Citrus paradisi*

Lime has light golden green leaves, thorny branches. Truly tropical. Good commercial crop on Key Largo and southward to Key West. Latin name means "golden-leaved."

Citrus aurantifolia

Gumbo Limbo has limbs that tend to billow horizontally, bring to mind big fire hoses. Bark is red-brown like bad sunburn, with thin tissue-like outer layer peeling off.

Bursera simaruba

Tiny wings at base of leaf are sign of all citrus fruits.

Mastic is one of the larger trees of the hammocks and Keys. Oval yellow fruit, size and shape of olive, is gummy, acid, pleasant to eat. *Sideroxylon foetidissimum*

Mahogany of the Keys is the true mahogany of the Amazon jungle. The dark red wood grows darker and richer with age. Florida trees are not large because biggest ones have been cut to build boats.

Swietenia mahogani

Luxuriant foliage of Sapodilla sprays out from end of branch.

Sapodilla is the chewing gum tree from South America, where there are 100 million in Yucatan and British

Honduras. Chicle comes from its milky latex. Wood makes iron-hard implement handles. *Achras sapota*

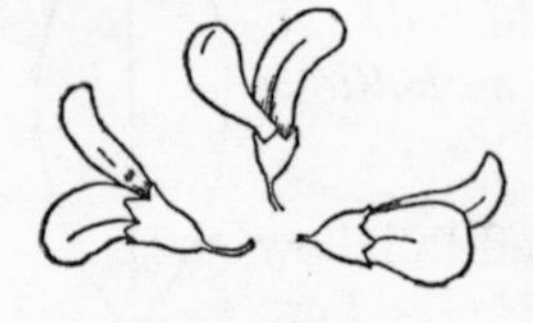

Jamaica Dogwood flowers resemble sweet peas.

Jamaica Dogwood arrests you with big clusters of pink sweet pea blossoms. Seminole Indians (tribe still lives in Everglades) discovered that bark is an opium-like drug and used infusion to stun fish, make them easy to catch. *Ichthyomethia piscipula*

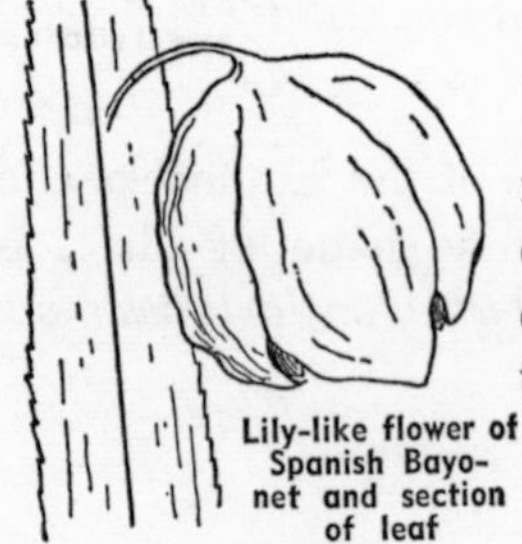

Lily-like flower of Spanish Bayonet and section of leaf

Spanish Bayonet is a lily that makes a slender tree up to 20 feet, capped by nodding, creamy flowers. Leaves clustered at base are the size and ferocity of bayonets. *Yucca aloifolia*

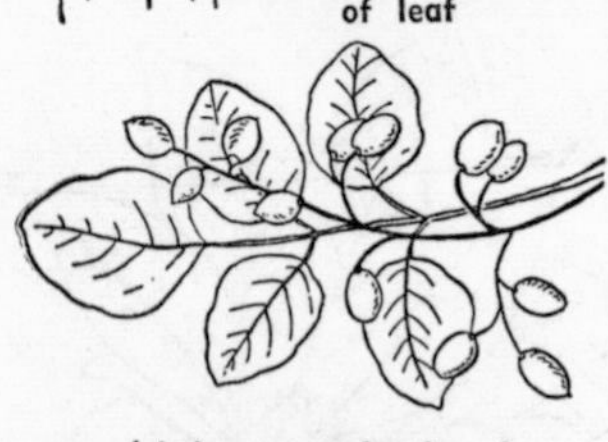

Admire orange berries of Poisonwood only from a distance.

Poison Wood (also called coral sumac) is common on the Keys, unfortunately. Exquisite smooth red-brown bark. Wood is colorful, yellow and white with heartwood mottled brown and red showing iridescent green and gold. Just read about this—*do not touch*. Sap is poisonous, like poison sumac. *Metopium toxiferum*

THE NORTHWEST

Sharp spires that give a saw-toothed edge to steep mountain slopes reveal a tree world utterly different from that of the Great American Woods of the East. Everyone who visits the Northwest should know the trees by name. They are too tall, too vivid, too much of everything there to call them just "trees" or "awfully big trees." These are Douglas fir, ponderosa pine, noble fir, western hemlock, and so on down the list of giants.

When you stand beside such a tree, you are an earthbound pygmy at the base of a sky-piercing tower. When you touch it, it feels solid as a cliff. When you stare upward, the incredible trunk has such straight lines they converge toward the vanishing point with the perspective of a railroad track. The tree runs into the sky and you cannot see the top. Yet this vast structure is alive. It expands steadily, creeps upward, timelessly growing, growing. Its massive material unfolds in mid-air, processed out of water and rock, activated by light. Just to be able to see this and think about it gives you a strong sense of enjoying your own share of eternity.

The types of trees in these northwestern spire forests have existed on earth millions of years longer than those of our broadleaf woods. What a contrast they are! Instead of bright green foliage, the prevailing color is dark blue-green that appears black against the sky.The crowns are high up and shadows are deep, down the length of the trunk. Instead of billowing, rounded treetops, the accent is that of sharp spearheads. Instead of the motion of broadleaf woods responding to the winds with branches swaying and leaves fluttering, these forests stand firm and vertical.

The Great American Woods of the East has infinite variety; colors change with the seasons; trees and shrubs blend together in seeming confusion. The ancient forests of the Northwest are uniform, and there are comparatively few kinds of trees growing together in one place.

Eastern trees are intimate; you can reach out and touch twig, bud and leaf. When you want to see the details of the big spires, you find their branches as high as a cloud. So you learn to know trees by all-over appearance of foliage, by bark, and by the position of the cones, which you squint to see, high on the tree. And you search the ground for an open cone cast off after it has discharged its seeds, or a closed one which a squirrel has cut off.

The vast extent of mountain slopes and canyons are the keynote of this part of our country, but the tree pattern of the whole region is like that of marble, with variegated colors. Swishing through the dark-blue areas of mountain forests are bright green strokes of the lowlands and streams, where grow the western versions of alder, poplar, maple, and oak. Between mountain ranges there are wide yellow plains. This is sagebrush country, where little rain falls because water carried in clouds from the Pacific is trapped by the mountains and spilled over the spires before it can reach the plains. This flat region is dotted with western juniper that creates beautiful red and golden wood out of the hot, dry sand.

The fourth area is a narrow strip along the ocean, crowded by the Coast Range forests of Douglas fir and western hemlock. Here a fascinating ribbon of dunes and rocky headlands bears Sitka spruce, and even in pure white sand, lodgepole pine, disguised as a fighting little tree called shore pine. Close to this shore line, just back of the dunes and headlands of southwestern Oregon are famous Oregon myrtle and the exquisite Port Orford cedar. In this place of sudden contrasts the beach road dips into a fern-floored rain forest, a natural sanctuary of western hemlock, at Short Sand State Park on the coast due west of Portland. Farther north, the coast route reaches one of the greatest rain forests at Olympic National Park in Washington.

The Cascade Range of the Northwest joins with the Sierra Nevada Mountains, the interior range of California. Moreover, the Coast Range is continuous from Washington and Oregon southward along the California coast. Along these mountain highways travel many of the trees which we here include under the Northwest; thus many trees in this section are outstanding trees of California. The intermingling of trees north and south through the Pacific Coast states is part of that phenomenon that has been called the footsteps of the forest. Seeds of southern trees dispersed toward the north eventually reach a natural barrier of climate, just as seeds of northern trees meet their climate barrier as they go south. By the same token, many of the Northwest trees become the trees of the Rocky Mountains.

DOUGLAS FIR

★★**Douglas Fir** is the highest expression of tree greatness of our time. You must know it, if only by reputation. This tree serrates the steep lines of western mountain slopes from British Columbia to central California, and flows over the Rockies from Canada to Mexico. A Douglas fir forest is amazingly uniform; tall, straight trunks stand so close together that, in continental perspective, they may be likened to a wheat field in density. Such a forest holds the darkness of night at noonday, but at a little distance the mountain side has a herring-bone pattern from the light on the upper foliage of myriad branches precisely at right angles to myriad peaks.

You can know Douglas fir as you drive through a forest by the heavy vertical ridges of the bark. These usually are solid cork, not flaky or split. Bark ridges are dark, with the deep fissures between suggesting the form of miniature mountain ranges.

Douglas fir is in a class by itself—it is not a true fir. Its many cones droop from branches and, when open, are cast off whole. This is in contrast to true firs whose cones stand erect on tree branches like big cylindrical Christmas candles. Pick up a Douglas fir cone from the ground; you'll see 3-pronged tongues sticking out between scales—the sure sign of a Douglas fir. If a branch has fallen from the altitudes, note how needles are soft, blunt, with

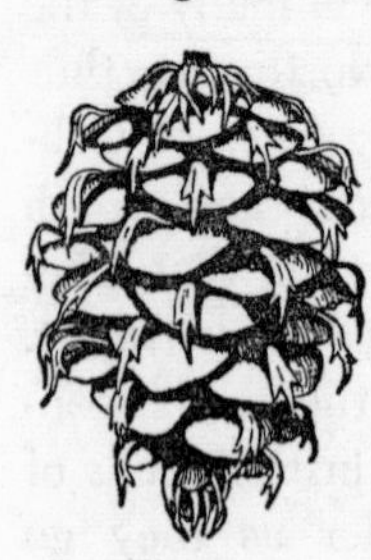

Douglas Fir

a rich tone. America's second tallest tree, next to sequoia, often outstrips the capacity of its water-lifting apparatus so that the peak is flattened. Two thirds of the lumber from the Northwest is Douglas fir. In the marketplace it is often called "Oregon pine." The strength of its streaming grain is revealed by its use as tall masts and spars. The power of a sea gale may bow an 8-inch mainsail boom, but the strength of Douglas fir never fails.

Pseudotsuga taxifolia

THE HEMLOCKS

Western Hemlock is one of the Northwest's aristocrats which everyone who knows our graceful eastern hemlock can recognize, but which is superbly different. Like sequoia, it is geographically pin-pointed by moisture. When the rainfall indicator touches 60 inches per year, the mighty western hemlock forms cool forests where skylight shafts slant down through shadowy vapors. These places are chiefly on the west slopes of the Cascades in Oregon and Washington, where the moisture of the ocean winds is released. Skipping the plains between mountain ranges, it reappears again at 60 inches of rain in the coast mountains. With its 150 feet of height and 5 feet of trunk thickness, western hemlock would rate as a giant except that it often makes its forests with Douglas fir. The huge dimensions of Douglas fir are emphasized when such a super tree as western hemlock appears in relation to it as an understory tree.

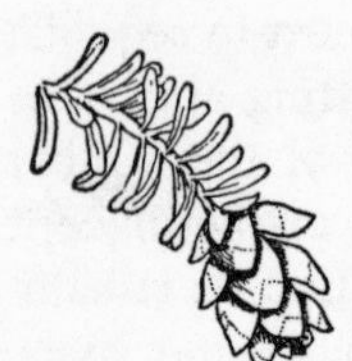
Western Hemlock

Needles resemble eastern hemlock, dark and shiny above, two white lines on underside. Cones are similar too; their little egg-shaped ovals dangling from flexible twig tips—they seem undersized for such a big tree. As the branches are usually out of reach, you can tell a western hemlock instantly when you drive by in a car by a glance at its peak. The top topples. About 12 inches of the tip flops over and dangles like a string. This doesn't prevent it from leading the tree straight up. The result is straight-grained, valuable wood unlike eastern hemlock, which is brittle and cross-grained. This western hemlock makes good floor lumber, topnotch boxes and crates, and it is the number-one paper pulp tree of the Northwest. *Tsuga heterophylla*

Mountain Hemlock takes first prize as the gayest, most sparkling of the evergreens. It's a wonderful tree to know for the colors of its details, and as a masterpiece of art in the way it fits, crisp and clear as mountain air, among rocks and snow patches. Mountain hemlock does not have the flexible, feathery branches of other hemlocks (although it has the flop-over leader that is the mark also of western hemlock). At first sight this tree might be taken for a spruce, with its angular, stabbing structure. Also like spruce, needles stick out around the twig, instead of in flat rows on either side of the twig. Mountain hemlock needles are oval in cross-section making them rounded, not flat. The topsides and undersides are uniform green; an interesting detail because needles of other evergreens have much lighter undersides. Other hemlocks have these white lines only on underside. Don't fail to note these distinctive needles, their plumpness, beautiful green, and the way they crowd together, especially on the upper side of the twig. See how each needle narrows to form its own stem and is attached to a little woody cushion on the twig. This makes hemlock twigs slightly rough where needles are off, but not so harshly rough as the projections of spruce twigs.

Purple cones hang in bunches that weigh down a branch. They often sparkle as though set with diamonds. This is due to the way mountain hemlock is bursting with marvelously fragrant resin, some of which crystallizes on the cones.

In the land of enormous timber, mountain hemlock is a small spire of 50 to 75 feet. This is one reason why you can enjoy it; it's not too far away in the sky. At timberline it is clear-cut, out in the open, glistening with resin crystals in the sunshine. Moderate size belies its age —many are 300 years old.

Mountain Hemlock

Everybody who visits Crater Lake National Park and Mt. Hood National Forest in Oregon, also Mt. Rainier and Olympic National Parks in Washington will find the exquisite mountain hemlock all around, the dominant tree at timberline. In Alaska it grows at sea-level and mounts higher and higher as it runs southward, reaching 10,000 feet in central California. *Tsuga mertensiana*

THE FIRS

If you would feel a special delight in rhythm and balance, with the bounce of outer branches turning upward in unison, go look for the firs. Oregon is their kingdom. A visitor from the East who knows the northwoods balsam fir will be astonished at the majesty of the northwestern firs. In contrast the soft, fragrant balsam is small and demure. There, in the Cascades, the super firs from Puget Sound meet those from the Rockies and northern California. You will see in the Crater Lake region and around Mt. Hood the sharpest, straightest tree spires in the world, the most harmoniously scalloped branches, the loveliest melody of flaring fronds. The broadly spread form of lower fir branches catches your eye. It is like a crinoline skirt, and turns up with a pagoda curve. This is seen where snow is the deepest in winter. The weight of snow stimulates needle growth to form a sort of fabric that will hold the weight up without breaking the branch.

You will have no problem in telling a true fir from the other tall timbers around. Glance at the top of the tree; if you see cones standing straight up on their branches, it's a fir. The cones of hemlock, spruce, pine, Douglas fir point down or out at angles, or dangle. Fir cones, even though high up, are big, fat cylinders with blunt round tops. When seeds are ripe, the handsome vault which held them vanishes, scales tumble off separately. A stark peg that was the core of the cone is all that is left, whereas other kinds of evergreens cast off whole cones which we pick up for decoration or fireplace purposes.

Fir needles are stemless, attached directly to the twig. The lower part is often compressed and twisted to act as a stem ending in a sort of suction cup. When needle is removed, this leaves a round scar flat on the twig. Other evergreens' twigs are rough with projections or bumps. Thus, a smooth twig, where needles are removed, is a sign of fir. Finally, fir bark has blisters that are wells of pure resin. Break one open; the fragrance on your fingers will be out of this world.

To call the different firs by name is more difficult. They even fool the experts. The easiest way to tell the kind of fir is by the place you are. They tend to congregate in their own communities, northward or southward, high up or on mid-mountain. Six common firs are abundant in their places; all are big, valuable, with overawing charm. You should know about this royal six. The first three (noble, alpine, and red) are seen on highest mountain locations and have dark, strong wood. The last three (grand, silver, and white) grow on lower mountain slopes, have white, weak wood, and all three are called "white fir" by lumbermen.

Alpine Fir resembles a Chinese pagoda.

Noble Fir has the fattest, dark purple, cones, concentrated at the top of the tree. These fat cylinders seem too big and heavy to be held erect on such a slender peak. In cross section needles are oval or four-sided in comparison to flat needles of other firs. Each needle is polished rich green and with a clean groove on top. Newest needles of lower branches usually have silvery tinge underneath, which shows up beautifully because noble fir needles dense on upper side of twig, sweep back with a wonderful wind-swept wave. Noble makes extensive forests in Cascades, high up on west sides facing the sea. It is the handsomest fir of Mt. Rainier. Great tall nobles cover Larch Mountain an hour's drive east of Portland, Oregon. (It ought to be called Noble Mountain, but lumbermen market noble fir in the name of "larch" by one of their quirks of misnaming.) If a squirrel cuts off a cone and lets it drop, you are lucky. Noble cone has curious pointed tongues that emerge from between the regular cone scales, and, bending down, lie flat, covering the dark cone with green shingles. *Abies nobilis*

Noble Fir

Alpine Fir is the smallest and highest up of the firs. Its cones are light brown tinged with purple, in contrast to the dark cones of noble. They are scattered on top branches instead of clustered at the very peak. Bark is interesting gray with a reddish tinge coming through from underneath, and with many aromatic resin blisters. Note the way long needles of this tree grow in bunches emphatically wind-blown and up-curving. Alpine is more widely distributed in the West than other firs. This is the only fir in Yellowstone Park, where it is abundant in the highest spots, above 7,000 feet. One of the best places to see it is on the broad shoulders of Mt. Hood and Mt. Rainier. Also it is common in Glacier National Park and in mountains of Colorado. *Abies lasiocarpa*

Alpine Fir

Corkbark Fir, a variety of Alpine, grows in southern Colorado, Arizona, New Mexico. It has singular soft, corky white bark

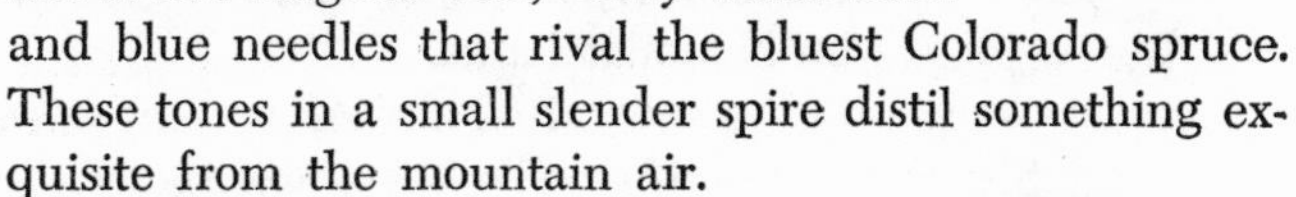

and blue needles that rival the bluest Colorado spruce. These tones in a small slender spire distil something exquisite from the mountain air.

Abies lasiocarpa var. arizonica

Red Fir is a California tree that has elaborated a variety called **Shasta Red Fir** which steps from Mt. Shasta over to Oregon, where it builds a mighty forest around Crater Lake. Shasta red rivals the biggest and best. High on the mountains, it might be mistaken for the regal noble fir. Both have big cones; both have deeply rough, red-brown bark. But here is an inside tip for distinguishing Shasta red from noble that is quick, easy, and takes no practice. A single needle tells you. The top of Shasta red needle has a neat straight ridge; the top of noble has a clean groove. Be a tree detective!

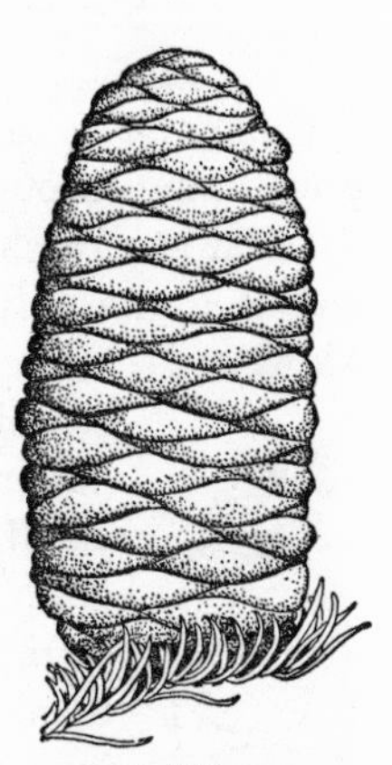

Red Fir

Shasta Red Fir

A vivid difference between Shasta red and the regular California red is that the former shingles its cone with wide green tongues, something like noble, while red fir does not have these peculiar tongues.

True California red is as big as the Shasta variety and one of the two tallest trees (the other is white fir) of the Sierra forests of central California. It makes the big forests above 7,500 feet in Yosemite, Sequoia, and Kings Canyon National Parks.

Red fir—*Abies magnifica*
Shasta red fir—*Abies magnifica var. shastensis*

Grand Fir is the handsome "white fir" with yellow-green cones around Puget Sound—the commonest fir in the State of Washington. In Oregon it climbs mountains, and it is the only fir which also makes lowland forest. Many are scattered through beautiful Willamette Valley.

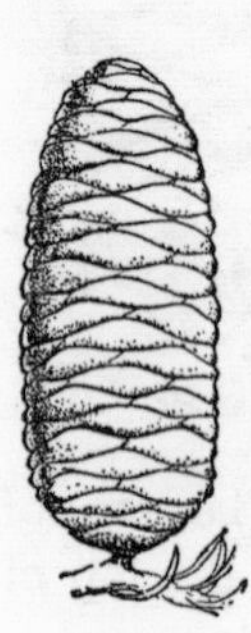
Grand Fir

Needles are deeply grooved on top, ridged underneath, and notched at tip. Something you'll never forget about grand fir is the diagram of these interesting needles: they are extra long and their bases twist so as to hold them out in flat rows on each side of the twig. On the twig segment of a year's growth they grow shorter at each end, longer in the middle, making a striking oval outline. As you run your eye along a branch, this series of ovals forms a wavy pattern. Grand fir sucks up so much water that a freshly cut log will hardly float. *Abies grandis*

Silver Fir (also called lovely fir) has the outstanding characteristic of vivid white undersides of all its needles, both new and old. (Noble fir has white undersides only on youngest needles but older ones turn yellow-green.) This white of silver fir needles contrasts conspicuously with dark green topsides. Note dense gray hairs on twigs. The quickest way to spot silver fir without stopping your car is by the gray bark with chalky white patches. This is a tree of the North, coming down from Alaska to the high Cascades in Oregon. It is the commonest of the firs in Olympic and Mt. Rainier National Parks.

Abies amabilis

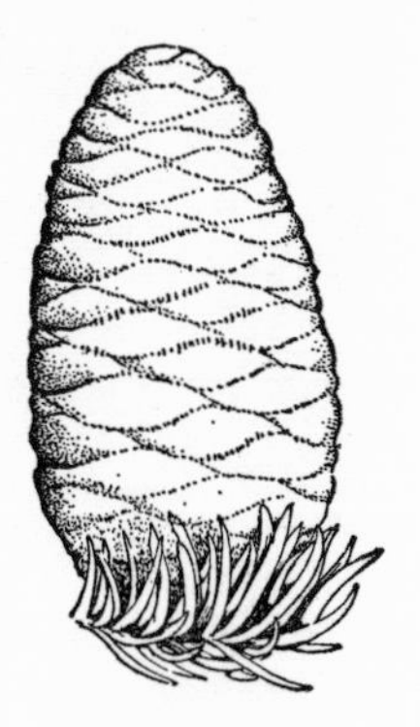

Silver Fir

White Fir is at its greatest in the California Sierras, where it builds 200-foot forests with red fir, its companion giant, in Yosemite, Sequoia and General Grant National Parks. Cones are extra big, dark green. The remarkable feature of white fir is the bright blue-green on the tops of many of its needle as well as on the undersides. Needles 2 or 3 inches long wave upward and spread out gaily at various angles as compared to other firs whose needles tend to be windswept together. White comes into southern California in small size. A good place to take in your hand and see the exquisite sweep of needles is around Oregon Caves National Monument, one of the most lush tree spots in the state. Colorado has a superb grove of this tree in North Cheyenne Canyon near Colorado Springs. *Abies concolor*

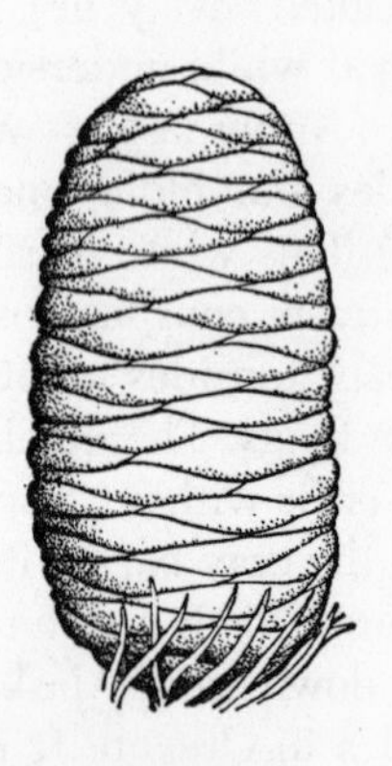

Cone of White Fir

"When man builds a structure, raw materials have to be converted into building materials, and then those materials have to be transported to their places. When a tree is built, the raw materials are air and water, with solutions of chemicals from the earth, and the building material is the cell. Then two miracles occur. One is that cells are never transported. No bricklayer ever places one on top of another. They simply occur in the right place and at the right moment by means of cell division. The other miracle is that, after cells have appeared at the right place, they are converted into specialized structural materials on the spot. It is as though bricks turned into plaster, roof, plumbing, and built-in cupboards."

from THIS GREEN WORLD

THE PINES

For surprise and discovery the pines of the Northwest exceed anything that our eastern and southeastern pines have to offer. Some rival the world's biggest trees; others grow horizontal instead of erect; some bear giant cones, others bear cones with eccentric or looped spirals of astonishing perfection; pine bark may be white—or black which magically turns to bright cinnamon red. Wherever you go in the Rockies and the northwestern mountains, you will find a pine with something diverting to show you. These pines are more cosmopolitan than other ruling evergreens there, and more dramatic. Pines in general are always easy to recognize because they have long, slender needles bundled together. The fun begins when you see with your own eyes the peculiar feature that tells you which kind of pine it is. The nine in the following list compose the story. The first four: sugar, ponderosa, western white, and lodgepole are widespread and common. The last five, whitebark, limber, Jeffrey, knobcone, and digger, are specialties which you may see, but, at least, have unusual features to read about.

Sugar Pine is the biggest pine tree in the world. In magnitude it qualifies for the society of sequoia and Douglas fir. The trunk streams into the sky more than 200 feet—clean, straight, against the law of gravity. At a far high point huge limbs are thrust out at right angles or on a downward slant forming a broad, flat crown in contrast to the sharp spires. These limbs are elbowed and lively, give a feeling that sugar pine is an articulate overlord of the forest. In thickness and length one of these limbs has the tonnage and dimensions of an ordinary good-sized tree. Suitable to this scale, sugar pine cones are enormous: a foot long, or even 20 inches. They dangle at the outer tips of branches, and the spectacle of these whopping cones hung high in the sky is the best identification of this tree. If you find a green cone on the ground, you're lucky, and should take it home to astonish your friends. Probably it was cut off by a squirrel that wanted to eat the seeds, proving the temerity and surefootedness of these little animals. Needles are wiry, catch highlights, and are clasped together in 5's.

Sugar Pine

Sugar pine belongs to a past age, like the elephant. There are not many young sugars coming along; the sweet seeds are too good to eat, by man and squirrel. Moreover, this is one of the world's top lumber trees. Straight, clear wood in a massive log has irresistible value. There are still many of these giants scattered, not making forests, in the Sierra Nevada Mountains of California, and in southern Oregon.

One of the greatest can be seen at Union Creek near Crater Lake, Oregon. They are at their finest a mile above sea level. Yosemite has plenty of sugar pine to offer you.

Pinus lambertiana

★★**Ponderosa Pine** (also called western yellow pine) is runner-up to Douglas fir as the backbone of the lumber industry of the Northwest. It covers a wider range than any other American cone-bearing tree. Usually humid regions of coast ranges and ocean-facing slopes of the Cascades and Sierras are the best breeding grounds of northwestern colossi, but ponderosa is a vivid exception. Its vast success is due to the way it grows on dry, sandy ground, high up in plenty of sun. You don't see it around Puget Sound, or along the coasts of Oregon and California. But on the east sides of inland ranges, ponderosa is everywhere. It makes the main forest growth of the Rockies from Canada to Mexico. Drive from Denver a few miles through Estes Park to Rocky Mountain National Park—ponderosa, with lodgepole pine, peppers the dry, stony hillsides. But those are small ponderosas compared to the 200-footers of Oregon and California.

Needles are long, up to 10 inches, clasped together in 3's. Cones seem ridiculously small.

Bark on big old ponderosa offers identification at a glance, at eye level. No other pine bark compares with this in color and form. Large smooth plates are cinnamon red. In sunlight the massive bole is a structure of luminous beauty. When you see that, don't rush by, especially if you have a

Ponderosa Pine

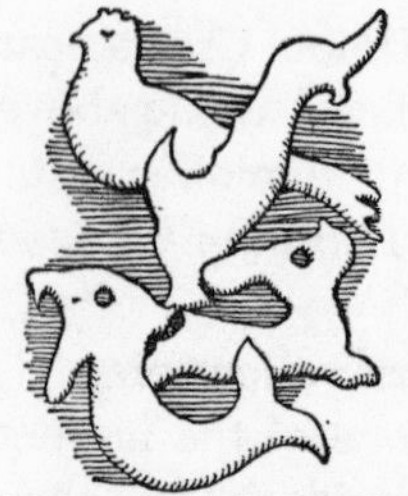
Ponderosa Pine bark scales come in all shapes.

sense of humor. At the base of the tree you'll find bark scales like pieces of a jig-saw puzzle. See the whimsical animals—little dogs barking, owl, long-necked horses, skunks with huge tails, wild geese, ad infinitum. Use a light touch—they are very brittle.

Pinus ponderosa

Lodgepole Pine is a little tree in the land of tall timber. But it's the best rebuilder after a forest fire. In the northern Rockies lodgepole is a straight, sharp spire up to 100 feet—and there's plenty of it with more growing fast to supply lumbering operations. Strangely, it appears again along the coast, as a picturesque beach pine.

Identifying lodgepole is elementary—it's the only pine of the region with 2 needles clasped together. Note how the egg-shaped cone curves so that the base forms an eccentric spiral.

In the Rockies and in Oregon where slopes facing eastward shade off into arid plains, lodgepole forms extensive forests with trees all about the same size. This is pioneer work after a fire. Lodgepole cones are sealed until a forest fire opens them like popcorn to release their seeds. In this respect it is like jack pine around the Great Lakes. Many trees will have kinks at the same level where the weight of snow bent them as saplings. A lodgepole forest has a peculiar aspect. Needles and branches are short; foliage is open so it casts little shade. There is no living ground cover, but the ground is littered with the carcasses of dead lodgepoles that glisten like big, silver jackstraws. Decay is negligible because hot sun floods the lodgepole forest. Exactly on the crest of the ridge the dry east slope meets the moist west slope. Here the cool, shadowy forest of Douglas fir and western hemlock begins along a sharply drawn line. Lodgepole pine is the commonest tree in Yellowstone Park. *Pinus contorta*

Western White Pine with plenty of moisture on western slopes rivals sugar pine in size and grandeur. The kingdom of this tree is in the last of the virgin forests of America, in northern Idaho. It is the finest pine in Glacier National Park, and a valuable timber tree of Washington State. The bark is ashy gray, stippled with small, rectangular plates. Cones are like the artistic eastern white pine cones, only larger. Indeed, western white pine can help a New Englander to step back to pioneer days and see a glorified vision of what eastern white pine (the great *Pinus strobus*) must have looked like before it was slapped down by the axe. *Pinus monticola*

Western White Pine

Whitebark Pine is the brightest star in the firmament of trees. It taps the essence of that eternal order to which all life must submit in order to be free. High on the mountain, touching the silent glacier, wind violence shakes boulders, and, in winter, it is a place of bitter, sterilizing cold. Here the whitebark carves out its own life vault and renders tumult and assault nil by intercourse with the basic serenity and power of sunlight. This wonderful tree flourishes on the highest, exposed places.

The whitebark pine exemplifies a truth to which arrogant man is often blind. He cannot deter life or change it; he must share it to survive eternally. He must relate himself to the cosmic life forces which constitute a vast integrated system from the farthest star to the bacteria in the earth under his feet. Only by discipline can a man be free. Through related effort with others and with nature, he finds fulfillment; and, missing that integration, he misses peace.

Whitebark pine draws on the purest mountain air, and the clearest light from the sky and the splendor of snow, and crystallized mineral elements from virgin rocks—its bark is white. Branches and twigs are so flexible the fiercest wind cannot hurt them. You can tie a knot in the twigs of this tree, which are segmented like the backbone of the human body. Each segment is about ¼ inch long, and that is a whole year's growth. Thus whitebark pine is created with meticulous regularity, slowly, with the rhythm of years. You can count 25 of these annual bumps on a few inches of twig. Needles are clasped in bunches of 5, clustered at the end of the twig. They stream together with a graceful swish.

Golden-mantle Squirrel sits on horizontal trunk of Whitebark Pine.

This tree may seem to be but an intellectual adventure to us, out of reach except to mountain climbers. But, in this day of roads to high places you can see whitebark pine in Yellowstone, Glacier, and Yosemite National Parks. In Mt. Rainier it is accessible at Yakima and along Skyline Trail. Mt. Hood has whitebark under its high ski tow. At Crater Lake National Park a marvelous whitebark with glistening white trunk sprawls over a big, flat boulder on the brink of a mountain cliff, as exposed and carefree as a bird in mid-air. In this instance, by merely substituting a horizontal for a perpendicular position, whitebark again obeys the natural order so that it lives indifferent to assault and retains its freedom and serenity. *Pinus albicaulis*

Limber Pine is the Rocky Mountain timberline tree with many of the qualities of whitebark pine, which is chiefly of the Cascades and high Sierras. Younger bark is light gray, but turns dark later; branches flex like ropes. This is a tree of drier places, the east side of mountains, the high mountains of the arid Southwest. A limber pine is modest in size but in San Isabel National Forest, Colorado, the largest evergreen tree in the state is recorded. You can see plenty of it at Mammoth Hot Springs in Yellowstone. *Pinus flexilis*

Jeffrey Pine is a marvelous tree, chiefly of the high dry Sierras of California, and there is a forest of it in the Siskiyou Mountains, southern Oregon. Long, 10-inch, needles are clasped in 3's, like ponderosa. The tree is wide and free in contrast to sharp spires of Douglas fir and hemlock around it. From its dynamic branches fall giant cones; huge ovals with tough, wide open scales, each of which bears a fierce prickle bent back so sharply that you can handle this cone. Take some home for the living-room table. But before you leave your Jeffrey pine, smell between the ridges of the rough bark—pineapple! A good place to see this pine is in the Glacier Point area of Yosemite National Park. *Pinus jeffreyi*

Jeffrey Pine

Knobcone Pine is born in the wake of a forest fire—the great paradox. Like lodgepoles it has adopted fire catastrophe for its regeneration, but lodgepole also propagates freely when its cones disintegrate with time. Knobcone holds its seeds viable half a century, sealed inside the hardest cone created by any living tree. Test it with your fingernail; it is like rock. This cone is bent at right angles, creating a right-angle spiral unrivaled for its geometric rhythm. Knobcone bears these cones in 3's directly on its trunk, not on branches. These cones are fastened there, unstirring, tightly locked, so many years that the growing trunk may swallow them. Or, if the tree dies, the cones remain fastened to the dead tree, unchanged, with their vital seeds inside. At length a fire destroys the forest and this is what knobcones have been waiting for. Their chance has come—they pop open, and a new forest is planted. This tree is fairly common on

Knobcone Pine

rocky slopes in southern Oregon and the Coast Ranges and Sierra of California. *Pinus attenuata*

Digger Pine is like a hot, dusty breath of the desert. It spreads widely with long gray needles (up to 12 inches) clasped in 3's. These are stiff, wiry, stand out at angles so that the tree casts almost no shade. This is its peculiarity, and claim to notoriety. The needles have a sheen which reflects sunlight like the bleached hair of a small boy who has been to summer camp. Digger is a California pine mingling with chaparral on the arid lower slopes of the Coast Ranges and the Sierras. In Oregon a healthy digger can be seen beside the road by a bridge over the Rogue River near Gold Hill. *Pinus sabiniana*

Cone of Digger Pine

If you drive a nail into a tree four feet above the ground, the nail stays there. It isn't lifted with the growth of the tree. Here is the explanation of why, as a tree grows in circumference and height, its wood does not pour up or stretch up. The bole is built horizontally. Once a cell is in position in the trunk it never shifts that position. Cells are never transported like bricks and placed one on top of another. They are created where needed—and stay put.

from THIS GREEN WORLD

THE CEDARS

The cedars are the tree surprise of the Northwest. Put them at the top of your list for discovery. When you ride through Oregon and Washington, it were better to take Douglas fir and ponderosa in your stride, better not to pause among the silver ghosts of lodgepole forest, if that is to find time to stay awhile with the cedars. Then you will touch, feel, and smell the exquisite tapestry of their foliage. You will see how lightly this lifts, rises and falls, like the breast of the breathing forest. You will see their fronds rise to a vertical position, then gently fan out, presenting a full surface to the sun with the serene gesture of a peacock's tail. Or, in the vagaries of small wind puffs, these fronds may pirouette or wave at you. Cedars have the most remarkable living motions of any trees in the world.

Cedar leaves are tiny, smooth scales laid uninterruptedly along the twig, which is a thread of wood that serves as a pipeline to bring nutrients to these scale leaves it bears. Such foliage conveys to its tree an overall softness and fluidity.

The name "cedar" is confusing because it does not apply to one type of evergreen as does pine, spruce, or hemlock. It is a bracket for juniper, arbor vitae, and cypress. America does not have a true native cedar, although various kinds are planted for elegance—for example, Atlas cedar from North Africa, cedar of Lebanon from Asia Minor, and India's deodar, a favorite ornament in southern California.

Western Red Cedar (also called giant arbor vitae) will be easily recognized by the eastern visitor who knows arbor vitae. But something extraordinary seems to have happened to the compact little brother with dense foliage almost to the ground. This is one of the giants. This enormity does not change the size of scale leaves or cones —they are the same as eastern arbor vitae. Half-inch cones seem ridiculously tiny on a 200-foot tree with a trunk 8 feet in diameter. Bark is brown-gray with loose stringy pieces; long bark fibers can be woven into mats and baskets. Big, old trunks are fluted with heavy, rounded ridges, and the base has huge flaring buttresses. It takes hundreds of years to erect a tree of tough, hard wood like this that lays hold of mother earth with such a mighty grasp.

Wood of western red cedar is fragrant and all but decay-proof and insect-proof. It is unsurpassed timber for shingles and boat hulls because it takes whatever weather or water is thrown at it.

Western Red Cedar

Western red cedar is a tree of the lower level forests in Washington and Oregon. It grows with Douglas fir and hemlock in the rain forest of Olympic National Park. You will see big specimens, even 12 feet in diameter, if you can pronounce "Ohanapecosh" when visiting the Mt. Rainier area, where there is a super cedar swamp. Also this marvelous tree is abundant in the northern Rockies, Idaho and Montana, as part of the deep, dark forest, which is the last of the big American forests with sections still unexplored. *Thuja plicata*

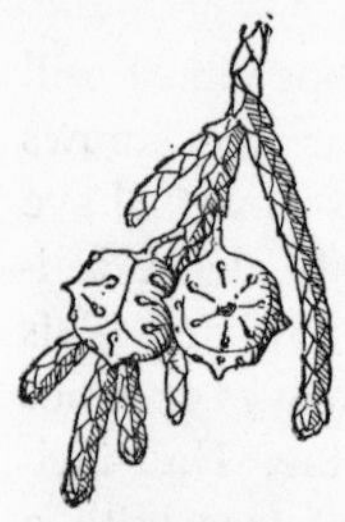
Alaska Cedar

Alaska Cedar remarkably enough looks like a tree from eskimo land, where on the fringe of the tundra it has been shaped by terrible wind and weighed down by snow. This is a comparatively small tree, seen beside the road on the edge of the forest, or as an understory about 75 feet high. It's a queer tree, which once seen you'll never forget. Foliage has a dusty look; wide fabric-like fronds turn down sharply and then revolve and close in toward the trunk. This makes the tree look squeezed; it is too sharp and narrow, like a collapsed tent. Cones are round, the size of shoe buttons.

In Oregon this is a tree of the northern Cascades. A short drive out of Portland you see it below Mt. Hood where Route 50 goes through Zig Zag and Government Camp. In Washington this cedar is common in the higher forests of the Cascades and Mt. Olympus, from there up the British Columbia coast it goes back to its home in Alaska. Alaska cedar has extremely durable light yellow wood that polishes beautifully. Furniture in Paradise Inn and Community House of Mt. Rainier National Park is made of this wood taken from fire-killed trees in the Silver Forest. *Chamaecyparis nootkatensis*

Incense Cedar is well named for its fragrance, although this is no more delicious than Alaska cedar and not so strong a perfume as that of western juniper. Dusty blue-green fronds, which collapsed on Alaska cedar are held upright on incense. They drop open and revolve with a significant motion. If you have imagination, this may suggest a Tibetan lama holding up a fan in each hand, trying to get your attention.

Incense cedar is largest in the Sierra Nevada of California. You see it in high gulches in Yosemite, Sequoia, and General Grant National Parks. Its trunk, unlike the tree columns that rise with almost parallel sides, tapers, and this reduces the height to around 100 feet. That takes 450 years to reach. In Oregon you see incense cedar south of Crater Lake near Union Creek, and many intimate incense trees around Oregon Caves. Study the scale leaves. They are put together in cycles of four, with the side pair like boat keels enclosing the face pair. These scales are longer than wide, contrasting with all other cedar scale leaves that are as wide as they are long. Incense's straight-grained wood has fine soft texture—makes good lead pencils.

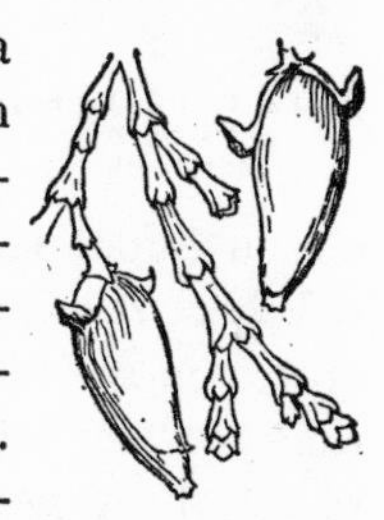
Incense Cedar

Libocedrus decurrens

Port Orford Cedar is one of those fascinating trees (like Monterey cypress) that by some delicate balance of circumstances grows only in one small locality in the world. This locality is close to the Pacific Coast in the southwestern corner of Oregon and the northwestern corner of California. It has an even climate the year round. Steep mountains condense water borne by Pacific winds. Ravines are deep, and coastal air is moist and cool; a

Port Orford Cedar has white crosses underneath.

sanctuary of many trees. The first prize of this tree treasury goes to Port Orford cedar.

In the mountains a few miles inland this is a huge, primeval tree with a trunk six feet in diameter and reaching 200 feet into the sky. These Port Orfords make their colonies in moist coves deep in Douglas fir forest. They are brought out in 8-foot lengths of log along with Douglas fir.

Where the Coast Highway, U.S. 101, runs through the area, you see lots of small Port Orfords with low foliage that you can touch and smell. It is bright yellow-green, so closely woven, so pliant that the fronds feel and look like golden cloth. The branches of the tree slant upward, while the soft foliage falls gracefully. The drapery of a branch is evenly disposed on each side, unlike other cedars whose fronds are irregular with more growth on one side of a branch. The most peculiar characteristic is the way a Port Orford frond, while draped longitudinally, also flexes at right angles in the center. This waves at you with the droll motion of a small child that holds up its fist, palm forward, and with fingers close together wags them up and down to say hello.

You probably have this cedar wood underneath yourself when you sit in your car, as this porous, acid-resisting wood is used for storage battery separators. The big logs are revolved and peeled to ⅛-inch thickness by a giant lathe that can handle 8-foot logs as great as 10 tons. As they peel, amazing fragrance fills the air—a unique perfume like witch hazel but sweeter and heavier.

Chamaecyparis lawsoniana

THE SPRUCES

What about spruces? You might suppose that the spire-with-prickly-needles-attached-to-pegs-on-the-twig would outdo itself in grandeur and abundance in the kingdom of the evergreens. But the big show has been taken over by fir, hemlock, and pine. Spruce plays a limited but highly distinctive and interesting part. Most widespread Engelmann spruce is a medium-sized tree to be seen all over the Rockies, and in spots in the Cascades. Three others are artistic and, in a sense, the most interesting spruces in the world. You should know about them, and if you go to the localities where they grow, be sure you don't miss them.

Engelmann Spruce expresses intense vigor disciplined into the form of a sharp spire. In the Northwest it is small and dense compared to the giants. Needles are square in cross-section, sharp, stiff, 1-inch long. Purple and yellow cones are so profuse that in the light of the sun they color the upper branches of a healthy Engelmann with a golden glow. Fallen cones carpet the ground beneath. Pick up some and shake them to

Cone of Engelmann Spruce

see one of the loveliest delicate tints hidden in trees. Chances are that unescaped seeds will drop out in your hand so that you can see their pink tissue paper wings.

Engelmann can be seen in a superb setting near Government Camp the south side of Mt. Hood, Oregon. It grows here around a wet meadow of blue gentian with snow-capped Mt. Hood rising behind its spires. In Mt. Rainier National Park this spruce is around White River camp ground. Engelmann is a Rocky Mountain tree, from Canada to Arizona. West of Denver, it forms dense forests on cool, moister north slopes. You see it just below timberline on Pike's Peak, and in every vista from transcontinental Route 40 around Granby, Colorado, and in Rocky Mountain National Park. *Picea engelmanni*

Sitka Spruce is the black-looking wind-blown tree along the shore line of Oregon and Washington. The strong west wind off the ocean streams upward with the slope of the Coast Range, and shapes the crown of this tree exactly in line with that flow. It is actually rigid and resistant, but in appearance like a torn banner flapping in the wind. Needles of Sitka are the longest (1½-inch), sharpest, and stiffest of any spruce. Unlike the typical spruce needle, they are flat. The blackness of the tree is the contrast of its silhouette against bright seascapes. Sitka is heavy and wide for a spruce. Its wood, seasoned by mighty winds, is so resistant, twangy, and strong that it is a leading wood for airplane construction. Sitka emerges from the north at Kodiak Is-

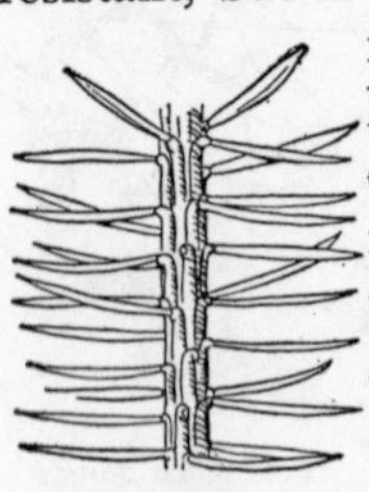

Sitka Spruce has longest and sharpest needles of any spruce. Cones are like Engelmann's.

land, Alaska, travels down the sea line to northern California. You see it around Puget Sound, and the west side of Olympic National Park, and along the entire Oregon coast. *Picea sitchensis*

Brewer Spruce (also called weeping spruce) is a solitary rarity with flexible dangling branches. This weeping is in contrast to the staccato, right-angled accent of all other spruces. It grows in a wild, unspoiled locality high in the Siskiyou Mountains, straddling the Oregon-California line, around a silent wilderness lake called Sanger. Before Brewer vanishes from our world, perhaps horticulture will use its natural magic to bring the pendulous beauty of this spruce to our parks and gardens. At present it is to be seen only by the most avid tree explorers. Needles on the flexing branches are curved. Fresh cones on the tree are rich purple and sparkle with crystals of resin as though set with diamonds. *Picea breweriana*

Weeping Spruce cone

Colorado Spruce is the State Tree of Colorado. It is abundant in the Rockies west of Denver, on moist slopes, and along streams. Needles point out at right angles to their twigs, and the bright blue tinge of younger needles has made this tree world-famous. It is planted so much in the East, you will find it listed in that section. When you go to Colorado, you will see this arresting tree in all its splendor in its natural range. *Picea pungens*

Note for mountain tree explorers: In a high dry place, around forests of big trees, you will see many skeletons of dead monarchs. The bark is gone and wood is twisted like silvery, satiny taffy. Slowly during the many years while these trees were alive, their trunks were slipping or stretching around beneath the bark. The tree grew longer branches on the sunny side, shorter branches on the shadier, mountain side, always reaching toward the light. This makes exposed mountain trees unsymmetrical. The prevailing wind is strong; pushes relentlessly against the bigger branches; thus, beneath its bark, the wood of the trunk revolves by sail action.

WESTERN LARCH

Western Larch has soft needles squirting from the ends of sturdy spurs, identical with larch of the Northeast. Here is another example, like arbor vitae, of a transcontinental pair that look alike in every respect, except that the western member is a giant. Western larch is a token of the great age of the Northwest spire forests. This larch mounts 180 feet in 700 years. Such slow growing makes the heaviest wood among evergreens. The bunch form of needles suggests pine, but larch needles are short, soft, and count around 20 in a bunch; pine needles are clasped tightly together in a sheath, and never more than 5 together. Larch needles turn yellow in the fall and drop off for the winter, again like eastern larch. Bark is fire-resistant, wood is decay-resistant, red-brown and white. But because it is scattered or remote in the depths of the big north Rocky Mountain forests, this distinctive, heavy wood has not been much used. Big western larch turns up in the Cascades of Washington and Oregon, but its chief fortress is the Rocky Mountains of northern Idaho and Montana. Abundant on lower west slopes of Glacier National Park; around Lake McDonald this is the chief forest tree. *Larix occidentalis*

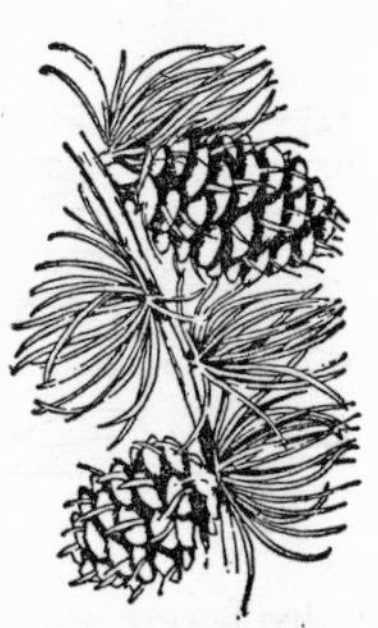

Cones and needle clusters of Western Larch

PACIFIC YEW

Pacific Yew is the most overlooked tree in the Northwest forests. It's underneath, in the shadows; it has no positive shape, but long-spreading branches sprawl out. Yew is worth seeing. Its needles are two tones of the richest green of any evergreen needles. Their tops are glossy dark; undersides, deep yellow-green. For comparison, larch needles have tiny sharp points, whereas fir are always blunt or notched. But the quickest way to spot yew is by the darkness of foliage. Pacific yew, contrasting with the little shrub yew of the East is a good-sized tree, 25 feet or higher. However, in the gigantic proportions of the western spire forest, where this is an understory tree, it looks comparatively miniature. Look for bright red berries instead of cones. Pacific yew is in the shadows of moist forests from Alaska to Monterey. There's plenty to be seen in Mt. Rainier National Park. Also you'll find it abundant as a large shrub in the deep woods on the west slope of Glacier National Park.

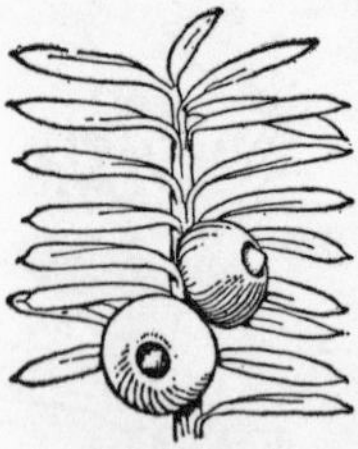

Pacific Yew

Taxus brevifolia

WESTERN JUNIPER

Western Juniper distills the gold and red of the arid sandy plains to construct some of the most brilliant wood that grows.

Across the broad sagebrush land you see almost nothing but western juniper. Its silhouette is black in the glaring sun. Its trunk is heavy and fluted and filled with the swirls of tortuous knots. Unlike the sharp spires of the mountains, this tree, surrounded by sunshine, seems to explode into the air, as broad as it is high. No matter how hot and thirsty you are, do not pass by the western juniper, though there is mile after mile of it, without stopping for a look at the details of its scale leaves. Each little scale glistens with what looks like a dew-drop. Touch it and see how viscous it is. This minute diamond of resin seals the breathing pore and helps prevent loss of precious moisture so that it can grow in such a dry place. Whether these droplets are fresh and clear or, on older scales, crystallized and crisp, they are marvelously fragrant. The balsam-like aroma fills the air. If you drive in central Oregon near Bend on Route 97, you will see beside a mesa ravine a hot grove called Peter Skene Ogden Park. Here is western juniper at its best, ready for your camera.

Western Juniper

Juniperus occidentalis

THE BROADLEAFS

With evergreens stealing the show, the broadleafs of the Northwest are too easily overlooked. The proportion of the Wagnerian landscape which they occupy is small. This is surprising to a visitor from the East where the green flood of the Great American Woods rolls over hill and dale. Northwestern broadleafs are confined to banks of streams, moist mountain ravines, and to the most interesting band of trees in the world that runs north and south along the Pacific coast of Washington, Oregon, and northern California.

Around towns and farms many trees familiar in the East have been planted—elm, horsechestnut, walnut, locust, catalpa, Lombardy poplar. Because you see these trees first, you may dismiss the broadleafs as not especially exciting or different from other parts of the country. This feeling is increased by the weeds that border the valley roadsides, Queen Anne's lace, mullein, hawkweed, tansy, yarrow, thistle, butter-and-eggs, St. Johnswort. This is the gauze of plants that appears wherever man disturbs the earth from Maine to California. Then, perhaps because maple leaves are so huge, you begin to discover the broadleaf trees of our Northwest.

The composition is simple. Alder, everywhere there's a moist place; easily recognized by those who know eastern alder, but with whiter bark, and growing as trees, not shrubs. Trembling aspen, the transcontinental tree; cottonwood; willows. After these irrepressibles, two unique maples, an occasional oak, ash, dogwood—and that's about all of the broadleafs except The Unique Four. (See pages 194-198.)

Bigleaf Maple is the outstanding shadetree and the only large maple of the Coast. Leaves are typically maple, but with big lobes, deep sinuses—the blade is often 12 inches long and 14 inches wide, and if you look for it, you can find an 18-incher. As a broad surface for sun-catching, this leaf is pure logic; at the edge of dark forest, the tree has to get its quota of sunlight from one side, so—it has leaves twice as big as the ordinary maple. The big leaves turn their backs on the shadows and face out, so that they catch your eye as you drive past. You see bigleaf at its finest around Puget Sound and in Western Oregon, and it extends into northern California. Everywhere in northwestern coastal towns it's a good street

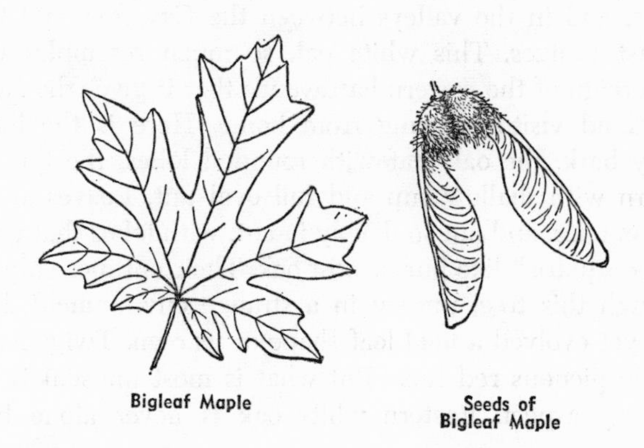

Bigleaf Maple

Seeds of Bigleaf Maple

Vine Maple

and park tree. Furry seeds hang on all summer in heavy clusters, yellow-brown, sticky. Their wings make nearly closed scissors. Wood is typical maple, deeper colored than eastern maple, more figured, with beautiful burls for fancy veneers. *Acer macrophyllum*

Vine Maple is a low edge-of-the-woods maple that is half tree, half shrub. Often slender trunks curve out, take root, make a vine maple thicket. Leaf is a pinwheel; it has about 9 radiating fingers almost exactly contained in a circle. In the fall these round leaves turn scarlet and yellow, rivaling Vermont's maples in brilliance. However, a low, understory tree can only lend dashes of color to a landscape which it far from dominates. *Acer circinatum*

Oregon White Oak wanders lonely near the Pacific coast and in the valleys between the Cascades and the Coast Ranges. This white oak so much resembles the sovereign of the eastern hardwoods that it gives the New England visitor a pang from home. Here is the light gray bark, the oak leaf with rounded lobes, the typical acorn with shallow cup and full oval nut. Leaves are a bit smaller, and not so deeply in-cut, with lobes that tend to be squarish like bur or post oak. Their outlines vary as though this tree, uneasy in a strange environment, has not yet evolved a final leaf shape of its own. Twigs have a conspicuous red fuzz. But what is most unusual is its solitary aspect. Eastern white oak is never alone but always in the vigorous company of white and black oaks. Oregon white oak is the only oak tree in the state of Washington and northern Oregon. It is fairly common on the prairie south of Tacoma and in the Yakima and Columbia River valleys. It is a part of the green landscape of Oregon's Willamette Valley. The tree is surprisingly small in this setting; its wood is only of local use for tool handles and ladders, but great for a log fire, with almost the heat value of coal. Oregon white oak does not climb much, except as a shrub. There is no oak in Mount Rainier National Park, nor around Mt. Hood or Crater Lake, and eastward. There is no oak in the vast deep forests of the northern Rockies, none in Glacier National Park and Yellowstone. This fact lends a certain accent to the only good looking oak in valleys near the Northwest coast. *Quercus garryana*

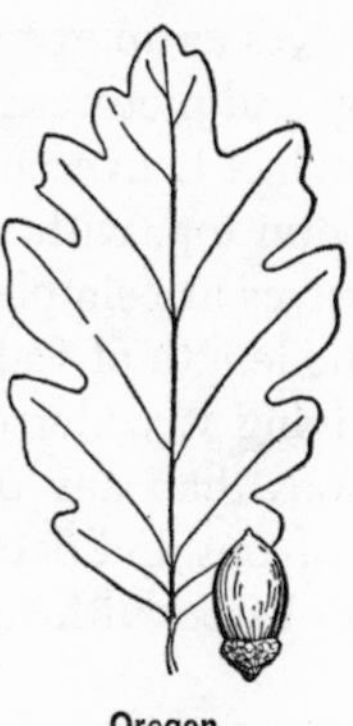

Oregon White Oak

Canyon Live Oak is the gold tree of Oregon and California. It grows beside the abandoned gear of gold prospectors in the Siskiyou Mountains of southwestern Oregon. The thick, broad-rimmed cup of its acorn is lined with bright golden fuzz, and a touch of this gold even tints the outside scales. On the under-surface of young leaves, you again discover gold, which turns to bluish white on older leaves. Canyon live oak, like the great live oak of our southern states, hold its

Canyon Live Oak

leaves as an evergreen. But this is a mountain tree, scrubby and picturesque or perhaps reaching 60 feet in a moist ravine. Leaves are small (1 to 2 inches), dark green, glossy on top, with spiney scallops like holly leaves, or older leaves are simple ovals without the spines. The tree goes the length of California on the Sierra Nevada Mountains, giving it wider distribution in a greater variety of locations than any other California oak. In the moist lower canyons and flats of Yosemite National Park, it is a beautiful tree with its dark holly-like foliage.

Quercus chrysolepis

California Black Oak is easily dismissed by the visitor from the East who wants to see different kinds of trees. To all appearances this one is like the black oak of the Atlantic states. Acorn cup is deep. Perhaps these two are listed as different types of oak because they were discovered and named by different botanists some 3,000 miles apart. Leaf of California black oak is the same size, with seven lobes, bristle-tipped and shiny, dark green. In Oregon and California, where there are few good-sized oaks, this is prized as a worthy broadleafed tree. It is part of the coastal green from southwestern Oregon to the Sierra and Coast Ranges of central California. In Yosemite National Park this is the commonest oak in the moist coves of ponderosa and sugar pine forest.

California Black Oak

Quercus kelloggi

Oregon Ash is another near duplicate of an eastern tree. It has the multiple leaves with 7 leaflets, opposite each other; the woven bark pattern; the artistic buds on heavy twig; and the paddle-shaped seed wings of the Pennsylvania red ash. The visitor from the East can skip this tree to marvel at the others. But you may wonder how ash could jump across prairies and mountains to turn up along the Pacific coast.

Fraxinus oregona

Berry cluster and leaf of Pacific Dogwood

Pacific Dogwood holds the spotlight of the coastal broadleaf belt. Westerners delight in their spring dogwood flowers as do easterners, all the more so because the gaiety of other eastern woodland trees such as redbud, shadblow, and red maple are missing. Pacific dogwood is larger than eastern flowering dogwood; it makes a good-sized understory tree in the Coast Ranges from British Columbia to San Francisco. It turns up in moist spots on western slopes of the Sierra Nevada; including Yosemite. An interesting point is that the showy, petal-like white bracts of the flowers usually count 6 instead of 4. Also the fruit clusters are larger, rounder, with many bright red little footballs. In a beauty contest Pacific dogwood might win over the stylish eastern dogwood.

Cornus nuttalli

Red Alder is one of the tree surprises of the Northwest. You won't have to search for it, as this is the commonest broadleaf of the region. Everywhere there's a damp place you see red alder. It's the first tree to start reconstituting a burnt or logged ground. The surprise is the size and quality of wood. Eastern alder is a weedy shrub of bog

Red Alder leaf and "cone"

thickets. Red alder is a tree 50 to 100 feet with a trunk a foot to three feet thick–considered the most important hardwood in the state of Washington. Leaves are dark and smooth on top, whitish underneath with some rusty hairs; edges curl under, teeth are coarse, irregular, giving leaf a rugged look. Bark is smooth light gray with black patches. You can always tell alder by the little oval cones (about ¾ inch long), easily mistaken for dainty pine cones. Wood is satiny white when fresh, but turns to cherry red, makes attractive furniture. This curious change of color is due to tannic acid in sap. Chewing inner bark turns saliva blood red. *Alnus rubra*

White Alder is an even larger tree than red. Its leaf is a blunter, broader oval with finer teeth, and shiny yellow-green underneath instead of whitish. Large white alders often line the banks of streams through hot, arid sage-brush country. Silver-gray bark reminds easterner of American beech. White alder is more common than red in the Coast Range valleys of northern California.
Alnus rhombifolia

Cascara is a widely known label on a bottle of medicine; in the Northwest it is a hardy, handsome native of the forest. Many people know it there who scarcely look at other trees, because stripping its bark is a profitable local industry in western Oregon and Washington. This is the understory tree with bigleaf maple and red alder, on the sunlit fringes of Douglas fir and hemlock forests. It is easily mistaken for alder, but look twice at the leaf and you may discover cascara. This leaf is a perfect oval without coarse teeth. Leaf edge appears smooth, but peer closely to see fine teeth; veins are straight, parallel, and conspicuous. Fruit is a small, shiny, black berry. Trunks a foot in diameter are rare today because stripping the bark kills the tree—the largest cascara you see will probably have a 6-inch thick trunk. Bark is various shades of brown, smooth or roughened with small scales. Cascara is native of the Northwest and of nowhere else in the world. It is cultivated for a park and garden tree in Oregon and Washington. Fortunately, stumps produce vigorous suckers that grow into a fresh crop so that trees and medicine keep coming. *Rhamnus purshiana*

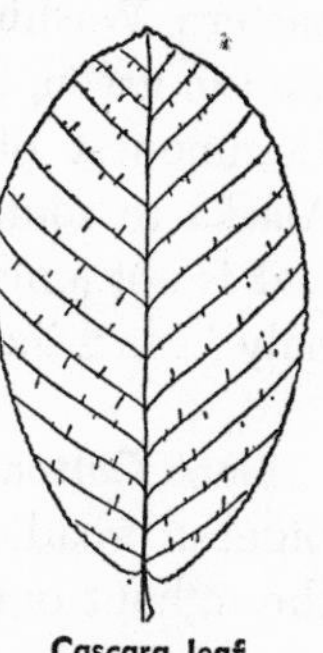

Cascara leaf

Willow is a ubiquitous broadleaf of the West Coast green belt. It comes in all sizes from slender withes to arching shrubs, and good sized trees. Willows have narrow, soft, weak leaves, and twigs that take root thrust in wet sand. Only an expert tries to recognize different kinds of willows. Well known is weeping willow, planted east and west. The biggest of the Northwest is 80-foot **Peachleaf Willow** which lines streams (with black cottonwood) and is planted around ranch houses, dry prairies of

Leaves of Nuttall Willow

eastern Washington and Oregon. **Black Willow** is common in green, fruit-bearing Willamette Valley of Oregon. Commonest of all willows on the Pacific coast from Alaska to southern California is the **Nuttall Willow.** Its leaf is not long and slender, but a wider oval and small—only 1½ to 2 inches. *Salix spp.*

Black Cottonwood is a poplar that wins the title as the biggest broadleaf of the Northwest. Poplars are common throughout our land. Trembling aspen shakes its leaves from coast to coast; Lombardy's exclamation catches your eye almost wherever you are, be it Boston, Denver, or Portland, Oregon; cottonwood snows under with its tassels the prairie states and eastward. But the king of all poplars grows only in the Northwest. It is said to reach 180 feet, but a casual 100-foot tree would overtop other poplars that line northwestern rivers. This is the biggest broadleaf of Alaska, the Yukon, and British Columbia. It marches down to northern California, spreading out over most of Washington and Oregon, and eastward through Rocky Mountain valleys in Idaho and Montana. Springing up around springs and streams in arid northwest prairies, this great tree spreads a wide crown of upreaching limbs to cast the only shade for a thousand miles. The beckoning of black cottonwood across the blistering sagebrush kept the pioneer wagon trains rumbling out their heartbreaking ten miles a day along the Oregon Trail. Black cottonwood wrote that chapter

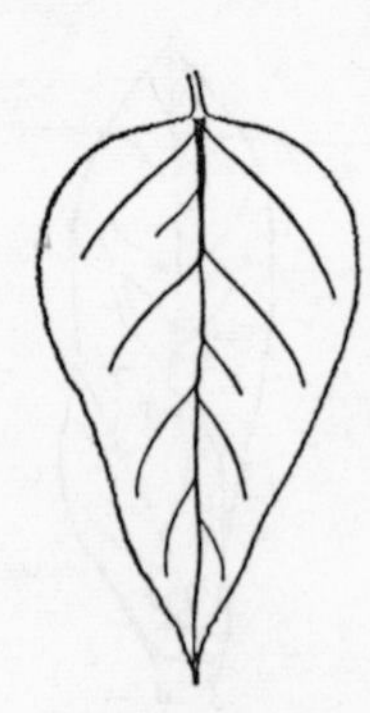

Black Cottonwood

of our country's history, when heat shriveled the wood of wheels, and alkali dust clogged and rotted the hooves of horses and cattle—and week after week it again appeared on the horizon to promise the only moist and shady spot to repair wheel rims and soothe sore feet.

Black cottonwood leaf is large, leathery; shadowy cool green on top, silvery underneath, turning to reddish brown in late summer. This is among the most graceful leaves of any tree, tapering like a pear, rounded at the bottom, and with fine rippling teeth on its margins. The stem is round in cross-section, not flattened in the way so typical of poplars, so that they wave instead of vibrate. The realm of the evergreen giants does not dispute the East's dominance of the leaf-dropping hardwoods; but, with bigleaf maple, red alder, and black cottonwood, it produces off the back of its hand, so to speak, something special even in that category. *Populus trichocarpa*

THE UNIQUE FOUR

The tree treasury of southwest Oregon, with its extension up and down the coast, has four remarkable trees found in no other part of the world. All four are broadleaf evergreens, that is, they are clothed with green leaves all winter, but unlike ordinary evergreens, have broad leaves instead of needles. They live together with sequoia, Port Orford cedar, and other ancient and honorable tree marvels in the Northwest's moist Pacific valleys—strongbox of the ages. From the viewpoint of the outside world these are rare trees, but this does not imply that only a connoisseur may find and enjoy them. They are abundant in their places, and every visitor who doesn't use a highway as a tunnel through the country can easily see them.

Oregon Myrtle (also called California laurel) is one of the great trees of the world, with arresting form and marvelous wood. When it can take its natural shape without interference, it forms a big bowl, upside down on a heavy pedestal. Its leaves which smell like bay rum, are dark and leathery, resembling eastern mountain laurel but broader ovals. These make such a dense head that from a little distance it appears that a gardener has clipped a giant boxwood to form a dome. Inside this dome are deep shadowy spaces among massive horizontal limbs, a bewitching place for a small boy to climb into and have a hideaway. The short trunk is almost as wide as it is tall, perhaps 5 feet in both dimensions, and it bulges with gnarls as though the wood were squeezed out by the great weight supported by the trunk. Because of perpetual shade, the hard gray bark is covered with moss and lichen so that it looks more like rock in a damp forest than part of a living tree.

The more gnarls there are on an Oregon myrtle log, the more valuable it is. They are the whirlpools, the comets, the frozen tornadoes of this marvelous wood. Such markings are not continuous strokes usual in wood grain, but they are short strokes with the aspect of showers of fast-moving sparks. Colors are gray-brown and silver, rich and distinctive in contrast to the yellow and reddish tones of most cabinet woods. It is so hard and polishes so smoothly it becomes like marble. This is ideal for superb wood-carving. Also this wood, fabricated to withstand the pressure of the dense tree, is used for house-moving rollers.

When you are near Coquille in southwestern Oregon, drive about ten miles to Myrtle Point to see fine specimens scattered around the fields. Around nearby Coos Bay you will find headquarters of myrtle wood carving. This tree extends southward, and the minute you cross the state line it becomes California laurel, prized for landscaping, and called by some people the handsomest "hardwood in the state." It is

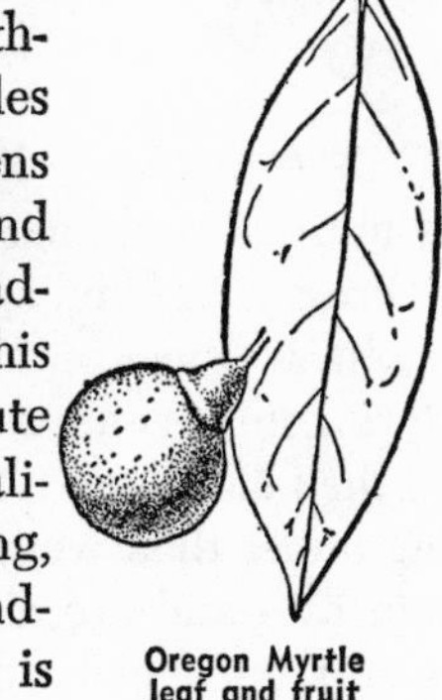

Oregon Myrtle leaf and fruit

planted as a street and park tree as far down as Santa Barbara. *Umbellularia californica*

Madrone will stop you with its color of bark—terra cotta and green patches that are a delight to see. Trees with snow white bark may catch the eye faster, but deep, rich colors in bark are more unusual. Madrone has sap chemicals which permeate the bark layers, so that each layer takes on a different wonderful color. Then these layers peel off fancifully in summer to expose the terra cotta and jade. Other layers show gradations of yellow and gray. A suede surface makes it all the richer with flat tones.

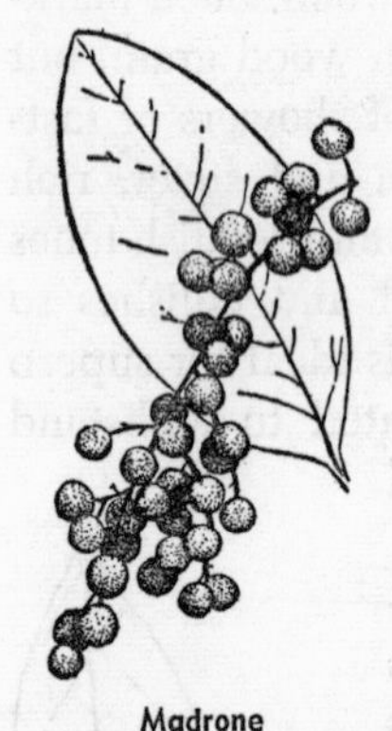

Madrone

Highlights in all trees are vital for gaiety and depth, where there is a gloss of bud, leaf, or bark. The sparkle of resin crystals, contrasting with shadows, make trees scintillate. Madrone has highlights on its leathery dark oval leaves that resemble rhododendron's. With its foreground of polished leaves and background of bark on limb and trunk that has no highlights, but the richest color, madrone is unusual and fine. You will stand and look.

Press your hand against the bark and feel its mysterious coolness. Even on a hot day it seems cold to the touch. Spring flowers are small, white globes held up in clusters. In the fall these are transformed into tiny oranges, drooping under their weight as brilliantly red as eastern mountain ash—and are also a feast for birds. Madrone wood is soft, turning hard, brittle, splitting easily when dry;

it makes good charcoal and tobacco pipes. But with its magic as a living tree, why think up uses for the wood? It grows in the coastal strip from Washington to below San Francisco. It does not transplant well outside those limits; but there's nothing like this as a park or garden tree in its home territory. *Arbutus menziesi*

Golden Chinquapin is part chestnut, part oak, and has evergreen leaves like mountain laurel. This combination of three kinds of trees makes one wonder whether this tree is evolving into a new type of oak or chestnut before our eyes. No one can ever answer this question because, to see the evolution of plants, we must telescope hundreds of thousands of years. In northern Oregon golden chinquapin is a shrub on the sunlit edges of ponderosa pine and western hemlock. A visitor who knows eastern trees is astonished to find the porcupine spines of chestnut burs on "mountain laurel." The mystery deepens at sight of golden sparkling scales on the underside of the leaf. Unlike true chestnut, the bur does not wholly cover the nut, which only peeks out, suggesting an acorn with a deep cup. The nut is sweet to eat. White flowers are often in bloom at the same time that nuts are ripening. It would be possible to have a bouquet of flowers and a bowl of good nuts from the same tree on your dinner table.

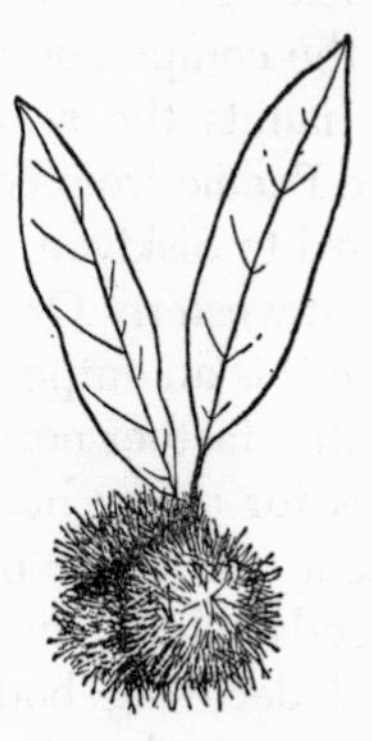
Golden Chinquapin

In southwestern Oregon, on humid mountain sides of the Siskiyous facing the Pacific, golden chinquapin is a hundred foot forest tree. Wood makes exquisite paneling, pale brown to roseate.

Castanopsis chrysophylla

Tanbark Oak, like golden chinquapin, is both oak and chestnut. Its leaves are small, evergreen, and with scallops sometimes so shallow that they hardly show. The fruit resembles an acorn but is more beautiful and exciting than acorns of true oaks. Its cup has long curly bristles like a chestnut bur and the nut is a handsome oval with soft fuzz across which play bluish and pinkish tints. The scientific name means "rock fruit" which aptly describes the hardness of the nut. This acorn is the chief feature of the tree from an artistic standpoint.

The name tanbark does not refer to the color of the bark but to the strong yellow tannic acid in the bark that is used for tanning leather. Tanbark oak is the companion of the famed redwood; it haunts the same humid valleys near the Pacific from central California northward to Siskiyou Mountain hideaways in southwestern Oregon. Across the state line it is an outpost of redwood, stepping a little farther north. If we could observe this for a few hundred years, we might see a new grove of energetic young redwoods where the acid from the leaves and decaying bodies of a tanbark outpost proved to be the best elixir for perpetuating these eternal trees.

Tanbark Oak

Lithocarpus densiflora

CALIFORNIA

California's trees are as diverse and dramatic as her mountains, canyons, deserts, and seacoast. Trunk, leaf, root, and fruit must strike a working balance with their environment. A great variety of trees results from combinations of hot and cold, wet and dry, sunshine and rock. Thus in a state-wide view California trees have no uniformity, but they add up to a vast exposition of all sorts of trees. They are the harmonious fourth dimension of this state which is 600 miles north to south, and from 160 feet below sea-level in Death Valley to 14 thousand feet above sea-level in the high Sierras.

Time also has made contrasts in California trees. Pacific Ocean currents stabilized the climate through thousands of years, so that trees belonging to a geologic past are still there for us to see. Close by are trees planted by man that have fallen swiftly into place to become as much a part of the scene as the old original trees.

It is impossible to list all the trees you will see in this exposition. However, the tree diagram is simple, broadly divided into three kinds of landscape: mountain, intermountain, and coast.

Two mountain ranges extend the length of the state; the Coast Range on the west side, paralleled by the Sierra Nevada inland on the east side. The forest trees of these mountains are the big spires of the Northwest described in the preceding section. Ponderosa pine, white fir, incense cedar run all the way down the state on these ranges. The big plus of the California mountains are the two sequoias.

Between the two ranges stretches an entirely different type of tree domain, consisting of plains and valleys where vineyards, and orchards are planted, and every community takes pride in its palms, eucalyptus, and ornamental trees. Southward the intermountain plain and the mountains themselves become arid, and the trees here are of the dry Southwest.

The third part of the California tree diagram is the coastal strip; a fantastic arboretum six hundred miles long and a few miles wide. This results from a mild climate its entire length, from the juxta-position of dunes, headlands, canyons, mountainsides, and from cool fogbathed to sunbathed land where trees transplanted from the most colorful subtropical areas of the world are perfectly at home. Along this coast also grow a few trees, almost forgotten in the discard of evolution—unique old trees such as Monterey cypress and Torrey pine that have clung to their tight little spots by the sea. Unlike the conventional arboretum, this one has been developed by a whole population wtih a high percentage of garden lovers and a sense of exultation in their climate and pride in their communities. An outstanding example of a community's love of trees is Santa Barbara. Anyone who wants to explore deeply the trees of southern California would do well to visit the Santa Barbara Botanic Garden which, with the city authorities publishes a beautifully illustrated guide to the trees of the region.

THE SEQUOIAS

The sequoias make you feel like a mite only momentarily living on earth. Entering a dusky sequoia grove, you do not see trees with the reality of trunk, branches, and leaves; you see broad, shadowy columns. Their contour lines are parallel above but down where you are they diverge gracefully to form a wide base. A black shadow at the ground line seems to detach this base from the earth; the vast roots are invisible; weight vanishes in the perfection of equilibrium. The big column seems to be balanced lightly in the air. Now examine the wonderful base closely and you will see bulging muscles. Sinews of wood and cordage of bark are tortured and taut, forming elbows and knees bent but firm under the downward thrust. This compression is the only apparent concession which sequoia makes to the law of gravity. All the rest is an uprush of wood around a perpendicular river of sap that flows hundreds of feet straight up into the air effortlessly, silently.

These dark columns took a thousand years or more to mount so that, seen through the distance of time, they are fixed and lifeless in our eyes, just as a swift star seems fixed when we see it through the distance of space. Moreover, this bole seems too wide, too silent, too immobile to be alive—yet it is the life of the ages. In a sequoia grove one trespasses in a place where there is no hurry or flutter, no measure of time, no wind, no sound. A dog does not bark. A person whispers.

The lowest branch of sequoia may be a hundred feet up, so that there is wide open space above your head.

This is not sky, it is a clerestory beneath the crown of needles and cones. This is broken by openings where shafts of sunlight slant through, accenting without dispelling the twilight. Often a sunshaft strikes a column so as to turn its parallel lines to gold; and again the searchlight will reach the floor of the forest where it reveals a clump of ferns, or throw a bright green spot on the carpet of wood sorrel.

There are two kinds of sequoia. *Redwood* is the tallest tree in the world and grows near the coast, where valleys are bathed in cool fogs from the Pacific. *Big tree* grows inland in the Sierra Nevada ranges; its nearest grove to San Francisco is about 150 miles due east. Big tree is the largest tree in the world in terms of tonnage of wood. Its trunk is more massive than redwood's. You will never confuse the two sequoias because they grow in such widely separated places.

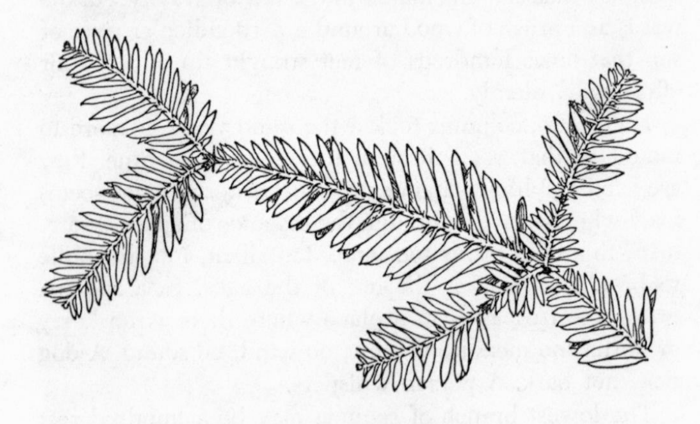

Redwood branch

Redwood is the world's tallest tree. The record holder has been measured as 349.3 feet high. A former record holder grows about 45 miles south of Eureka, California, near U. S. Route 101. Like a bug at the base of a tall corn stalk, you will see a tremendous trunk; but its diameter of 20 feet, supporting tons of timber drawn upward 264 feet straight as a plumb line is one of nature's easy miracles. It would take ten of the gigantic Parthenon columns created by the Greeks, one on top of another, to reach as high as this redwood. The world's tallest tree started growing about Julius Caesar's time, and before its hidden valley was reached, the Dark and Middle Ages had come and gone; the changes of thought, art, literature, society from the ancient to the modern world took place; America's history to our day was made. From our limited viewpoint sequoias never die of old age; old trees are fireproof, with bark a foot deep, and even more important, disease-proof. While man respects it, storms spare it, and the climate holds, the world's tallest tree should keep right on from here going up and up with serene indifference to us and our confusion.

For all its greatness redwood is in delicate balance. So much of its trunk is a standpipe of water that the tree needs 50 to 60 inches of rain per year plus dripping fog every night, with hot days, cool nights, and little winter freezing. This precise combination pins down redwood to the northerly valleys of California's Coast Range. The most southern grove is near Carmel, but north of San Francisco redwood is the chief tree of the big forests. San Francisco visitors in a hurry can see redwoods in Muir Woods a few miles across Golden Gate Bridge.

Redwood is not easily transplanted although Santa Barbara has quite a few. Somehow six redwoods are growing in South Carolina, and Norfolk, Virginia, has one planted in 1860, now 75 feet tall. Even in its own citadel it doesn't grow well from seed. One-inch cones look too small, and their seeds are not usually fertile. Fortunately redwood possesses such wonderfully potent wood that the tree will sprout without seeds. No other cone-bearing evergreen will do this but when a redwood is slain by man or storm, a circle of suckers springs out of the stump and keeps right on growing. Also the knotty whirlpools of wood, known as burls, produce so many treelets that a redwood burl in a saucer of water in your house sprouts fern-like houseplants and would become trees if the burl were to sprout in a redwood forest. There is no present fear of extinction.

There is yet enough redwood so that we can cut some into little pieces to fit into our world. Wood is red-brown, beautiful for trim and practically decay-proof for shingles, foundations, and posts.

Many of the finest groves are protected from the saw. Take Redwood Highway north to see something you'll find nowhere else in the world. *Sequoia sempervirens*

Big Tree is what everybody calls this tree, and that sums it all up. It's the perfect name because it relieves the pressure of trying to find words to describe it. People who take other trees for granted are stopped in their tracks by big tree. The result is that today the people own 92% of all big trees ten feet thick or more—so that they can be sure that the trees will just stand there to be looked at.

The pioneers who first jogged on horseback into the groves of big trees around 1853 were quick to sense that they had discovered something with a truly American appeal. Hunters had brought back reports which were not believed until two adventurers finally went to look. They had the P. T. Barnum instinct; knew that there is money in astonishing. Because in those days the people couldn't come to the trees, it was decided to bring a piece of a tree to the people, and the first big tree was cut down. Men who had coped with the continental wilderness were up against a job to fell just one big tree. To have at a trunk some 35 feet thick (with bark 2 feet thick) by swinging at it with an axe would be as insufficient as a woodpecker trying to fell an oak by pecking at it. So four men working for 22 days bored holes, and finally upset the tree with wedges. A section was gotten to New York a year later and put on exhibition. After that, the promoters felt it would be more profitable to transport bark than wood, so they painstakingly stripped off the bark of a trunk 92 feet in circumference and over 300 feet tall and sold the bark alone for a thousand dollars for exhibiting in Europe. Meanwhile a double bowling alley was built on the prone log of the first big tree felled, and gold prospectors and their friends from Sacramento and San Francisco visited it to be awed and entertained. These were the first of the tourists who today by the thousands go to see the groves of big tree in Yosemite.

If big tree's size saved it for showmanship, it also saved it from destruction in the days of ruthless cutting. Around 1890

Redwood cone

big trees looked like a fabulous vein of gold to lumbermen. Why not? One big tree alone has a volume of 600 thousand board feet, enough to build 80 five-room houses. With such a concentration of wealth it only remained to help oneself to lumber fast and plenty. Fortunately, it was still the era of the woodsman with the hand axe. So the destruction of big trees was slowed up until the people were aroused that here was something unique on the face of the earth.

Big trees are in 26 isolated groves in eastern California from Lake Tahoe to Bakersfield, a tiny sector of only 200 miles on our earth's surface. They like it over a mile high, with deep winter snows. Cones are larger than redwood, about the size of a hen's egg. They produce plenty of vital seed, and young big trees are coming along. Big tree does not reproduce from burl and stump suckers. Pollen is ripe in mid-winter and dusts the enormous crowns with golden gauze. Bark grows two feet deep, with massive furrows and fluting; like redwood, bark texture is shreddy, and because it lacks resin, it is practically fireproof. Roots of big tree are unseen marvels. Redwood growing in the bottom of a valley where sediments are deep plunges its roots a hundred feet downward, but big tree in rocky ravines and high sandy basins forms an enormous horizontal system a mere 8 feet deep. Roots of a single tree may occupy three acres.

Big tree transplants fairly well. Six are growing in Roanoke, Virginia. The Dupont estate in southeastern Pennsylvania has planted an avenue of big trees. A big tree at Bristol, Rhode Island, is nearly 100 feet tall; you can see it from the main road near the Mount Hope bridge. Clayton Pinetum, Roslyn, Long Island has a flourishing little big tree. The oldest and finest in the East is at Tyler Arboretum, Philadelphia. But these are pygmy captives compared to the real thing. Mariposa Grove at south end of Yosemite National Park is one of the largest. South Calaveras Grove, a few hours' run eastward from San Francisco, is one of the least despoiled. Giant Forest in Sequoia National Park has the awesome General Sherman with its top broken off by lightning but which goes right on defying the ages after living 3800 years in the same spot—its diameter 36 feet. One branch, held horizontal high above the ground, is 6½ feet in diameter and 150 feet long, larger than our loftiest American elm.

Sequoiadendron giganteum

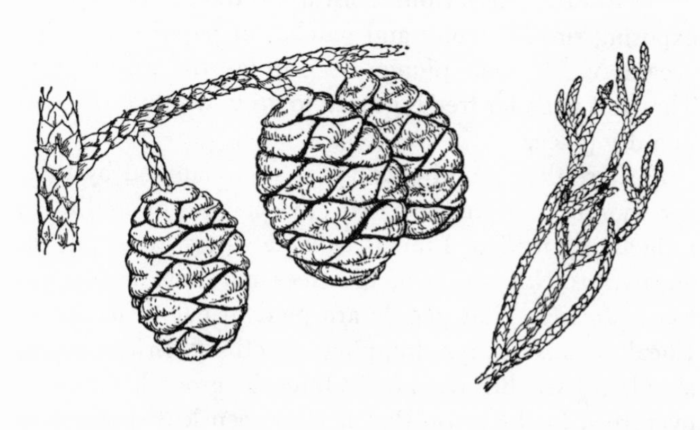

Big tree cones and branch

THE EUCALYPTI

Eucalyptus is the most conspicuous tree in towns, along roads, and as windbreaks in many parts of California. You see it everywhere around San Francisco and on the Peninsula. Sparse foliage casts little shade, lifted high above houses and other trees on a tall, often leaning, trunk. Leaves are long and slender like willow. They dangle in graceful blue-green clusters; on a hot day leaves coil lengthwise, turning their edges instead of the flat blade toward the sun, thus reducing evaporation. Foliage is arranged to let moisture from fogs and light drizzles drip through, thus collecting more than twice as much water as other trees from moisture in the air. Bark peels, exposing smooth white and patches of pastel colors like sycamore. Big roots plunge deep to tap the water table. Thus this peculiar tree is geared to grow with weed speed in a dry place.

Early settlers found eucalyptus so undaunted by rainless months and hot days that city planners offered a tax reduction for San Francisco landowners who put in eucalyptus. Now the huge old trees and their suckers are too aggressive, and people are paid to cut them down. Eucalyptus is always dropping something. Brittle twigs, shreds of bark, lids from fruits litter the ground. Although evergreen in the sense that it has green leaves the year 'round, leaves drop off in flocks at irregular intervals adding to the litter. All eucalypti come from Australia.

Be on the lookout for the following:

Blue Gum is the eucalyptus you are most likely to

see. Young leaves are smoky blue, and bark patches have delicate bluish tinge. Numerous long peeling strips give an unkempt look to trunk. Leaves are aromatic when crushed, and are the source of eucalyptus oil sold in drugstores for irritated mucous membrane.

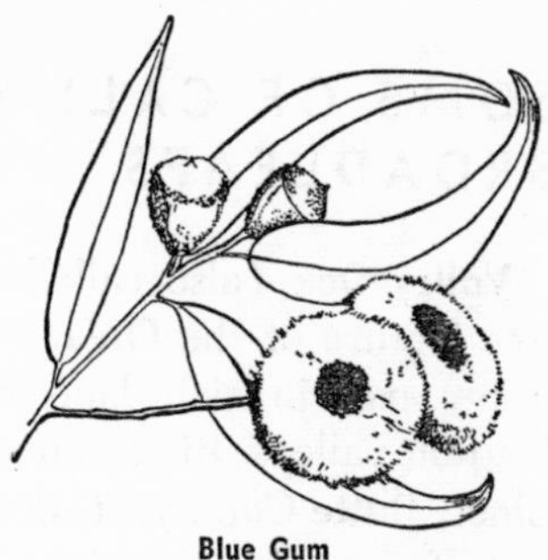

Blue Gum

Eucalyptus globulus

Red Gum is a big, valuable Australian timber tree often planted as shade tree and for windbreaks around Los Angeles. Twigs are red. Bark is gray, furrowed, doesn't peel off as much as others. *Eucalyptus rostrata*

Red Flowering Gum is the most popular decorative eucalyptus in southern California. Pink and red flowers in bright clusters bloom July through September. Small tree for a eucalyptus, with furrowed bark peeling little, and broader leaves. *Eucalyptus ficifolia*

Red Ironbark has hard red-brown bark. Often planted in hotel grounds because white flowers (one variety has pink) bloom from November to February. This shows its origin in Southern Hemisphere where our winter is summer. *Eucalyptus sideroxylon*

Lemon-scented Gum is most graceful of all. Bark is beautiful white suede. Leaves are lemon fragrant, their oil used to perfume soap. Much cultivated in gardens, one of finest is at Ellwood Ranch, near Ellwood.

Eucalyptus citriodora

SOME OF CALIFORNIA'S OWN BROADLEAFS

Valley Oak (also called California white oak) is the tree feature of the Great Valley. You see it as a broad, heavy oak in rich land of the Sacramento and San Joaquin valleys. Biggest one is near Route 32 just east of Chico, Butte County. Its dome covers 15 thousand square feet of ground, where in a good acorn season it deposits a blanket of acorns weighing a ton. California's first-prize leaf-dropping hardwood is to be seen along hundreds of miles of highways, especially near Jolon, Monterey County; Visalia, Tulare County; Fair Oaks, Sacramento County. Stop your car to see the fine acorn. A cartridge 2¼ inches long, chestnut brown shading to rich mahogany, rests in a round, deep, heavily pebbled cup. Valley oaks in San Bernardino County are our country's tallest white oaks; Connecticut's tallest eastern white oak, the great *Quercus alba,* takes second place. *Quercus lobata*

Blue Oak has a deep, plunging root system, a downy blue leaf, and a flaky, white trunk to balance with arid, rocky conditions where ordinary trees surrender. In such a place it's a companion of dusty digger pine. Because California has vast dry areas on lower slopes of both mountain ranges, blue oak is the state's most abundant and widespread oak. Acorn production is astronomical. If you camp out near blue oaks, you can hear pop, pop of acorns falling on the hard dry sand all night long. Averaging 20 per square foot and a high fat content, this is a feast for fattening cattle—perhaps a million tons a year of free food for the grazing, produced by a dauntless oak in a seemingly sterile place. *Quercus douglasii*

Coast Live Oak is the feature tree of the landscape along the coast from San Francisco Bay southward. It's evergreen, with small, holly-like leaves. You see its dark, rounded crowns dotting the coastal hills and valleys when you drive down the Peninsula from San Francisco, around San Mateo and Palo Alto. This is also the common tree around Monterey, Santa Barbara, and San Diego. Unusual bark is alive and moist until it is about 2 inches thick. Acorns are sometimes delicious to eat, but quality varies and you have to crunch them to find out. Coast live oak is a great real estate promoter; it is easy to grow, disease-proof, carefree; a valuable shade tree. *Quercus agrifolia*

Interior Live Oak is the common oak in Yosemite and elsewhere on Sierra slopes just below big timber where chaparral begins. It has a vivid black silhouette made by small evergreen leaves, some with smooth edges, some

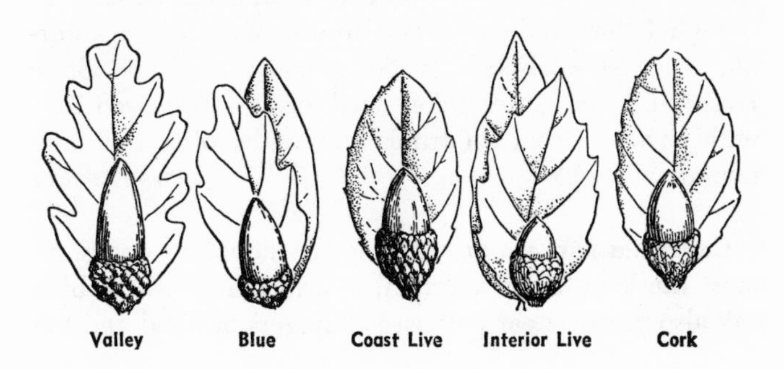

scalloped. The acorn is small, sharp, narrow—its feature is a long deep cup that fits half of the nut like a glove, with thin red-brown overlapping scales. Acorns, produced in profusion, are rich and fattening for animals, but big crop is mostly wasted because interior live oaks often grow in rough, inaccessible canyons.

Quercus wislizenii

Cork Oak is interesting tree to see around southern California towns; a healthy, broad-headed shade tree with dark oval evergreen leaves, white-hairy on undersides. Bark of old trees has high market value for cork. Takes 20 years for first stripping of virgin bark which is only good for tannin, or outside siding for rustic, picturesque house; ten years later is stripped for fishnet floats or insulation. In fifty years tree produces high grade cork. Champagne corks are good example of best material—unique in the vegetable kingdom for compressibility, elasticity; frictional on glass yet smooth—and highly impervious to air and water. Trees continue to bear cork for 200 years, quality becoming better and better after each 10-year stripping. American impatience is stumbling block to important cork producing industry although 4 thousand cork oaks are now mature in California. Biggest cork oak is on grounds of Napa State Hospital, Napa, a few miles north of San Francisco Bay, with a heavy coat on trunk and limbs of a thousand pounds of cork. *Quercus suber*

California Buckeye grows on lower mountain slopes, almost the length of California, in arid places where blue oak also grows. Leaf pattern like fingers of hand and big

California Buckeye

round seeds with shiny brown jackets resemble horse-chestnut and Ohio buckeye. This small tree or big shrub is eye-catcher when you are sightseeing. Leaves come out in February, then profusion of white and pink flowers in May and June. Leaves drop off with hot days, leaving branches bare all summer except for thousands of big, round capsules dangling like ornaments all over tree. Capsules split open when buckeyes are ripe in November; buckeyes cover ground or roll down into piles in gullies.

Aesculus californica

Western Sycamore is the widest-reaching, toughest, leaf-dropping tree from central California into Mexico (Baja California). Bark has white patches like eastern sycamore; button balls dangle in groups of 4 to 6; leaves come 10 inches wide on long stem that wears a cute collar at base. Anyone who knows maple-like pattern of sycamore leaf will recognize these, but they are fancier, gayer than formal leaf of eastern sycamore. This massive tree shakes its fists at you with huge, crooked limbs across shimmering hot sand and rock country where it grows by a watercouse. Sycamore on Juan y Lolita Rancho, Santa Ynez Valley, just north of Santa Barbara, with 158-foot spread, may be broadest tree in the U. S.

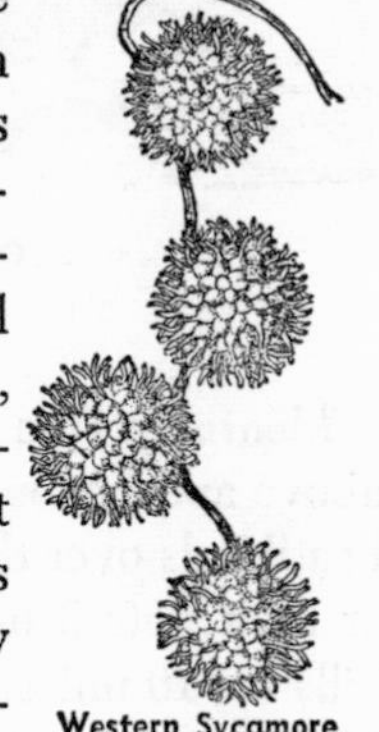
Western Sycamore fruits

Platanus racemosa

FOUR SURPRISING EVERGREENS

Monterey Cypress has less than a square mile of the earth's surface, the smallest native home of any American tree. When near Carmel, don't miss the two tiny groves, at Cypress Point and Point Lobos. See rare tree gems, picturesque and tortured, pouring out of rocky headlands, twisted, contorted, as though about to plunge into the sea, or with flattened tops streamlined like flags in a strong wind. This old relic grows fast in cultivation from seed and is now commonly seen in California planted for hedges, windbreaks, park trees. But these cultivated trees are threatened by a fatal fungus disease; it appears that this dauntless warrior of the ages won't be hurried by our feverish ways.

Monterey Cypress

Cupressus macrocarpa

Monterey Pine forms a belt of rich, dark green pines above and beyond the Monterey cypress, which hugs the headlands over the sea. Its natural range is slightly greater as it gets 3 miles from the coast and runs along the hills for 10 miles. Tops are flat and picturesquely broken. Monterey pine is another forest fire phoenix (like jack and knobcone); its cones remain closed until touched by fire. Strangely, this patriarch that has clung to earthly existence in such a narrow strongbox has become one of the chief timber trees of New Zealand and Australia. It grows fast and tall when seeds are taken from Carmel and planted in the Southern Hemisphere. *Pinus radiata*

Torrey Pine is another of the marvelous only-place-in-the-world trees. Its refuge is 8 miles of coast from La Jolla to Del Mar, just north of San Diego. Needles are 10 inches long, gray-green, stiff, in clusters of 5. Torrey pines are a remarkable sight with radiating balls of long needles on much-branched, sprawling, contorted trees. Some limbs make complete loops, responding to unseen forces that cause violent changes in direction. Torrey pines are an oasis of evergreen on treeless hills covered with dry, dusty grass. Transplanted for years, it often turns up around California as a garden and street tree. Ten miles south from Santa Barbara in Carpinteria on Route 101, be on lookout for world's biggest sample of this remarkable tree. *Pinus torreyana*

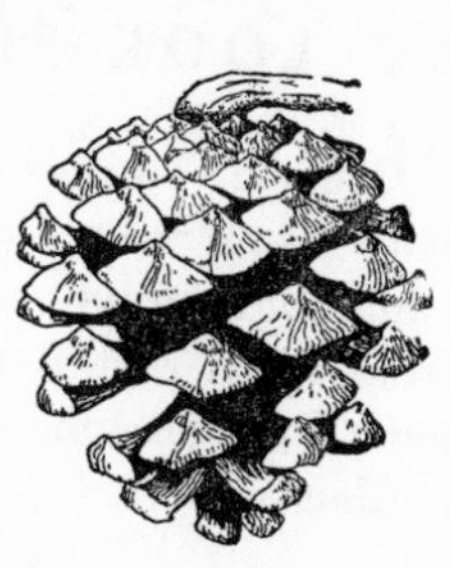
Torrey Pine cone

Big Cone Spruce is the long-limbed tree that gives a forest touch to dry canyons and gulches above Pasadena and Los Angeles. Common in San Gabriel and San Bernardino Mountains where it raises real estate values. Looks like a tree in an amateur's first attempt to paint, because it has ungainly long lower limbs that go out horizontally and then droop, while short upper branches go up. This is a relative of the lordly Douglas fir. It has tongues of Douglas fir peeking out between scales. Many of these trees of ungainly beauty have been destroyed by chaparral fires in recent years. *Pseudotsuga macrocarpa*

SOME DECORATIONS TO LOOK FOR

Camphor Tree is ornamental tree of exceptional beauty, with evergreen leaves, bright green in April. Leaves have camphor odor when crushed; commercial camphor comes from wood of this tree. Extensively cultivated in Pasadena and elsewhere in southern California in streets, gardens and parks. *Cinnamomum camphora*

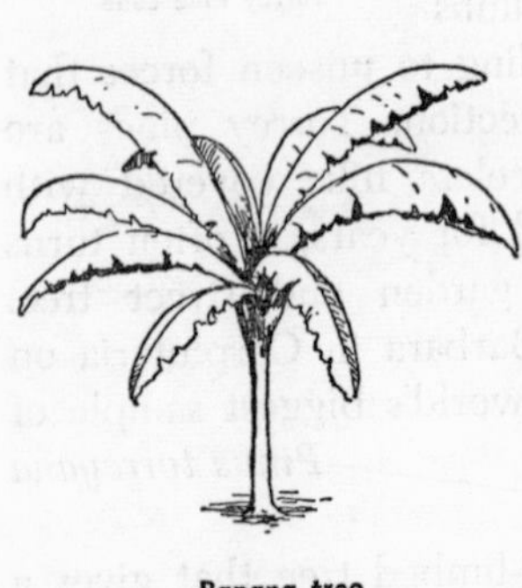
Banana tree

Banana Tree's huge leaves 10 feet long on short trunk might be taken for palm; but this is tree with its own family. Stands out in parks in cities like Berkeley and around courthouse grounds and wherever choice trees are planted. Interesting tree to know and point out as producer of bananas. *Musa paradisiaca*

Moreton Bay Fig is wide-reaching tree with big, shiny, oval rubber-plant leaves. Passengers arriving at Southern Pacific Station, Santa Barbara, see great one with spread of 135 feet, and gnarled roots protruding from earth a hundred feet around, like angry throng of partly buried snakes. *Ficus macrophylla*

Orange Pittosporum is aromatic healthy evergreen, whose dark, glossy leaves clustered at tips of twigs remind you of orange leaf except that margins are wavy. Fruit is exquisite half-inch seed box, smooth to touch, rich red-brown color. Orange blossom fragrance of white flowers makes pittosporum famous on an early spring evening. This delightful tree is seen throughout southern California—in tree-rich Santa Barbara it is planted more than any other tree or shrub. *Pittosporum undulatum*

Pepper Tree is one of California's outstanding shade trees. Like eucalyptus and carob, it makes a healthy shade tree in a dry, hot spot without irrigation because of deep digging roots. First pepper tree from Peru was planted in Santa Barbara Mission ground in 1825, and, ever since, pepper has been making itself more and more at home. Street planners with more trees to choose from today wish there were not so many peppers. They have abundant red berries and lacy foliage, but branches are low and berries litter sidewalk. *Schinus molle*

Jacaranda (also called green ebony) is an exciting street and park tree not to miss. Its popularity in southern California is great. Ten-inch leaves are made of dozens of tiny spine-tipped leaflets. Leaves drop off in spring instead of in fall because habits were formed in Brazil where seasons are reversed. Eye-catching 2-inch flowers come in big lavendar or blue clusters. These are more luxurious, last three times longer, than the flowers of paulownia. Fruit is a unique, squashed eccentric capsule. *Jacaranda acutifolia*

THE ACACIAS

This is the tree or shrub with golden cataracts of flowers in tiny balls, and silvery gray foliage. Along California streets acacias catch the eye in early spring as though a yellow spotlight has been turned on. Here are three of the most conspicuous of tree acacias:

Black Acacia is a curious exception to the usual acacia style. A big tree up to 70 feet, abundant in coastal communities. Instead of feathery leaves, this tree has flattened leaf stems about 4 inches long which serve as leaves. Its flowers, instead of golden yellow are white, appear late in spring. Los Angeles has more black acacias on its streets than any other tree. *Acacia melanoxylon*

Bailey Acacia is slender tree with feathery gray-toned foliage. Often cultivated for spring flower shows. Nurserymen say it's their most popular. *Acacia baileyana*

Silver Wattle is good-sized, fast-growing tree wherever there is water and sunshine in southern California. Silvery fuzz on leaf gives name. This has become naturalized in places, that is, grows from its own seed outdoors.
Acacia decurrens var. *dealbata*

THE PALMS

Around Chicago or Boston palms are houseplants and greenhouse curiosities; around Los Angeles they are as much a part of the outdoors as the sunshine. Palms have a peculiar blueprint. Unlike most of the trees of our country, the trunk does not taper from bottom to top, but rises with more or less parallel sides like a pillar. This often bulges slightly and spreads out at the base. This trunk is not made of wood in the usual sense. There are no annual rings, but black fibres scattered through spongy cells make the trunk tough, and a bit elastic. Palm trunks, reversing the wood from usual trees, are hard on the outside, soft in the center.

No branch grows from the palm pillar, but huge sprays of leaves spring from its top. These come in two styles: feather-leaves, and fan-leaves. In recognizing a palm tree, its type of leaf is the first point to check. Of many kinds of palms those you are most apt to see in California are the following:

Canary Island Date Palm is most conspicuous feather-type palm throughout California. Short, thick trunk is rough with heavy projections where leaves of past years were attached. Big clusters of orange fruit are conspicuous. Huge, dark leaves, 20 feet long, spring upward and curve down to form imposing dense dome. Fine specimens in Beverly Hills, Oakland, Palo Alto, and many communities of central and southern California. *Phoenix canariensis*

Canary Island Palm

Queen Palm is the common feather-type palm of streets and parks in San Diego, Los Angeles, and Santa Barbara.

Its tall, smooth, gray trunk reminds the easterner of royal palm in Florida, but queen palm has conspicuous dark rings on the cement-like surface. The spray of leaves, held high, gives this tree the local name of "feather duster." To see a stately double row, drive along Santa Barbara Street in Santa Barbara.
Arecastrum Romanzoffianum

Piccabeen Palm (also called king palm) is an exquisite street palm that first catches the eye by its slenderness and the delicate spray of feathers at its crest. Smooth gray trunk is ringed with rounded ridges. Eye-catching feature, the lavender flowers that dangle from the trunk, a distance below the crown of leaves. Fanciful thought is how such flowers can grow out of a concrete pillar. They turn to scarlet berries. *Archontophoenix Cunninghamiana*

Washington Palm is famous for great size (up to 80 feet) and for the fact that its native home is in southern California. Palm Canyon near Palm Springs has a thousand in their wild, picturesque ravines—a feature of the state. Fan-leaf crown seems inadequate for such a great tree. Fans poke out at odd angles, and old ones flop down covering trunk, giving an ungainly look. This is a desert tree, with amazingly deep roots that must tap plenty of underground water. You can see it planted extensively, giving romantic South Sea Island look to streets, parks, and hotel grounds from Beverly Hills southward. *Washingtonia filifera*

ORCHARD TREES

Avocado has large oval leaves of rich green so typical of other laurels as oregon myrtle, camphor tree, and the eastern sassafras. In southern California avocado is a crop of increasing value with the rising popularity of this nourishing salad fruit that cannot be cooked, canned or dried—must always be served fresh. Air shipping modernizes this style of fruit, yet avocado is oldest American tree crop, a legacy from the Aztecs. *Persea americana*

Date Palm is a stately tree with trunk roughened by old leaf bases. Its crown is open and feathery; 15-foot leaves reach up in the form of huge wine glasses. Set out in orchards, the rows of this tree are an impressive sight. The king of the desert oases has become a valuable crop in the arid Riverside and Imperial Counties.

Phoenix dactylifera

Olive is dainty orchard tree with creamy white fragrant flowers, of Sacramento Valley and southward. To the owner it is producer of olives and olive oil. To the passing motorist it offers surprising color effect of dark purple-black fruits against silver flashes from undersides of leaves. A flourishing orchard is near Corning, Route 99W. Old gnarled trees in California Spanish Mission grounds still produce good olives. You can see it as park tree in Pasadena and Phoenix, Arizona.

Olea europaea

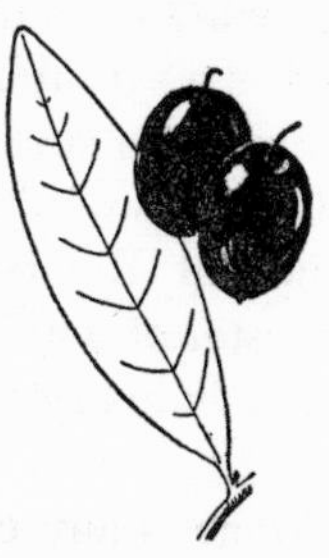

Ripe fruit and leaf of Olive tree

English Walnut (also called Persian walnut) is a strong hardwood resembling black walnut except that the nuts have thin shells. English walnuts sometimes line highways, and a hundred thousand acres of orchards stretch from Los Angeles into Oregon. Valuable invention was machine to stamp brand name on rough surface of each nut at rate of 2 thousand nuts a minute. *Juglans regia*

Lemon trees are small with thorny branches; white blossoms have purple tinge on outside of petals. Many groves near coast between San Diego and Los Angeles; and lemons are most valuable orchard crop of Santa Barbara County. Lemon crops in southern California are commercial triumph of recent years. Fruit is picked year 'round, but is best in mid-winter. *Citrus limonia*

Orange trees make green hundreds of thousands of acres of irrigated valleys. Best groves east of Los Angeles. When frost threatens, hundreds of smudge pots are lighted; dancing light of highlights on polished leaves is eerie night spectacle. Because soot settles on fruit, electric wind machines are replacing smudge pots. California makes year 'round shipments with only two varieties: Valencia in summer, Navel in winter. A tree imported in 1873 grows with regal rights behind ornamental iron fence at Riverside and still bears good crop. This is ancestor of 9 million orange trees lined up in a half billion dollar industry of sunshine and leaves. *Citrus sinensis*

Prune is any cultivated plum tree with so much sugar that it can be dried without removing pit. Leaf and flower look like those of our familiar cherry tree. Sacramento Valley has 200 thousand acres of plum trees waiting for fruit to drop off. Plum on ground is picked up, dried in sun until it wrinkles, glossed up with glycerine or fruit syrup, and lo, a prune! *Prunus spp.*

Almond is a peach relative whose fruit is not plump with juicy pulp, but has thick skin and big, crisp, delicious kernel—unlike the bitter stone of ordinary peaches. Pink flowers cover branches before leaves come out in February. Orchards developed since 1900 throughout California have 5 million trees, produce more almonds than we import. *Prunus amigdalus*

Carob (also called St. John's bread) is a drought-resisting ornamental tree with great commercial possibilities. It has tiny red flowers, evergreen leaves with 4 or 5 oval leaflets along a midrib, and a tough, lumpy, dark red pod like a locust tree. That pod contains food value for human bread, cereal, candy, syrup—and is great for fattening calves. You see it as a common street tree throughout southern California. Pasadena has 3 thousand carobs—see the fantastic contortions of the branches! Carob will grow in steep, arid ground with orange-tree climate. Carob orchards are being tried out successfully in Coachella and Imperial Valleys. *Ceratonia siliqua*

THE SOUTHWEST

From a transcontinental plane you can see how much of the Southwest looks like the biggest baldspot of our land. The bordering states of Colorado, Oklahoma, and Texas have trees from the Great American Woods, especially hackberry, black willow, honey locust, box elder, green ash, elm, post oak. Trees from the South march in via the Gulf Coast—for example, live oak, palmetto, bald cypress. High mountain ranges penetrate deep into the Southwest bringing ponderosa pine, Douglas fir, Englemann spruce from the Northwest. Trees planted around towns are a mixture from all quarters. Southern California contributes trees to Phoenix, El Paso, Albuquerque. In fact, camphor tree and Washington palm get all the way over to New Orleans. Rivers winding over the Southwest are green ribbons of Fremont cottonwood and sandbar willow.

The baldspot itself is far from being an unbroken wild of sterile sand. The Great Basin of Nevada is strewn with sagebrush. Southward, mesas and plains, the driest, hottest part of our country, are peppered with creosote bush. Only small areas which glare white with alkaline flats are plantless. Even Death Valley, where the temperature reaches 134°, produces the ephedra shrub, greasewood, and sage. So dauntless is the living cell to fashion some sort of device to grow anywhere that there are even a few trees on the hot desert among the creosote bushes. These are unlike trees anywhere else. To see them feels like seeing the sort of contrivances that might grow on another planet.

Pinyon (also called nut pine) covers the dry southern Rockies with a stubby, robust forest. Long ridges reach into the Southwest with dark fingers of this commonest tree of Utah, Arizona, New Mexico. Needles are short, twisted apart in clusters of 2's. Cones are small, flaring, with big, delicious seeds. Wood smells like beeswax. Dead limbs with crisp gray lichens add to the picturesque look of this daughty tree that strikes a balance with heat and frost, snow and drought. You can see much pinyon around Santa Fe and on the brink of the Grand Canyon. *Pinus edulis*

Oneleaf Pinyon (also called nut pine) is unique among pines because needles are in bundles of one. Heavy cone scales swing out, discharging edible nut sold for good eating throughout United States. This is the most abundant and valuable tree of Nevada, a state divided into sagebrush plains and broad slopes covered with oneleaf pinyon and juniper. Pines are scattered, bushy; look black as though burned, but are exceedingly welcome with nourishing nuts and tough wood for corral building. *Pinus monophylla*

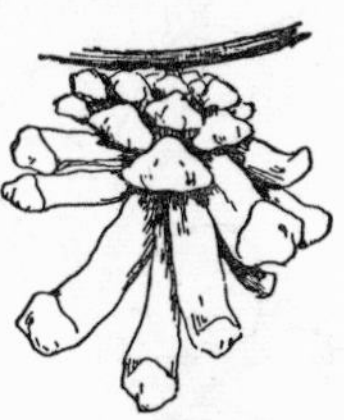
Pinyon Pine cone

Mesquite rises above the creosote brush as a large shrub or small tree, conspicuous all across the vast, shim-

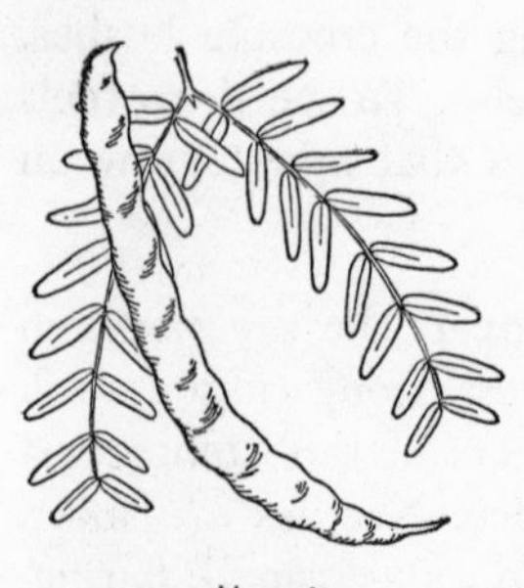
Mesquite

mering desert. The most important tree from Texas to southern California. Thorny branches, feathery gray leaves, masses of yellow flowers, and honey-sweet pods. Wide branches cast thin, hot shade for fifty feet, where dry gravel is covered with beans avidly eaten by animals. One kind, called screw-bean, bears pods tightly twisted into spiral coils like a piece of rope. It takes water to produce so much good food, so mesquite is an indicator of ground water in the desert—though it may be hard to dig as deep as roots go. *Prosopis juliflora*

Blue Palo Verde

Blue Palo Verde has interlocking spiny branches, dense head; a beautiful tree of the desert washes and canyons from California across southern Arizona. The blue in its name is from the soft, glowing blue-green of foliage. In late March the tree is a mass of golden yellow flowers visible for miles. This remarkable tree has plenty of leaves in the brief rainy season, but they all fall off with drought, so water is not lost through leaves during hot summer. It then uses chlorophyll in green trunk and branches to make food and serve as leaves. Palo verde means "green stick." One kind of palo verde grows with saguaro (see below). Another kind of palo verde is much planted around southwestern towns and farms. You'll know it by gorgeous yellow flowers or bright green trunk and branches. *Cercidium floridum*

Saguaro, the giant cactus, pronounced sa-wáro, points up its weird cylinders like giant fingers. This majestic symbol of the Sonoran Desert may reach fifty feet. Today a bacterial disease threatens the existence of saguaro. Its best stand is called the Saguaro National Monument, 20 miles east of Tucson, Arizona. You'll always dream about it if you visit it. *Carnegiea gigantea*

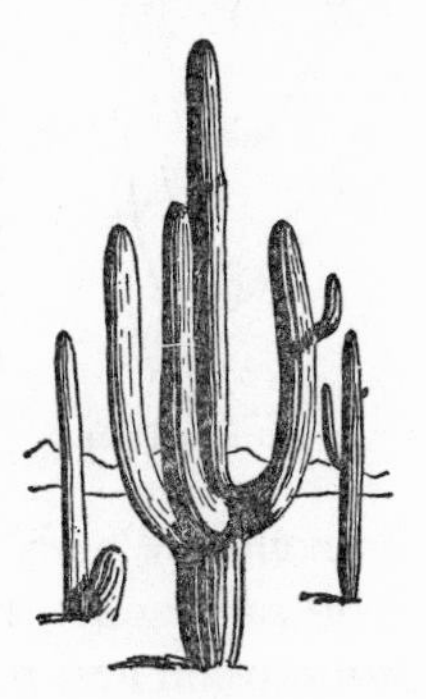

Saguaro

Joshua Tree is actually a 25-foot lily with heavy branches ending in round balls of sharp, slender leaves 10 inches long. Leaves also cover trunk. The thing looks like a purely imaginative tree, unreal in our world. Infinitely slow-growing, of unknown great age, Joshua tree has its roots so amalgamated with the desert sand that it cannot be transplanted or raised elsewhere. Although gradually disappearing, there are many groves of Joshuas to enjoy in southern California and Arizona. Best display is in Mojave Desert due east of Los Angeles—take Route 60 or 70 through Cajon Pass to Joshua Tree National Monument. *Yucca brevifolia*

Joshua tree

Crucifixion Thorn

Crucifixion Thorn is unbelievable tree which one might expect to seek in Samarkand or Mongolia, but it actually grows on mesas and in canyons of southern Utah and in washes of Arizona desert between Flagstaff and Phoenix. Tree has no leaves. Trunk is green like palo verde; branches are long, green, elastic thorns that stick out more or less parallel to each other, in curious geometric pattern. Flowers are in greenish-white bunches at base of branches. Woody fruit and leafless thorny branch give little satisfaction to grazing animals, but tree helps control erosion and rouses curiosity on desert landscape.

Canotia holacantha

Desert Ironwood

Desert Ironwood is a fine tree of the deep desert with lavender sweet-pea flowers and blue-green foliage. Gray, stringy bark distinguishes it from palo verde when flowers are not showing. The latter has green bark. Wood is rock-heavy, dulls tools, and can hardly be cut with saw. Desert souvenirs are made of this wood.

Olneya tesota

THREE LITTLE TREES OF TOWN AND FARM

Chinaberry (one form is Texas umbrella tree) lines streets of southwestern towns like rows of big beach umbrellas, making dense shade during hot dry summer. Yellow seed pods bedeck branches after leaves fall off; these contain shiny, smooth, bead-like seeds. Tree came from Greek missions where beads were used for rosaries. *Melia azedarach*

Russian Olive is tough and pretty, indifferent to drought or cold. White flowers are fragrant, but chief feature is the silver leaves—you tell it from afar by the way it glints in the sun. The unmistakable Russian olive is seen in many western towns from North Dakota to Texas. *Eleagnus angustifolia*

Oleander turns from a tall shrub into a graceful tree in a hot moist place—perfumes the air with pink, white and purple flowers. Leaves are long, slender, rich blue-green. Galveston, Texas, is the "Oleander City." Its streets are made luxuriant and fragrant by this tree in a way a visitor never forgets. *Nerium oleander*

A GUIDE TO THE QUICK IDENTIFICATION OF TREES

The Great American Woods

Evergreens of the West

This Guide is designed to help you name a tree when you have a leaf or evergreen needle, cone, or twig in your hand, or when you notice an unusual bark or fragrance. By comparing your leaf with the very generalized silhouette in the Guide, your search is narrowed to a few trees. These are listed below in order of the size of the *average* leaf – thus the first tree listed is likely to have small leaves, the last tree on the list probably has large leaves. But leaves, even on the same tree, vary greatly in both size and shape – some are even listed under two or more shapes. Leaves on young sprouts are often abnormally large. So you must always remember that these little drawings are only visual approximations to direct you more quickly to the full description of the tree elsewhere in the book.

SINGLE LEAVES

OF THE GREAT AMERICAN WOODS

s —smooth-edged t —toothed

w—wavy-edged tt—doubled-toothed

t Trembling aspen
tt River birch
tt Paper birch
tt Crab apple+
w White poplar+
t Bigtooth aspen
t Balsam poplar
t Mulberry+
s Catalpa+
s Paulownia+

s Live oak
t Silverbell
t Pin cherry
t Sweet cherry
s Tupelo
s Sassafras+
s Laurel oak
s Shingle oak
t Sorrel tree
s Fringe tree
s Magnolias
  Southern
  Cucumber tree
  Sweet bay
  Umbrella

t Shadblow
tt Crab apple+
t Chokecherry
t Wahoo
t Black cherry
s Osage orange
s Persimmon
s Dogwood

+ Leaves so marked are listed throughout this section under more than one shape.

SINGLE LEAVES
OF THE GREAT AMERICAN WOODS

s Redbud
s Catalpa+
s Paulownia+

tt Yellow birch
tt Sweet birch
t Hop hornbeam
t Blue beech
tt Slippery elm

t Hackberry
tt American elm
w Witch hazel
t Basswood+

t Beech
w Chinquapin
t Chestnut

s Water oak
w Chestnut oak
s Pawpaw

tt Gray birch
t Lombardy poplar
tt Hawthorn
t Cottonwood

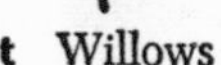

t Willows
s Willow oak

w Ginkgo

t Sweet gum

s Sassafras+
t Mulberry

LOBED LEAVES
OF THE GREAT AMERICAN WOODS

r—rounded tips
s—sharp tips

5 lobes or more
- Sycamore
- London plane tree
- Maples:
  - Silver
  - Sugar
  - Black
  - Norway
  - Schwedler
  - Sycamore
  - Japanese+

Oaks:
- r White
- r Post
- r Swamp white
- r Bur
- s Red
- s Black
- s Pin
- s Scarlet
- s Scrub
- s Spanish
- s Overcup

3-5 lobes
- Striped maple
- Mountain maple
- Red maple
- White poplar+
- Crab apple+

4 lobes
- Tulip tree

MULTIPLE LEAVES
OF THE GREAT AMERICAN WOODS

3-5 leaflets
- Box elder
- Wafer ash
- Pignut+
- Shagbark hickory

5-11 leaflets
- Bitternut+
- Ash
- Pignut
- Mockernut
- Yellowwood
- Pecan+

9-27 leaflets
- Mountain ash
- Black locust
- Sumac
- Pecan+
- Walnut
- Ailanthus
- Butternut+

Honey locust+
Kentucky coffeetree
Chinaberry
Hercules' club

Japanese maple+
Buckeye
Horse chestnut

SEEDS

SEEDS WITH WINGS

Ash

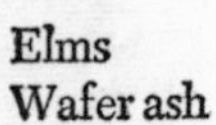
Elms
Wafer ash

Ailanthus

Maple

Basswood

PRICKLE-BALLS

Sweet gum
Sycamore
Chinquapin
Horse chestnut (shell)
Buckeye (shell)

PODS

Redbud
Kentucky coffeetree
Catalpa
Black locust
Honey locust

TASSELS

Birches
Poplars
Willows

NUTS

Beech

Buckeye

Hickory

Black walnut

Oak

Butternut

Horse chestnut

Sumac

Tulip

Magnolia

BERRIES AND FRUITS

Basswood	Paulownia
Mountain ash	Crab apple
Witch hazel	Persimmon
Hackberry	Pawpaw
Holly	Peach
Tupelo	Apple
Sassafras	Orange
Wild cherry	Osage orange
Mulberry	
Hawthorn	
Ginkgo	
Cherry	

Note that the berries and fruits in the left-hand column are approximately half natural size. Those in the right-hand column are about one-fifth natural size.

TWIGS

MILKY SAP

Sumac
Norway maple
Osage orange
Mulberry

CHAMBERED PITH

Black gum
Blackberry
Black walnut
Butternut
Paulownia

CORKY RIDGES

Wahoo
Sweet gum
Winged elm

THORNS

Osage orange
Hercules club
Black locust
Honey locust
Hawthorn
Crab apple

TWIG COLORS

Sassafras – green
Box elder – green, purple-red
Osage orange – yellow
Sweet bay – green
Poplar – orange-gray
Willow– golden yellow
Ailanthus – orange
Sweet birch – rich brown

SMELL

Ailanthus – rank
Basswood – sweet
Black walnut – aromatic
Balsam – fragrant
Juniper – piney
Sweet gum – resinous

TASTE

Wafer ash – bitter
Cherry – bitter
Sweet birch – wintergreen
Yellow birch – wintergreen
Sassafras – aromatic
Sorrel – sour

TREE FLOWERS

WHITE
Yellowwood
Shadblow
Fringe tree
Black locust
Silverbell
Mountain ash
Basswood
Hercules' club
Dogwood
Horse chestnut
Catalpa[3]

PINK, WHITE
Fruit trees
Crab apple
Hawthorn
Magnolia
Dogwood

RED
Pawpaw

YELLOW
Witch hazel[1]
Buckeye

PINK, PURPLE
Redbud
Paulownia

GREENISH
Sassafras
Tulip[2]

1. blooms in fall
2. with orange splashes
3. with brown spots

Dogwood

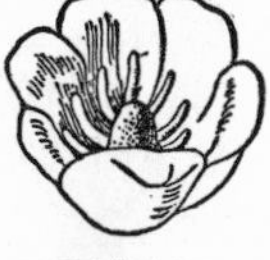
Tulip tree

Catalpa

Southern magnolia

Sorrel

Shadblow

Silverbell

Apple

BARK

Persimmon — chunky squares
*Sycamore — white patches
*Paper birch — chalky white
*Gray birch — light gray
Sweet birch — glossy, dark red
Yellow birch — gold, shreddy
Old willow — deeply sculptured
Black locust — deep furrows
Striped maple — white lines on green
*Chestnut oak — deep ridges
Ash — diamond crisscrosses
Hop-hornbeam — shreddy
Shagbark hickory — loose strips
*Beech — smooth gray
Trembling aspen — light green
Blue beech — smooth, muscular

* See also photographs following page 128

EASTERN EVERGREENS

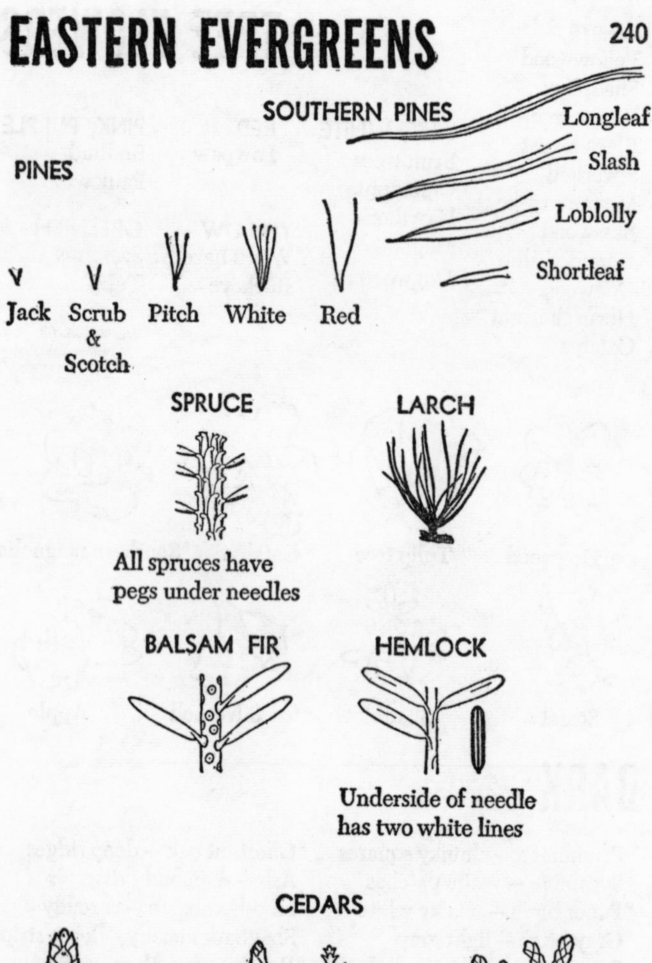

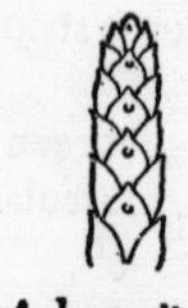

Arbor vitae

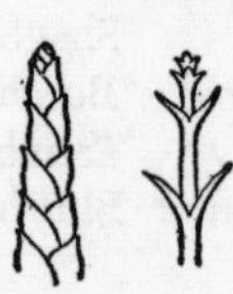

Red cedar

Southern white cedar

WESTERN EVERGREENS

PINES

Monterey Torrey Jeffrey Ponderosa Digger

Oneleaf Pinyon Lodgepole Limber & Whitebark Sugar & Western white Knobcone

SPRUCES

Engelmann Sitka

FIR

HEMLOCK

LARCH

YEW

JUNIPER

DOUGLAS FIR

CEDARS

Western red

Alaska

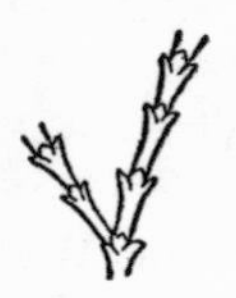

Incense

Port Orford

CONES OF EAST AND WEST

EASTERN PINES

Longleaf
6-10 in.

White
4-8 in.

Shortleaf 2 in.
Loblolly 2-6 in.
Slash 2-6 in.

Jack
1-2 in.

Red 1-2 in.
Scrub 2-3 in.
Pitch 2-3 in.

FIRS

Balsam 2-4 in.
Alpine 2-4 in.
Red 6-9 in.
Grand 2-4 in.
Silver 3-6 in.
White 3-5 in.

Noble 4-6 in.
Shasta red
8 in.

SPRUCES

Black 1 in.
Red 1½ in.
White 2 in.

Engelmann
2 in.
Sitka 2-4 in.

Norway
4-6 or 7 in.

CEDARS

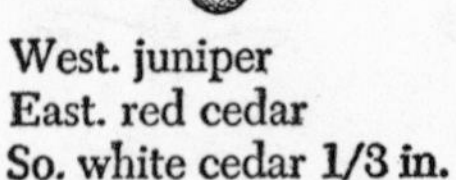

West. juniper
East. red cedar
So. white cedar 1/3 in.

Alaska
cedar
½ in.

Port
Orford
cedar
1/3 in.

Arbor vitae
Western red
cedar ½ in.

Incense
cedar
1 in.

YEW

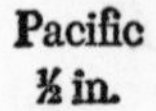

Pacific
½ in.

LARCHES

Eastern
¾ in.

Western
1½ in.

DOUGLAS FIR

¾ in.

HEMLOCKS

Eastern
¾ in. max.
Western
1 in.

Mountain
1¼-3 in.

INDEX

OTHER BOOKS BY RUTHERFORD PLATT

THIS GREEN WORLD

This book is the world of nature about us today.

"Such a vivid presentation of nature's technocracy and functionalism, especially when so excellently illustrated as is this book with many of Mr. Platt's photographs in black and white and in color—and scores in drawing—gives this book a wide appeal and should assure it lasting popularity."

—Richardson Wright in *New York Herald Tribune*.

"Superb in its plan and masterly in its execution, this book is a record of a true naturalist. It is a book for the bird-lover as well as the lover of plants, for more and more we are coming to realize the interdependence of all life. . . . All nature lovers must unite . . . in thanking Mr. Platt for this unusual book." —*Audubon Magazine*.

OUR FLOWERING WORLD

This book is the origins of the world of nature—how the earth, through the eons of time, acquired its green mantle of plants and flowers and trees.

"This beautiful, unusual, richly informative book is a trail-blazer in its special field. . . . The author fits the great, panoramic, overlapping time-pictures together in straight-forward and occasionally beautiful prose. . . . The author has accomplished what many have tried to do. He makes the past live as he tells the over-all story of plant life on this planet." —*The New York Times*.

"The author has written a truly great book in that he takes his readers out of the stuffy libraries and classrooms and shows them the trees living the present but reflecting the past."—*Organic Gardening*.